William Alexander Parsons Martin

The Chinese: their Education, Philosophy, and Letters

William Alexander Parsons Martin

The Chinese: their Education, Philosophy, and Letters

ISBN/EAN: 9783744718042

Printed in Europe, USA, Canada, Australia, Japan

Cover: Foto ©ninafisch / pixelio.de

More available books at **www.hansebooks.com**

THE CHINESE

THEIR

EDUCATION, PHILOSOPHY, AND LETTERS

BY

W. A. P. MARTIN, D.D., LL.D.

PRESIDENT OF THE TUNGWEN COLLEGE, PEKING

NEW YORK

HARPER & BROTHERS, FRANKLIN SQUARE

1881

TO

PROFESSOR W. D. WHITNEY, LL.D.

THE MAINSTAY
OF THE AMERICAN ORIENTAL SOCIETY, AND
A DISTINGUISHED LEADER IN ORIENTAL STUDIES, THIS
LITTLE VOLUME, WHICH, IN SOME SENSE
OWES ITS EXISTENCE TO HIM

Is Respectfully Inscribed

BY HIS FRIEND

THE AUTHOR

PREFACE.

My dear Professor Whitney,—

The earliest of the following essays was written at your instance twenty years ago; and you will recognize several of the others as having passed through your hands on their way to the A. O. S., or to the magazines in which they made their first appearance.

You will, I trust, welcome them as old friends, and for their sake give a favorable reception to those which are now, for the first time, introduced to your attention.

The contents of this volume, though somewhat miscellaneous, are yet connected by a certain unity; falling naturally into three divisions, treating respectively of the education, philosophy, and letters of the Chinese—in a word, of their intellectual life.

I call them Hanlin* Papers, not merely because the first three discuss educational processes which culminate in the Hanlin Academy, but more especially because the Hanlin is confessedly the highest embodiment of Chinese intellectual life.

No one of these papers throws any light on your favorite field of research,† and none of them pretends to be exhaustive of its special subject; they are offered to you and the public only as a bundle of *Beiträge*—a small contribution towards the better understanding of China and the Chinese.

Yours truly, W. A. P. Martin.

Peking, *March* 24, 1880.

---

* The title of the first edition, printed in China.

† Philology.

CONTENTS.

APPENDIX.

CONTENTS

THE CHINESE:

THEIR EDUCATION, PHILOSOPHY, AND LETTERS.

THE HANLIN YUAN, OR IMPERIAL ACADEMY.

NEAR the foot of a bridge that spans the Imperial Canal a few rods to the north of the British Legation, the visitor to Peking may have noticed the entrance to a small *yamen.* Here are the headquarters of the Hanlin Academy, one of the pivots of the Empire, and the very centre of its literary activity.

On entering the enclosure, nothing meets the eye of one who is unable to read the inscriptions that would awaken the faintest suspicion of the importance of the place. A succession of open courts with broken pavements, and covered with rubbish; five low, shed-like structures, one story in height, that have the appearance of an empty barn; these flanked by a double series of humbler buildings, quite inferior to the stables of a well-conducted farmstead—some of the latter in ruins; and dust and decay everywhere. Such is the aspect presented by the chief seat of an institution which is justly regarded as among the glories of the Empire. A glance, however, at the inscriptions on the walls—some of them in Imperial autograph—warns the visitor that he is not treading on common ground.*

---

* This paper appeared originally in the *North American Review*, July, 1874. Since that date the buildings here described have undergone a few slight repairs, but are not otherwise changed.

This impression is confirmed when, arriving at the last of the transverse buildings, it is found to be locked, and all efforts to obtain an entrance fruitless. Its yellow tiling is suggestive; and the janitor, proof against persuasion, announces, with a mysterious air, that this is a pavilion sacred to the use of the emperor. There, concealed from vulgar eyes, stands a throne, on which his Majesty sits in state whenever he deigns to honor the Academy with his presence.

Sundry inscriptions in gilded characters record the dates and circumstances of these Imperial visits, which are by no means so frequent as to be commonplace occurrences. A native guide-book to the "lions" of the capital, devoting eighteen pages to the Hanlin Yuan, dwells with special emphasis on the imposing ceremonial connected with a visit of Kienlung the Magnificent in the first year of the cycle which occurred after the commencement of his reign.

From this authority we learn that the rooms of the Academy, having fallen into a state of decay, were rebuilt by order of the Emperor, and rededicated, with solemn rites, to the service of letters. His Majesty appeared in person to do honor to the occasion, and conferred on the two presidents the favor of an entertainment in the Imperial pavilion. Of the members of the Academy not fewer than one hundred and sixty-five were present. "Among the proudest recollections of the Hall of Gems" (the Hanlin), says the chronicler, "for a thousand years there was no day like that."

The Emperor further signalized the occasion by two conspicuous gifts.

The first was a present to the library of a complete set of the wonderful encyclopædia called the *T'u-shu-chi-ch'eng*. Printed in the reign of Kanghi, on movable copper types, and comprehending a choice selection of the most valuable works, it extends to six thousand volumes, and constitutes of itself a library of no contemptible magnitude.

The other gift, less bulky, but more precious, was an original ode from the Imperial pencil. Written as an impromptu effusion in the presence of the assembled Academicians, it bears so many marks of premeditation that no one could have been imposed on by the artifice of Imperial vanity. It is engraved after the original autograph on a pair of marble slabs, from which we have taken a copy.

In their native dress these verses are worthy of their august author, who was a poet of no mean ability; but in the process of translation they lose as much as a Chinaman does in exchanging his flowing silks for the parsimonious costume of the West. At the risk of producing a travesty instead of a translation, we venture to offer a prose version.

ODE

COMPOSED BY THE EMPEROR KIENLUNG ON VISITING THE HANLIN YUAN IN 1744.

On this auspicious morning the recipients of celestial favor,
Rank after rank, unite in singing the hymn of rededication.
Thus the birds renew their plumage, and the eagle, soaring heavenward, symbolizes the rise of great men.
Those here who chant poems and expound the Book of Changes are all worthies of distinguished merit.
Their light concentres on the embroidered throne, and my pen distils its flowery characters,
While incense in spiral wreaths rises from the burning censer.
Before me is the pure, bright, pearly Hall;
Compared with this, who vaunts the genii on the islands of the blest?
A hundred years of æsthetic culture culminate in the jubilee of this day.
To maintain a state of prosperity, we must cherish fear, and rejoice with trembling.
In your new poems, therefore, be slow to extol the vastness of the Empire;
Rather by faithful advice uphold the throne.
I need not seek that ministers like Fu-Yuih shall be revealed to me in dreams;
For at this moment I am startled to find myself singing the song of Yau (in the midst of my ministers).
In my heart I rejoice that ye hundreds of officers all know my mind,

And will not fan my pride with lofty flattery.
Happy am I to enter this garden of letters,
In the soft radiance of Indian summer;
To consecrate the day to the honor of genius,
And to gather around my table the gems of learning;
But I blush at my unworthiness to entertain the successors of Fang and Tu.
Why should Ma and Tsieu be accounted solitary examples?
Here we have a new edition of the ancient Shih-chü (library of the Hans).
We behold anew the glorious light of a literary constellation.
But the shadow on the flowery tiles has reached the number eight;
Drink till you are drunk; three times pass round the bowl.
When morning sunlight fell on the pictured screen,
We opened the Hanlin with a feast,
The members assembling in official robes.
We took a glance at the library—enough to load five carts and fill four storehouses.
We visited in order the well of Lew and the pavilion of Ko.
We watch the pencil trace the gemmy page,
While the waters of Ying-chau (the Pierian Spring) rise to the brim; and in flowery cups we dispense the fragrant tea.
Anciently ministers were compared to boats which crossed rivers;
With you for my ministers I would dare to encounter the waves of the sea.

From this effusion of Imperial genius we turn again to the august body in whose honor it was written, and inquire, Where are the apartments in which those learned scribes labor on their elegant tasks? Where is the hall in which they assemble for the transaction of business? Where the library supplied by Imperial munificence for the choicest scholars of the Empire? These questions are soon answered, but not in a way to meet the expectations of the visitor. The composing-rooms are those ranges of low narrow chambers on either hand of the entrance, some of them bearing labels which indicate that it is there the Imperial will puts on its stately robes; but they are empty, and neither swept nor garnished.

Those of the members who have special functions are employed within the precincts of the palace, while the large class known as probationers prosecute their studies in a separate college called the *Shu-ch'ang-kwan.* Common hall, or assembly-room, there is none. The society holds no business meetings. Its organization is despotic; the work of the members being mapped out by the directory, which consists of the presidents and vice-presidents. In an out-of-the-way corner, you are shown a suite of small rooms, which serves as a vestry for these magnates, where they drink tea, change their robes, and post up their records. For this purpose they come together nine times a month, and remain in session about two hours.

As for the other members, they convene only on feast-days as marked in the rubrics of the State, and then it is merely for the performance of religious rites or civil ceremonies. The ritual for both (or rather the calendar) is conspicuously posted on the pillars of the front court, suggesting that the sap and juice of the Academy have dried up, and that these husks of ceremony are the residuum.

So far as this locality is concerned, this is true; for though the Academy exists, as we shall see, in undiminished vigor, the work intended to be done here is transferred to other places; and but for occasions of ceremony these halls would be as little trodden as those of the academies of Nineveh or Babylon. Of the ceremonies here performed, the most serious is the worship of Confucius, before whose shrine the company of disciples arranged in files, near or remote, according to their rank, kneel three times in the open court, and nine times bow their heads to the earth. A more modern sage, Han-wen-kung, whose chief merit was an eloquent denunciation of Buddhism, is revered as the champion of orthodoxy, and honored with one third this number of prostrations.

Besides the temples to these lights of literature, there is another shrine in which incense is perpetually burning before the tablets of certain Tauist divinities, among them the god of the North Star.

The juxtaposition of these altars illustrates the curious jumble of religious ideas which prevails even among the educated classes. If Confucianism, pure and simple, calm and philosophic, were to be found anywhere, where should we expect to meet with it if not in the halls of the Hanlin Yuan?

As to the library, it must have been at least respectable in the palmy days of Kienlung—that Emperor having replenished it, as we have seen, by a gift of six thousand volumes. Copies of a still larger collection of works, the *Sze-k'u-ch'uen-shu*, printed in the earlier part of the same reign, were deposited there, as also a manuscript copy of the immense collection known as *Yung-lo-ta-tien.* But in China, libraries are poorly preserved; books have no proper binding, the leaves are loosely stitched, the paper flimsy and adapted to the taste of a variety of insects, while their official guardians often commit depredations under the influence of an appetite not altogether literary.

Through these combined influences, the Hanlin library has dwindled almost to a vanishing-point. Two of the book-rooms being within the sacred enclosure of the Imperial pavilion, the writer was not permitted to see them. The greater part of the books have been transferred elsewhere; and the condition of those that remain may be inferred from that of the only book-room that was accessible. Its furniture consisted of half a dozen cases, some locked, some open—the latter empty; the floor was strewn with fragments of paper, and the absence of footprints in the thick deposit of dust sufficiently indicated that the pathway to this fountain of knowledge is no longer frequented.

But things in China are not to be estimated by ordinary rules. Here the decay of a building is no indication of the decadence of the institution which it represents. The public buildings of the Chinese are, for the most part, mean and contemptible in comparison with those of Western nations; but it would not be less erroneous for us to judge their civilization by the state of their architecture than for them, as they are prone to do, to measure ours by the tape-line of our tailor. With them architecture is not a fine art; public edifices of every class are constructed on a uniform model; and even in private dwellings there is no such thing as novelty or variety of design. The original idea of both is incapable of much development; the wooden frame and limited height giving them an air of meanness; while the windowless wall, which caution or custom requires to be drawn around every considerable building, excludes it from the public view, and consequently diminishes, if it does not destroy, the desire for æsthetic effect. Materialistic as the people are in their habits of thought, their government, based on ancient maxims, has sought to repress rather than encourage the tendency to luxury in this direction. The genius of China does not affect excellence in material arts. With more propriety than ancient Rome she might apply to herself the lines of the Roman poet:

> "Excudent alii spirantia mollius æra
> . . . regere imperio populos . . .
> Hæ tibi erunt artes; pacisque imponere morem."

For not only is the Chinese notoriously backward in all those accomplishments in which the Roman excelled, but, without being warlike, he has equalled the Roman in the extent of his conquests, and surpassed him in the permanence of his possessions. With him the art of government is the "great study;" and all else—science, literature, religion—merely subsidiary.

For six hundred years, with the exception of a brief interval, the Hanlin has had its home within the walls of Peking, witnessing from this position the rise of three Imperial dynasties and the overthrow of two. Under the Mongols it stood, not on its present site, but a little to the west of the present drum-tower. Kublai and his successors testified their sense of its importance by installing it in an old palace of the Kin Tartars. Eo-yang-ch'u, a discontented scholar of a later age, alluding to the contrast presented by the quarters it then occupied, laments in verse

"The splendid abode of the old Hanlin,
The glittering palace of the Prince of Kin."

The Ming emperors removed it to its present position, appropriating for its use the site of an old granary. The Tsing emperors had a palace to bestow on the Mongolian lamas, but allowed the Hanlin to remain in its contracted quarters, erecting at the same time, in immediate contiguity, a palace for one of their princes. This is now occupied by the British Legation, whose lofty chimneys overlook the grounds of the Academy, and so menace the *fung-shuy* (good luck) of the entire literary corporation. If this were the whole of its history, the Hanlin would still enjoy the distinction of being more than twice as ancient as any similar institution now extant in the Western world; but this last period—one of few vicissitudes—covers no more than half its career. Its annals run back to twice six hundred years, and during that long period it has shared the fortunes and followed the footsteps of the several dynastics which have contended for the mastery of the Empire. From its nature and constitution attached to the court, it has migrated with the court, now north, now south, until the capital became fixed in its present position. At the beginning of the fifteenth century, the Academy was for a few years at Nanking, where Hungwu made his capital. During the period of the Crusades it accompanied the court of the Southern Sungs as they retired before the invading Tartars, and fixed at Hangchau the seat of their semi-empire. For two centuries previous it had shed its lustre on Pienliang, the capital of the Northern Sungs.

During the five short dynasties (907–960) it disappears amidst the confusion of perpetual war, though even then each aspirant for "The Yellow" surrounded himself with some semblance of the Hanlin, as a circumstance essential to Imperial state; but its earliest, brightest, and longest period of repose was the reign of the Tangs, from 627 to 904, or from the rise of Mahomet till the death of Alfred. For China this is not an ancient date;

but it was scarcely possible that such a body, with such objects, should come into existence at any earlier epoch. Under the more ancient dynasties the range of literature was limited, and the style of composition rude. It is not till the long reign of the house of Han that the language obtains its full maturity; but even then taste was little cultivated—the writers of that day being, as the native critics say, more studious of matter than of manner. During the short-lived dynasties that followed the Han and Tsin, the struggle for power allowed no breathing-time for the revival of letters; but when the Empire, so long drenched in blood, was at length united under the sway of the Tangs, the beginning of the new era of peace and prosperity was marked by an outburst of literary splendor.

For twenty years Kaotsu, the founder, had been involved in sanguinary conflicts. In such circumstances valor was virtue, and military skill comprised all that was valued in learning. In the work of domestic conquest, his most efficient aid was his second son, Shemin. Destined to complete what his father had begun, but with a genius more comprehensive and a taste more refined, this young prince was to Kaotsu what Alexander was to Philip, or Frederick the Great to the rough Frederick William. Studying the poets and philosophers by the light of his camp-fires, he no sooner found himself in undisputed possession of the throne than he addressed himself to the promotion of learning. In this he was only reverting to the traditions of an empire which from the earliest times had always been a worshipper of letters. But Taitsung (the name by which he is called in history) did not confine himself to the beaten path of tradition; he issued a decree that men of ability should be sought out and brought to court from their retired homes and secret hiding-places. His predecessors had done the same; but Taitsung formed them into a body under the name of Wen-hio-kuan, and installed them in a portion of his palace, where, the historian tells us, he was accustomed, in the intervals of business and late in the hours of the night, to converse with these learned doctors. The number of these eminent scholars was eighteen, in allusion possibly (though a Confucian would repudiate the idea) to the number of Arhans or disciples who composed the inner circle of the family of Buddha—Buddhism being at that time in high repute. Among these the most prominent were Fang-yuenling and Tu-juhui, who were afterwards advanced to the rank of ministers of State. We have already seen their names in the Ode of Kienlung, where they are alluded to as the typical ancestors of the literary brotherhood. This was the germ of the Hanlin Yuan.

Under previous reigns letters had been valued solely as an aid to politics, and scholarship as a proof of qualification for civil employment. But from this time letters began to assume the position of a final cause, and civil employment was made use of as an incentive to encourage their cultivation. Previously to this the single exercise of answering in writing a series of questions intended to gauge the erudition and test the acumen of the candidate was all that was required in examinations for the civil service; but from this epoch taste presided in the literary arena, and compositions, both in prose and verse, in which elegance of style is the chief aim became thenceforth a leading feature in the curriculum. That wonderful net which catches the big fish for the service of the Emperor, and allows the smaller ones to slip through, was during this dynasty so far perfected that in the lapse of a thousand years it has undergone no very important change. As might have been expected, the epoch of the Tangs became distinguished above all preceding dynasties as the age of poets. Litaipe—whose brilliant genius was believed to be an incarnation of the golden light of the planet Venus—Tufu, Hanyu, and others shed lustre on its opening reigns. Their works have become the acknowledged model of poetic composition, from which no modern writer dares to depart; and, under the collective title of the poetry of Tang, they have added to the Imperial crown an amaranthine wreath such as no other dynasty has ever worn. Litaipe was admitted to the Academy by Minghwang or Huentsung; the Emperor, on that occasion, giving him a feast, and, as native authors say, condescending to stir the poet's soup with the hand that bore the sceptre.

It is not a little remarkable that the art of printing made its appearance almost simultaneously with the formation of the Academy and the reorganization of the examination system. Originating in a common impulse, all three interacted on each other, and worked together as powerful agencies in carrying forward the common movement. The method of stamping characters on silk or paper had no doubt been discovered long before; but it was under this dynasty that it was first employed for the reproduction of books on a large scale. It was not, however, so employed in the reign of Taitsung. That monarch, resolving to found a library that should surpass in extent and magnificence anything that had been known in the past, was unable to imagine a more expeditious, or, at least, a more satisfactory, method of producing books than the slow process of transcription. For this purpose a host of pencils would be required; and Taitsung, in the interest of his library, made a fresh levy of learned men who were elegant scribes as well as able scholars. To these, Huentsung, one of his successors, added another body of scholars, and, combining the three classes into one society, called it by the name of *Hanlin*, or the "Forest of Pencils"—a designation that was now more appropriate than it would have been when the number of its members fell short of a score.

When the printing-press was introduced as an auxiliary in the manufacture of books, it relieved the Imperial scribes of a portion of their labors, but it did not supersede them. Released from the drudgery of copying, they were free to devote their leisure to composition; and in China in the eighth century, as in Europe in the fifteenth, the art of printing imparted a powerful stimulus to the intellectual activity of the age.

Rising, as we have seen, in the halcyon days of Taitsung, the Hanlin Yuan was not long in attaining its full development. In the reign of Huentsung it received the name by which it is now known, and through twelve centuries, from that day to this, it has undergone no essential modification, either in its objects, membership, or mode of operation; if we except, perhaps, the changes required to adapt it to the duplicate official system of the present dynasty. Its constitution and functions, as laid down in the *Ta-ts'ing-hwui-tien*, or Institutes of the Empire, are as follows:

1. There shall be two presidents—one Manchu and one Chinese. They shall superintend the composition of dynastic histories, charts, books, Imperial decrees, and literary matters in general.

2. The vice-presidents shall be of two classes; namely, the readers, and the expositors to his Majesty the Emperor. In each class there shall be three Manchus and three Chinese.

3. Besides these, the regular members shall consist of three classes—namely, Siuchoan, Piensieu, and Kientao—in all of which the number is not limited. These, together with the vice-presidents, shall be charged with the composition and compilation of books, and with daily attendance at stated times on the classic studies of his Majesty.

4. There shall be a class of candidates on probation, termed Shuki shi, "lucky scholars," the number not fixed. These shall not be charged with any specific duty, but shall prosecute their studies in the schools attached to the Academy. They shall study both Manchu and Chinese. Their studies shall be directed by two professors—one Manchu and one Chinese—assisted by other members below the grade of readers and expositors, who shall act as divisional tutors. At the expiration of three years they shall be tested as to their ability in poetical composition, the Emperor in person deciding their grades, after which they shall be admitted to an audience; those of the first three

grades being received into full membership, and those of the fourth grade, which comprises the remainder, being assigned to posts in the civil service, or retained for another three years to study and be examined with the next class.

5. There shall be two recorders—one Manchu and one Chinese. These shall be charged with the sending and receiving of documents.

6. There shall be two librarians—one Manchu and one Chinese. These shall be charged with the care of the books and charts.

7. There shall be four proof-readers—two Manchus and two Chinese. These shall attend to the revision and collation of histories, memorials, and other literary compositions.

8. There shall be forty-four clerks—forty Manchus and four from the Chinese Banners. These shall be employed in copying and translation.

9. The expositors at the classic table (of the Emperor) shall be sixteen in number—eight Manchus and eight Chinese. The Manchus must be officers who have risen from the third rank or higher. The Chinese also must be of the third rank or higher, having risen from the Academy. These shall be appointed by the Emperor on the recommendation of the Academy. The classic feasts shall take place twice a year—namely, in the second and the eighth month; at which time one Manchu and one Chinese shall expound the Book of History, and one Manchu and one Chinese shall expound the other classics, to be selected from a list prepared by the Academy. The subject and sense of the passages to be treated on these occasions shall in all cases be arranged by consultation with the presidents of the Academy, and laid before the Emperor for his approval. When the Emperor visits the "Palace of Literary Glory," these expositors, together with the other officers, shall perform their prostrations at the foot of the steps, after which their going in and out shall be according to the form prescribed in the Code of Rites. When

they shall have finished their expositions, they shall respectfully listen to the discourses of the Emperor.

10. The daily expositors shall be twenty-eight Manchus and twelve Chinese. They shall be above the grade of Kientao and below that of president, and may discharge this duty without resigning their original offices.

11. Prayers and sacrificial addresses for several occasions shall be drawn up by the Hanlin and submitted to the Emperor for his approval. These occasions are the following: namely, at the Altar of Heaven; the Ancestral Temple; the Imperial Cemeteries; the Altar of Agriculture; sacrifices to mountains, seas, and lakes, and to the ancient sage Confucius.

12. The Hanlin shall respectfully prepare honorary titles for the dowager empresses: they shall also draw up patents of dignity for the chief concubines of the late emperor; forms of investiture for new empresses and the chief concubines of new emperors; patents of nobility for princes, dukes, generals, and for feudal states; together with inscriptions on State seals—all of which shall first be submitted for the Imperial approbation.

13. The Hanlin shall respectfully propose posthumous titles for deceased emperors, together with monumental inscriptions and sacrificial addresses for those who are accorded the honor of a posthumous title—all of which shall be submitted to the Emperor for approval.

14. The presidents of the Hanlin shall be *ex officio* vice-presidents of the Bureau of Contemporary History, in which the Hanlin of subordinate grades shall assist as compilers and composers, reverentially recording the sacred instructions (of the Emperor).

15. Prescribes the order of attendance for the Hanlin when the Emperor appears in public court.

16. Prescribes the number and quality of those of the Hanlin who shall attend his Majesty during his sojourn at the Yuen-Ming-Yuen (Summer Palace).

17. Provides that those members of the Hanlin whose duty it is to accompany his Majesty on his various journeys beyond the capital shall be recommended by the presidents of the Academy.

18. Provides that when the Emperor sends a deputy to sacrifice to Confucius, certain senior members of the Academy shall make offerings to the twelve chief disciples of the Sage.

19. The Hanlin, in conjunction with the Board of Rites, shall copy out and publish the best specimens of the essays produced in the provincial and metropolitan examinations.

20. Prescribes the form to be used in reporting or recommending members for promotion, and provides that when an examination is held for the selection of Imperial censors, the Piensieu and Kientao, on recommendation, may be admitted as candidates.

21. Regulates examinations for the admission of probationary members.

22. Admits probationers, after three years of study, to an examination for places in the Academy or official posts elsewhere.

23. Provides for examinations of regular members in presence of the Emperor, at uncertain times, in order to prevent their relapse into idleness.

24. Provides for the promotion of members who are employed as instructors or probationers.

Such is the official account of the Hanlin as at present constituted; but what information does it convey? After all we have done in the way of explanation in connection with a rather free translation, it still remains a confused mass of titles and ceremonies, utterly devoid of any principle of order; and without the help of collateral information, much of it would be altogether unintelligible. Interrogate it as to the number of members, the qualifications required for membership, the duration of membership, the manner of obtaining their seats (a term which must be used metaphorically of an association in which all but a few are expected to stand), and it is silent as the Sphinx. Should one, with a view to satisfying curiosity on the first point, attempt to reckon up the number of classes or divisions, to say nothing of individuals, the number being in some cases purposely indefinite, he would certainly fail of success. Some who are enumerated in those divisions are official employés of the society, but not members; and yet there is nothing in the text to indicate the fact: e. g., the proof-readers are Hanlins, the copyists and translators are not; the librarians are Hanlins, the recorders are not. We shall endeavor briefly to elucidate these several points.

Unlike the academies of Europe, which are voluntary associations for the advancement of learning under royal or imperial patronage, the Hanlin is a body of civil functionaries, a government organ, an integral part of the machinery of the State: its mainspring, as that of every other portion, is in the throne. Its members do not seek admission from love of learning, but for the distinction it confers, and especially as a passport to lucrative employment. They are consequently in a state of perpetual transition, spending from six to ten years in attendance at the Academy, and then going into the provinces as triennial examiners, as superintendents of education, or even in civil or military employments which have no special relation to letters. In all these situations they proudly retain the title of member of the Imperial Academy; and, in their memorials to the throne, one may sometimes see it placed above that of provincial treasurer or judge.

There are, moreover, several *yamens* in the capital that are manned almost exclusively from the members of the Hanlin. Of these the principal are the *chan-shih-fu* and the *ch'i-chü-ch'u;* both of which are, in fact, nothing more than appendages of the Academy. The former, the name of which affords no hint of its functions, appears to bear some such relation to the heir-apparent as the Hanlin does to the Emperor. The beggarly building in which its official meetings are held may be seen on the banks of the canal opposite to the British Legation. It is, nevertheless, regarded as a highly aristocratic body, and gives employment to a score or so of Academicians. The other, which may be described as the Bureau of Daily Record, employs some twenty more of the Hanlins in the capacity of Boswells to the reigning Emperor, their duty being to preserve a minute record of all his words and actions.

Among the Imperial censors, who form a distinct tribunal, a majority perhaps are taken from the ranks of the Hanlin, but they are not exclusively so; while the higher ranks of the Hanlin, without being connected with the censorate, are *ex officio* counsellors to his Majesty. Of those whose names are on the rolls as active members of the Academy in regular attendance on its meetings, the number does not exceed three or four score; though on great occasions, such as the advent of an emperor, the ex-members who are within reach are called in and swell the number to twice or thrice that figure. Besides these are the probationers or candidates, to the number of a hundred or more, who pursue their studies for three years under the auspices of the Academy, and then stand examination for membership. If successful, they take their places with the rank and file of the Imperial scribes; otherwise, they are assigned posts in the civil service, such as those of sub-prefect, district magistrate, etc., carrying with them in every position the distinction of having been connected, for however brief a time, with the Imperial Academy. Without counting those rejected candidates, whose claim to the title is more than doubtful, the actual and passed members probably do not fall short of five hundred.

The qualifications for membership are two—natural talent and rare acquisitions in all the departments of Chinese scholarship; but of these we shall treat more at length hereafter. The new members are not admitted by vote of the association, nor appointed by the will of their Imperial master. The seats in this Olympus are put up to competition, and, as in the Hindoo mythology, the gifted aspirant, though without name or influence, and in spite of opposition, may win the immortal *amreet.* None enter as the result of capricious favor, and no one is excluded in consequence of unfounded prejudice.

The Hanlin Yuan has not, therefore, like the Institute of France, a long list of illustrious names who acquire additional distinction from having been rejected or overlooked; neither does it suffer from lampoons such as that which a disappointed poet fixed on his own tombstone at the expense of the French Academy—

> "Ci-gît Piron, qui ne fut rien,
> Pas même académicien."

In the Chinese Academy the newly initiated has the proud consciousness that he owes everything to himself, and nothing to the complaisance of his associates or the patronage of his superiors.

Of the duties of the Hanlin, these official regulations afford us a better idea—indicating each line of intellectual activity, from the selection of fancy names for people in high position up to the conducting of provincial examinations and the writing of national histories; but the advancement of science is not among them. They do nothing to extend the boundaries of human knowledge, simply because they are not aware that after the achievements of Confucius and the ancient sages any new world remains to be conquered. Towards the close of the last year the Emperor, by special decree, referred to the Academy the responsibility of proposing honorific titles for the Empress-dowager and the Empress-mother. The result was the pair of euphonious pendants, Kangyi and Kangking, with which the Imperial ladies were decorated on retiring from the regency; and we are left to imagine the anxious deliberations, the laborious search for precedents, the minute comparison of the historical and poetical allusions involved in each title, before the learned body were able to arrive at a decision.

The composition of prayers to be used by his Majesty or his deputies on sundry occasions, and the writing of inscriptions for the temples of various divinities, in acknowledgment of services, are among the lighter tasks of the Hanlin. They are not, however, like that above referred to, of rare occurrence. Ambitious of anything that can confer distinction on their respective localities, the people of numerous districts petition the throne to honor the temple where they worship by the gift of an Imperial inscription. They ascertain that some time within the past twenty years the divinity there worshipped has interfered to prevent a swollen river from bursting its banks; to avert a plague of locusts, or arrest a protracted drought; or, by a nocturnal display of spectral armies, to drive away a horde of rebels. They report the facts in the case to their magistrates, who verify them, and forward the application to the Emperor, who in turn directs the members of the Hanlin to write the desired inscription. Cases of this kind abound in the Peking gazette; one of those best known to foreigners being that of Sze-tai-wang at Tientsin, whose merit in checking, under the avatar of a serpent, the disastrous floods of 1871 obtained from the Emperor the honor of a commemorative tablet written by the doctors of the Hanlin.

If to these we add the scrolls and tablets written by Imperial decree for schools and charitable institutions throughout the Empire, we must confess that the Hanlin Yuan might earn for itself the title of Academy of Inscriptions in a sense somewhat different from that in which the term is employed in the Western World. Indeed, so disproportionate is the space allotted in the constitution to these petty details that the reader, judging from that document alone, would be liable to infer that the Academicians were seldom burdened with any more serious employment. But let him go into one of the great libraries connected with the court (unhappily not yet accessible to the foreign student), or even to the great book-stores of the Chinese city, and he will learn at a glance that the Hanlin is not a mere piece of Oriental pageantry. Let him ask for the Book of Odes; the salesman hands him an Imperial edition in twenty volumes, with notes and illustrations by the doctors of the Hanlin. If he inquire for the Book of Rites, or any of the thirteen canonical books, the work is shown him in the same elegant type, equally voluminous in extent, and executed by the hands of the same inexhaustible editors. Then there are histories without number; next to the classics in dignity, and far exceeding them in extent.

If the poems of India, such as the Mahâbhârat, in length outmeasuring half a score of Iliads, suggest the idea of the infinite, the histories of China are adapted to produce a similar impression. There are in the capital, at this present time, no fewer than four bureaus or colleges of history, constantly occupied, not, as might be supposed, with the history of other countries and distant ages, but with the events of the present reign and those of its immediate predecessor. These are all conducted by members of the Hanlin; and the scale on which they execute their tasks may be inferred from the fact that the Bureau of Military History recently reported the completion of a portion of its labors in seven hundred and twenty books, or about three hundred and sixty volumes. These only cover the Taiping and Nienfei rebellions, leaving the Mahometan and foreign wars of the last seventeen years to be spun out probably to an equal extent.

Here is a paragraph from the instructions of one of these bureaus, which, in respect to the laborious minuteness which they exact, may be taken as a sample of the whole:

"They (the scribes) are to take note of the down-sitting and uprising of his Majesty, and to keep a record of his every word and action. They are to attend his Majesty when he holds court and gives audience; when he visits the Altar of Heaven or the Temple of Ancestors; when he holds a feast of the classics, or ploughs the sacred field; when he visits the schools or reviews the troops; when he bestows entertainments, celebrates a military triumph, or decides the fate of criminals. They must follow the Emperor in his hunting excursions, and during his sojourn at his country palace. They will hear the Imperial voice with reverence, and record its utterances with care, appending to every entry the date and name of the writer. At the end of every month these records shall be sealed up and deposited in a desk, and at the close of the year transferred to the custody of the Inner Council."

Besides these dynastic histories, there are topographical histories of provinces, prefectures, districts, and even of towns and villages, in number and extent to which we have no parallel. In most of these the government takes a direct interest, and as far as possible they are edited by members of the Hanlin; e. g., a supplement is now being made at Paotingfu to the history of the province of Chihli, bringing it through the troubled days of the Taiping rebellion and foreign invasion, down to the present time. It is executed under the superintendence of a Hanlin Piensieu, whose services were not obtained without a special application to the throne by the Viceroy Li Hung Chang.

In addition to work of this kind, which is constant as the stream of time, the Hanlin supplies writers and editors for all the literary enterprises of the Emperor. Some of these are so vast that it is safe to say no people would undertake them but those who erected the Great Wall and excavated the Grand Canal; nor would China have had the courage to face them had she not kept on foot as a permanent institution a standing army of learned writers.

Two of these colossal enterprises distinguish the brilliant prime of the present dynasty; while a third, of proportions still more huge, dates back to the second reign of the Mings. This last is the *Yung-lo-ta-tien*, a cyclopædic digest of the Imperial library, which at that time contained 300,000 volumes.

There were employed in the task 2169 clerks and copyists, under the direction of a commission consisting of three presidents, five vice-presidents, and twenty sub-directors. The work, when completed, contained 22,937 books, or about half that number of volumes. It was never printed as a whole, and two of the three manuscript copies, together with about a tenth part of the third, were destroyed by fire in the convulsions that attended the overthrow of the Mings.

In the reign of Kanghi (latter part of the seventeenth century) a similar compilation was executed, numbering 6000 volumes, and beautifully printed on movable copper types, with the title of *T'u-shu-chi-ch'eng.*

About a century later, under Kienlung, a still larger collection, intended to supplement the former, and preserve all that was most valuable in the extant literature, was printed on movable wooden types with the title of *Sze-k'u-ch'uen-shu.* These two collections reproduce a great part of the preceding; nevertheless, great pains have been taken to copy out and preserve the original work. A commission of members of the Hanlin was appointed for this purpose by Kienlung, and a copy of the work, it is said, now forms a part of the Hanlin library. In this connection we may mention two other great works executed under the Mings, which have been reproduced by the present dynasty in an abridged or modified form. While the codification of the laws found in Yunglo a Chinese Justinian, it found its Tribonians among the doctors of the Academy. The Encyclopædia of Philosophy, compiled by the Hanlin under Yunglo, the second of the Mings, was abridged by the Hanlin, under Kanghi, the second of the Tsings. A still more important labor of the Hanlin, performed by order of the last-named illustrious ruler, was the dictionary which bears his name—a labor more in keeping with its character as a literary corporation.

Thiers speaks of the French Academy as having *la mission à régler la marche de la langue.* It did this by publishing its famous dictionary; and about the same time the members of the Hanlin were performing a similar task for the language of China, by the preparation of the great dictionary of Kanghi—a work which stands much higher as an authority than does the *Dictionnaire de l'Académie Française.* A small work, not unworthy of mention in connection with these grave labors, is the Sacred Edict, which goes under the name of Kanghi. It is not, however, the composition of either Kanghi or Yung-cheng, but purely a production of Hanlin pencils. In the Memoirs of the Academy we find a decree assigning the task and prescribing the mode of performance:

"'Taking,' says the Emperor, 'the sixteen edicts (or maxims of seven words each) of our sacred ancestor surnamed the Benevolent for a basis, we desire to expand and illustrate their meaning, for the instruction of our soldiers and people. Let the members of the Hanlin compose an essay, of between five and six hundred characters, on each text, in a plain and lucid style, shunning alike the errors of excessive polish and rusticity. Let the same text be given to eight or nine persons, each of whom will prepare a discourse, and hand it in in a sealed envelope.'"

From this it appears that the sixteen elegant discourses which compose the body of that work are selections from over a hundred—the picked performances of picked men.

In the early part of the Manchu dynasty, the Hanlin were much engaged in superintending the translation of Chinese works into Manchu, a language now so little understood by the Tartars of Peking that those voluminous versions have almost ceased to be of any practical value. Under the present reign the learned doctors have been working somewhat in a different direction, showing that the Chinese are not so incapable of innovation as is usually supposed. A minority reign naturally suggested the want of a royal road to the acquisition of knowledge; our Hanlin doctors were accordingly directed to supply his Majesty with copies of History *made easy* and the Classics *made easy*. The mode of making easy was a careful rendering into the Mandarin or court dialect—a style which these admirable doctors disdain as much as the mediæval scholars of Europe did the vernacular of their day. May we not hope that these works, after educating the Emperor, will, like those prepared by the Jesuits *in usum Delphini*, be brought to the light for the instruction of his people?

As it is intended here to indicate the variety rather than the extent of the literary labors of the Hanlin, these remarks would be incomplete if they did not refer to their poetry. They are all poets; each a laureate, devoting his talents to the glorification of his Imperial patron. Swift said of an English laureate,

> "Young must torture his invention
> To flatter knaves, or lose a pension."

In China the office is not held on such a condition. Sage emperors have been known to strike out with their own pen the finest compliments offered them by their official bards. Kienlung, as we have seen, felt it necessary to warn the Hanlin against the prevailing vice of poets and pensioners. In China poetry is put to a better purpose; Imperial decrees and official proclamations being often expressed in verse, for the same reason that induced Solon to borrow the aid of verse in the promulgation of his laws. Didactic compositions in verse are without number, and for the most part as dry as Homer's catalogue of the fleet. A popular cyclopædia, for instance, in over a score of volumes, treats of all imaginable subjects in a kind of irregular verse called *fu*.

Employed as scribes and editors, it would be too much to expect that the Hanlin should distinguish themselves for originality. It is a rare thing for an original work to spring from the brain of an Academician. In imitation of Confucius, they might inscribe over their door, "We edit, but we do not compose."

"On entering this hall," said M. Thiers, taking his seat in the

French Academy forty years ago, "I feel the proudest recollections of our national history awakening within me. Here it is that Corneille, Bossuet, Voltaire, and Montesquieu, one after another, came and took their seats; and here more recently have sat Laplace and Cuvier. . . . Three great men, Laplace, Lagrange, and Cuvier, opened the century; a numerous band of young and ardent intellects have followed in their wake. Some study the primeval history of our planet, thereby to illustrate the history of its inhabitants; others, impelled by the love of humanity, strive to subjugate the elements in order to ameliorate the condition of man; still others study all ages and traverse all countries, in hopes of adding something to the treasures of intellectual and moral philosophy. . . . Standing in the midst of you, the faithful and constant friends of science, permit me to exclaim, happy are those who take part in the noble labors of this age!"

In this passage we have a true portraiture of the spirit that animates the *peerage* of the Western intellect; they lead the age in every path of improvement, and include in their number those whom a viceroy of Egypt felicitously described, not as *peers*, but as *les têtes couronnées de la science.* How different from the drowsy routine which prevails in the chief tribunal of Chinese learning! Of all this the Chinese Academician has no conception; he is an anachronism, his country is an anachronism, as far in the rear of the world's great march as were the people of a secluded valley, mentioned in Chinese literature, who, finding there an asylum from trouble and danger, declined intercourse with the rest of mankind, and after the lapse of many centuries imagined that the dynasty of Han was still upon the throne.

It is doing our Hanlin a species of injustice to compare him with the Academicians, or even with the commonalty of the West, in a scientific point of view; for science is just the thing which he does not profess, and that general information which is regarded as indispensable by the average intelligence of

Christendom is to the Hanlin a foreign currency, which has no recognized value in the market of his country; nevertheless, we shall proceed to interrogate him as to his information on a few points, merely for the sake of bringing to view the actual condition of the educated mind of China.

In history he can recite with familiar ease the dynastic records of his own country for thousands of years; but he never heard of Alexander or Cæsar or the first Napoleon. Of the third Napoleon he may have learned something from a faint echo of the catastrophe at Sedan, certainly not from the missions of Burlingame or Ch'unghau—events that are yet too recent to have reached the ears of these students of antiquity, who, whatever their faults, are not chargeable with being *rerum novarum avidi.*

In geography he is not at home even among the provinces of China proper, and becomes quite bewildered when he goes to the north of the Great Wall. Of Columbus and the New World he is profoundly ignorant, not knowing in what part of the globe lies the America of which he may have heard as one among the Treaty Powers. With the names of England and France he is better acquainted, as they have left their record in opened ports and ruined palaces. Russia he thinks of as a semi-barbarous state, somewhere among the Mongolian tribes, which formerly brought tribute, and was vanquished in conflict—her people being led in triumph by the prowess of Kanghi.*

In astronomy he maintains the dignity of our native globe as the centre of the universe, as his own country is the middle of the habitable earth—a conviction in which he is confirmed by the authority of those learned Jesuits who persisted in teaching the Ptolemaic system three centuries after the time of Copernicus. Of longitude and latitude he has no conception; and re-

---

* The Siberian garrison of Albazin were brought to Peking, where their descendants still reside.

fuses even to admit the globular form of the earth, because an ancient tradition asserts that "heaven is round and the earth square." To him the stars are shining characters on the book of fate, and eclipses portents of approaching calamity.

In zoology he believes that tigers plunging into the sea are transformed into sharks, and that sparrows by undergoing the same baptism are converted into oysters; for the latter metamorphosis is gravely asserted in canonical books, and the former is a popular notion which he cares not to question. Arithmetic he scorns as belonging to shopkeepers; and mechanics he disdains on account of its relation to machinery and implied connection with handicraft.

Of general physics he nevertheless holds an ill-defined theory, which has for its basis the dual forces that generated the universe, and the five elements which profess to comprehend all forms of matter, but omit the atmosphere. Of the nature of these elements his text-book gives the following luminous exposition: namely, that "the nature of water is to run downward; the nature of fire is to flame upward; the nature of wood is to be either crooked or straight; the nature of metals is to be pliable, and subject to change; the nature of earth is to serve the purposes of agriculture." *

So weighty is the information contained in these sentences that he accepts them as a special revelation, the bed-rock of human knowledge, beneath which it would be useless, if not profane, to attempt to penetrate. It never occurs to our philosopher to inquire *why* water flows downward, and *why* fire ascends; to his mind both are ultimate facts. On this foundation human sagacity has erected the pantheon of universal science. This it has done by connecting the five elements with the five planets, the five senses, the five musical tones, the five colors, and the five great mountain-ranges of the earth; the

* From the Hungfan in the Shuking.

quintal classification originating in the remarkable observation that man has five fingers on his hand, and setting forth the harmony of nature as a connected whole with a beautiful simplicity that one seeks for in vain in the Kosmos of Humboldt.

This system, which our Hanlin accepts, though he does not claim the merit of having originated it, is not a mere fanciful speculation; it is a practical doctrine skilfully adapted to the uses of human life. In medicine it enables him to adapt his remedies to the nature of the disease. When he has contracted a fever on shipboard or in a dwelling that has a wooden floor, he perceives at once the origin of his malady, or his physician informs him that "wood produces fire;" earth is wanted to restore the balance, i. e. life on shore, or outdoor exercise.

In the conduct of affairs it enables him to get the lucky stars in his favor, and, through the learned labors of the Board of Astronomy, it places in his hands a guide-book which informs him when he should commence or terminate an enterprise, when he may safely venture abroad, and when it would be prudent to remain at home. It enables him to calculate futurity, and obtain the advantages of a kind of *scientia media*, or conditional foreknowledge; to know how to arrange a marriage so as to secure felicity according to the horoscope of the parties; and ascertain where to locate the dwellings of the living or the resting-places of the dead, in order to insure to their families the largest amount of prosperity.

These occult sciences the Hanlin believes implicitly, but he does not profess to understand them—contented in such matters to be guided by the opinion of professional experts. A Sadducee in creed and an epicure in practice, the comforts of the present life constitute his highest idea of happiness; yet he never thinks of devising any new expedient for promoting the physical well-being of his people. Like some of the philosophers of our Western antiquity, he would feel degraded by occupation with anything lower than politics and ethics, or less refined than poetry and rhetoric. "Seneca," says Lord Macaulay, "labors to clear Democritus from the disgraceful imputation of having made the first arch; and Anacharsis from the charge of having contrived the potter's wheel." No such apologist is required for our doctors of the Hanlin, inasmuch as no such impropriety was ever laid to their charge.

The noble motto of the French Institute, *Invenit et perfecit*, is utterly alien from the spirit and aims of the Academicians of China. With them the Golden Age is in the remote past; everything for the good of human society has been anticipated by the wisdom of the ancients.

"Omnia jam ferme mortalibus esse parata."

Nothing remains for them to do but to walk in the footsteps of their remote ancestors.

Having thus subjected our Academician to an examination in the elements of a modern education, we must again caution our readers against taking its result as a gauge of mental power or actual culture. In knowledge, according to our standard, he is a child; in intellectual force, a giant. A veteran athlete, the victor of a hundred conflicts, his memory is prodigious, his apprehension quick, and his taste in literary matters exquisite.

"It is a dangerous error," says an erudite editor of Sir W. Hamilton, "to regard the cultivation of our faculties as subordinate to the acquisition of knowledge, instead of knowledge being subordinate to the cultivation of our faculties. In consequence of this error, those sciences which afford a greater number of more certain facts have been deemed superior in utility to those which bestow a higher cultivation on the higher faculties of the mind."

The peculiar discipline under which the Hanlin is educated, with its advantages and defects, we shall indicate in another place. Before quitting this branch of the subject, we may remark, however, that its result as witnessed in the Hanlin is not, as generally supposed, a feeble, superficial polish which unfits its recipient for the duties of practical life; on the contrary, membership in the Hanlin is avowedly a preparation for the discharge of political functions, a stepping-stone to the highest offices in the State. The Academician is not restricted to functions that partake of a literary character; he may be a viceroy as well as a provincial examiner; a diplomatic minister as well as a rhymester of the court.

In glancing over the long catalogue of the academic Legion of Honor, one is struck by the large proportion of names that have become eminent in the history of their country.

We have had occasion more than once in the preceding pages to refer to the Memoirs of the Academy. These records, unfortunately, extend back no further than the accession of the present dynasty, in 1644; and they terminate with 1801, comprising only a little more than one and a half of the twelve centuries of the society's existence. Published under Imperial auspices in thirty-two thin volumes, they are so divided that the books or sections amount to the cabalistic number sixty-four, the square of the number of the original diagrams which form the basis of the *Yih-king*, the national Book of Divination.

The first thing that strikes us on opening these pages is the spirit of imperialism with which they appear to be saturated. The transactions of his Majesty constitute the chief subject; the performances of the members are mentioned only incidentally; and the whole association is exhibited in the character of an elaborate system of belts and satellites purposely adjusted to reflect the splendor of a central luminary. Cast your eye over the table of contents, and see with what relief this idea stands out as a controlling principle in the arrangement of the work.

The first two books are devoted to what are called *Sheng Yu*, Holy Edicts, i.e. expressions of the Imperial mind in regard to the affairs of the society in any manner, however informal.

Six books are given to *T'ien-chang*, or Celestial Rhetoric, i. e. productions of the vermilion pencil in prose and verse. Eight books record the imposing ceremonies connected with Imperial visits; six books commemorate the marks of Imperial favor bestowed on members of the Academy; sixteen of the remaining forty-two are occupied with a catalogue of those members who have been honored with appointments to serve in the Imperial presence, or with special commissions of other kinds. In the residuary twenty-six we should expect to find specimens of the proper work of the Academy, and so we do; for no less than three books are taken up with ceremonial tactics; forms to be observed in attendance on the Emperor on sundry occasions, the etiquette of official intercourse, etc.; these things occupying a place among the serious business of the society. Fourteen are filled with specimens of prose and verse from the pens of leading members, and one is assigned to a high-flown description of the magnificence of the academical buildings; the rest contain a meagre catalogue of official employments and literary labors.

What a picture does this present—a picture drawn by themselves—of the highest literary corporation in the Empire! Yet, notwithstanding the enormous toadyism with which they are inflated, we do not hesitate to say that the twenty-two books especially devoted to the emperors are by far the most readable and instructive portion of the Memoirs. They throw light on the personal character of these monarchs, exhibit the nature of their intercourse with their subjects, and illustrate the estimation in which polite letters are held in the view of the government.

The first chapter opens with the following:

"Shunche, the founder of the Imperial family, in the tenth year of his reign, visited the Inner Hall of the Academy, for the purpose of inspecting the translation of the Five Classics. On this occasion, his Majesty said, 'The virtues of Heaven and the true method of government are all recorded in the Book of

History; its principles will remain unalterable for ten thousand generations.' "

The translation referred to was into the Manchu language; it was made for the purpose of enabling the conquering race the more speedily to acquire the civilization of the conquered.

The young sovereign, then only sixteen years of age, shows by this brief speech how thoroughly he had become imbued with the spirit of the Confucian books. The record proceeds:

"In the fifth moon of the same year, his Majesty again visiting the Inner Hall, inquired of the directors why the writers had ceased from their work so early. The Chancellor Fan replied, 'This is the summer solstice; we suspend our labors a little earlier on that account.'

"The Emperor, looking round on his attendant officers, said, 'To take advantage of some peculiarity of the season to make a holiday is natural; but if you wish to enjoy repose, you must first learn to labor; you must aid in settling the Empire on a secure basis, and then your days of rest will not be disturbed. If you aim only at pleasure without restraining your desires, placing self and family first and the Empire second, your pleasure will be of short duration. Behold, for example, *our* course of conduct, how diligent we are in business, how anxiously we strive to attain perfection. It is for this reason *we* take pleasure in hearing the discourses of these learned men; men of the present day are good at talking, but they are not so good at acting. Why so? Because they have no settled principles; they act one way to-day and another to-morrow. But who among mortals is free from faults? If one correct his faults when he knows them, he is a good man; if, on the contrary, he conceal his faults and present the deceptive aspect of virtue, his errors multiply and his guilt becomes heavier. If *we*, and you, our servants, are diligent in managing the affairs of state, so that the benefit shall reach the people, Heaven will certainly vouchsafe its protection; while on those who do evil without inward examination or outward reform, Heaven will send down calamity. . . . If your actions were virtuous, would Heaven afflict you? Ch'engt'ang was a virtuous ruler, yet he did not spare pains in correcting his faults; on the contrary, Chengteh, of the Ming dynasty, had his heart set on enjoyment, and clung to his own vices, while he was perpetually finding fault with the shortcomings of his ministers. When the prince himself refuses to reform, the reformation of his people will be impossible, however virtuous his officers may be.'"

This little sermon, excepting the preceding brief encomium on the sacred books, is all that the Academy has thought fit to preserve of the discourses of Shunche. His son, the illustrious Kanghi, fills a large space in the Memoirs. Here are a few extracts, by way of specimens:

"The Emperor Kanghi, in the ninth year of his reign (the fifteenth of his age), said to the officers of the Board of Rites, 'If one would learn the art of government, he must explore the classic learning of the ancients. Whenever *we* can find a day of leisure from affairs of state, we spend it in the study of the classics. Reflecting that what is called Classic Feast and Daily Exposition are important usages, which ought to be revived, you are required to examine and report on the necessary regulations.'"

In his twelfth year, his Majesty said to the Academician Futali,

"To cherish an inquiring mind is the secret of progress in learning. If a lesson be regarded as an empty form, and, when finished, be dismissed from the thoughts, what benefit can there be to heart or life? As for *us*, when our servants (the Hanlin) are through with their discourses, *we* always reflect deeply on the subject-matter, and talk over with others any new ideas we may have obtained; *our* single aim being a luminous perception of the truth. The intervals of business, whether the weather be hot or cold, *we* occupy in reading and writing."

So saying, his Majesty exhibited a specimen of his penmanship, remarking that calligraphy was not the study of a prince, but that *he* found amusement in it.

In the ninth moon of the same year, his Majesty said to Hiong-tsze-lü, "The precept in the *Tahio*, on the study of *things*, is very comprehensive; it is not to be limited to mathematical inquiries and mechanical contrivances."

Again he said, "Heaven and earth, past and present, are governed by one law. Our aim should be to give our learning the widest possible range, and to condense it into the smallest possible compass."

In the fourteenth year, his Majesty, on reading a paper of the Hanlin, and finding himself compared to the Three Kings and Two Emperors (of ancient times), condemned the expression as a piece of empty flattery, and ordered it to be changed.

In the sixteenth year, his Majesty said, "Learning must be reduced to practice in order to be beneficial. You are required to address me with more frankness, concealing nothing in order to aid me in carrying into practice the principles to which I have attended."

In the nineteenth year, the Emperor, in bestowing on members of the Hanlin specimens of his autograph, remarked that in ancient times sovereign and subject were at liberty to criticise each other, and he desired them to exercise that liberty in regard to his handwriting, which he did not consider as a model.

In the twenty-first year, in criticising certain specimens of ancient chirography, his Majesty pointed to one from the pen of Lukung, remarking, "In the firmness and severity of these strokes I perceive the heroic spirit with which the writer battled with misfortune."

In the twenty-second year, his Majesty ordered that the topics chosen for the lectures of the Classic Feast should not, as hitherto, be selected solely with reference to the sovereign, but that they should be adapted to instruct and stimulate the officers as well.

In the twenty-third year, his Majesty was on a journey, when, the boat mooring for the night, he continued reading until the third watch. His clerk—a member of the Hanlin—had to beg his Majesty to allow himself a little more time for repose; whereupon his Majesty gave a detailed account of his habits of study, all the particulars of which are here faithfully preserved.

In the forty-third year, his Majesty said to the High Chancellor and members of the Academy, "From early youth I have been fond of the ink-stone; every day writing a thousand characters, and copying with care the chirography of the famous scribes of antiquity. This practice I have kept up for more than thirty years, because it was the bent of my nature. In the Manchu I also acquired such facility that I never make a mistake. The endorsements on memorials from viceroys and governors, and Imperial placets, are all written with my own hand, without the aid of a preliminary draft. Things of any importance, though months and years may elapse, I never forget, notwithstanding the endorsed documents are on file in the respective offices, and not even a memorandum left in my hands."

In the fiftieth year, his Majesty said to the High Chancellors, "In former generations I observe that, on occasion of the Classic Feast, the sovereign was accustomed to listen in respectful silence, without uttering a word. By that means his ignorance was not exposed, though he might not comprehend a word of the discourse. The usage was thus a mere name without the substance.

"As for me, I have now reigned fifty years and spent all my leisure hours in diligent study; and whenever the draft of a discourse was sent in, I never failed to read it over. If by chance a word or sentence appeared doubtful, I always discussed it with my literary aids; for the Classic Feast is an important institution, and not by any means to be viewed as an insignificant ceremony."

Of Yungcheng, the son and successor of Kanghi, the Memoirs

have preserved but a single discourse, and of that only its opening sentence is worth quoting. His Majesty said to the members of the Hanlin, "Literature is your business, but we want such literature as will serve to regulate the age and reflect glory on the nation. As for sonnets to the moon and the clouds, the winds and the dews—of what use are they?"

The next Emperor, Kienlung, far surpassed his predecessors in literary taste and attainments; and his reign being long (sixty years), his communications to the Hanlin are more than proportionally voluminous. Space, however, compels us to make our extracts in the inverse ratio. Many of the preceding and some which follow have nothing to do with the Academy, save that they were speeches uttered in the hearing of the Hanlin, and by them recorded. This, however, is to the point.

In the second year his Majesty said to the general directors, "Yesterday we examined the members of the Academy, giving them for a theme the sentence 'It is hard to be a sovereign, and to be a subject is not easy.' Of course there is a difference in the force of the expressions 'hard' and 'not easy,' yet not one of them perceived the distinction." Here follows an elaborate exposition from the vermilion pencil, which I must forego, at the risk of leaving my readers in perpetual darkness as to the momentous distinction. It is, however, but just to say that the Emperor intends the paper, not as a scholastic exercise, but as a political lesson.

In the fifth year, his Majesty says he has remarked that the addresses of the Hanlin contain a large amount of adulation, and a very small amount of instruction. He accordingly recommends them to modify their style. Two years later he complains that "the Hanlin often make a text from the sacred books a stalking-horse for irrelevant matters; e. g. Chow-changfah, in lecturing on the Book of Rites, took occasion to laud the magnificence of our sacrifice at the Altar of Heaven as without a parallel for a thousand years." "Before the sacrifice," he says,

"'Heaven gave a good omen in a fall of snow, and during its performance the sun shone down propitiously.' Now these rites were not of my institution; moreover, the soft winds and gentle sunshine on the occasion were purely accidental; for at that very time the Province of Kiangnan was suffering from disastrous floods, and my mind tormented with anxiety on that account. Let Chow-changfah be severely reprimanded, and let the other Hanlin take warning."

Among the remaining speeches of Kienlung, there are three that do him credit as a vindicator of the truth of history. In one of them he rebukes the historiographers for describing certain descendants of the Mings as usurpers, observing that they came honestly by their titles, though they were not able to maintain them. In another he criticises the ignorance and wilful perversions of facts exhibited by Chinese historians in their account of the three preceding Tartar dynasties—namely, the Liau, Kin, and Yuen. And in the last he reproves his own writers of history for omitting the name of a meritorious individual who had fallen into disgrace.

Among the communications of the next Emperor, Kiaking (the Memoirs close with the fourth year of his reign), I find nothing of sufficient interest to be worth the space it would occupy.

Thus far the emperors; what the Hanlin say to them in conversation or formal discourse is not recorded. But we know that they are so situated as to exert a more direct influence on the mind of their master than subjects of any other class. They are the instructors of his youth, and the counsellors of his maturer years; and this, the fixing of the views and moulding of the character of the autocrat of the Empire, we may fairly regard as their most exalted function.

But if they influence the Emperor, we see in the preceding paragraphs how easy it is for the Emperor to influence them. Herein is our hope for the rehabilitation of the Academy. Far from being decayed or effete, it contains as many and as active minds as at any previous period. At present they spend much of their time in making "sonnets to the moon;" but if the Emperor were so disposed, he could change all that in a moment. He could employ the Hanlin in translating out of English as well as into Manchu—in studying science as well as letters.

Nor are indications wanting that this change in the direction of their mental activity is likely to take place. Some years ago Prince Kung proposed that the junior members of the Hanlin should be required to attend the Tungwen College, for the purpose of acquiring the languages and sciences of Europe. Wojin, a president of the Hanlin and teacher of the Emperor, presented a counter-memorial, and the measure failed. But such is the march of events that the same measure, possibly in some modified form, is sure to be revived, and destined to be finally successful.

When that time arrives, the example of the Academy will have great weight in promoting a radical revolution in the character of the national education.

COMPETITIVE EXAMINATIONS IN CHINA.*

The reform proposed in the organization of our civil service, which contemplates the introduction of a system of competitive examinations, makes an inquiry into the experience of other nations timely. England, France, and Prussia have each made use of competitive examinations in some branches of their public service. In all these states the result has been uniform—a conviction that such a system, so far as it can be employed, affords the best method of ascertaining the qualifications of candidates for government employment. But in these countries the experiment is of recent date and of limited application. We must look farther East if we would see the system working on a scale sufficiently large and through a period sufficiently extended to afford us a full exhibition of its advantages and defects.

It is in China that its merits have been tested in the most satisfactory manner; and if in this instance we should profit by their experience, it would not be the first lesson we have learned from the Chinese, nor the last they are capable of giving us. It is to them that we are indebted, among other obligations, for the mariner's compass, for gunpowder,† and probably also for a remote suggestion of the art of printing. These arts have been of the first importance in their bearing on the advancement of society—one of them having effected a complete revolution in the character of modern warfare, while the others have imparted

* Reprinted from the *North American Review* for July, 1870. Read originally before the American Oriental Society at Boston, October, 1868.

† China's claim to the discovery of gunpowder has been vigorously combated, but, in my opinion, not set aside.

a mighty impulse to intellectual culture and commercial enterprise. Nor is it too much to affirm that, if we should adopt the Chinese method of testing the ability of candidates, and of selecting the best men for the service of the State, the change it would effect in our civil administration would be not less beneficial than those that have been brought about by the discoveries in the arts to which I have referred.

The bare suggestion may perhaps provoke a smile; but does any one smile at the idea that we might improve our polity by studying the institutions of Egypt, Rome, or Greece? Are, then, the arrangements of a government that arose with the earliest of those states, and still exists in undecaying vigor, to be passed as undeserving of attention? The long duration of the Chinese government, and the vast population to which it has served to secure a fair measure of prosperity, are phenomena that challenge admiration. Why should it be considered derogatory to our civilization to copy an institution which is confessedly the masterpiece in that skilful mechanism—the balance-wheel that regulates the working of that wonderful machinery?

In the arts which we have borrowed from the Chinese we have not been servile imitators. In every case we have made improvements that astonish the original inventors. We employ movable type, apply steam and electricity to printing, use the needle as a guide over seas which no junk would have ventured to traverse, and construct artillery such as the inventors of gunpowder never dreamed of. Would it be otherwise with a transplanted competitive system? Should we not be able to purge it of certain defects that adhere to it in China, and so render it productive of good results which it fails to yield in its native climate? I think, therefore, that I shall serve a better purpose than the simple gratification of curiosity if I devote a brief space to the consideration of the most admirable institution of the Chinese Empire.

Its primary object was to provide men of ability for the service of the State, and, whatever else it may have failed to accomplish, it is impossible to deny that it has fulfilled its specific end in a remarkable degree. The mandarins of China are almost without exception the choicest specimens of the educated classes. Alike in the capital and in the provinces, it is the mandarins that take the lead in every kind of literary enterprise. It is to them the Emperor looks to instruct as well as to govern his people; and it is to them that the publishers look for additions to the literature of the nation—nine tenths of the new books being written by mandarins. In their social meetings, their conversation abounds in classical allusions; and instead of after-dinner speeches, they are accustomed to amuse themselves with the composition of impromptu verses, which they throw off with incredible facility. It is their duty to encourage the efforts of students, to preside at the public examinations, and to visit the public schools—to promote, in short, by example as well as precept the interests of education. Scarcely anything is deemed a deeper disgrace than for a magistrate to be found incompetent for this department of his official duties. So identified, indeed, are the mandarins with all that constitutes the intellectnal life of the Chinese people that foreigners have come to regard them as a favored caste, like the Brahmins of India, or as a distinct order enjoying a monopoly of learning, like the priesthood in Egypt.

Nothing could be further from the truth. Those stately officials, for whom the people make way with such awe-struck deference, as they pass along the street with embroidered robes and imposing retinue, are not possessors of hereditary rank, neither do they owe their elevation to the favor of their sovereign, nor yet to the suffrages of their fellow-subjects. They are self-elected, and the people regard them with the deeper respect, because they know that they have earned their position by intellectual effort. What can be more truly democratic than thus to offer to all "the inspiration of a fair opportunity?" In this genuine democracy China stands unapproached among the nations of the earth; for whatever imperfections may attach to her social organization or to her political system, it must be acknowledged that China has devised the most effectual method for encouraging effort and rewarding merit. Here at least is one country where wealth is not allowed to raise its possessor to the seat of power; where the will even of an emperor cannot bestow its offices on uneducated favorites; and where the caprice of the multitude is not permitted to confer the honors of the State on incompetent demagogues.

The institution that accomplishes these results is not an innovation on the traditional policy of the Empire. It runs back in its essential features to the earliest period of recorded history. The adherence of the Chinese to it through so many ages well illustrates the conservative element in the national character; while the important changes it has undergone prove that this people is not by any means so fettered by tradition as to be incapable of welcoming improvements.

The germ from which it sprang was a maxim of the ancient sages, expressed in four syllables—*Chü hien jin neng*—"Employ the able and promote the worthy;" and examinations were resorted to as affording the best test of ability and worth. Of the Great Shun, that model emperor of remote antiquity, who lived about B.C. 2200, it is recorded that he examined his officers every third year, and after these examinations either gave them promotion or dismissed them from the service. On what subjects he examined them at a time when letters were but newly invented, and when books had as yet no existence, we are not told; neither are we informed whether he subjected candidates to any test previous to appointment; yet the mere fact of such a periodical examination established a precedent which has continued to be observed to the present day. Every third year the government holds a great examination for the trial of candidates, and every fifth year makes a formal inquisition into the record of its civil functionaries. The latter is a poor substitute for the ordeal of public criticism to which officials are exposed in a country enjoying a free press; but the former, as we shall have occasion to show, is thorough of its kind, and severely impartial.

More than a thousand years after the above date, at the commencement of the Chow dynasty, B.C. 1115, the government was accustomed to examine candidates as well as officers; and this time we are not left in doubt as to the nature of the examination. The Chinese had become a cultivated people, and we are informed that all candidates for office were required to give proof of their acquaintance with the five arts—music, archery, horsemanship, writing, and arithmetic; and to be thoroughly versed in the rites and ceremonies of public and social life—an accomplishment that ranked as a sixth art. These "six arts," expressed in the concise formula *li*, *yo*, *shay*, *yu*, *shu*, *su*, comprehended the sum total of a liberal education at the period, and remind us of the *trivium* and *quadrivium* of the mediæval schools.

Under the dynasty of Han, after the lapse of another thousand years, we find the range of subjects for the civil-service examinations largely extended. The Confucian Ethics had become current, and a moral standard was regarded in the selection of the competitors—the district magistrates being required to send up to the capital such men as had acquired a reputation for *hiao* and *lien*—"filial piety" and "integrity"—the Chinese rightly considering that the faithful performance of domestic and social duties is the best guarantee for fidelity in public life. These *hiao-lien*, these "filial sons and honest subjects," whose moral character had been sufficiently attested, were now subjected to trial in respect to their intellectual qualifications. The trial was twofold—first, as to their skill in the "six arts" already mentioned; and, secondly, as to their familiarity with one or more of the following subjects: the civil law, military affairs, agriculture, the administration of the revenue, and the geography of the Empire with special reference to the state of the water communications. This was an immense advance on the meagre requirements of the more ancient dynasties.

Passing over another thousand years, we come to the era of the Tangs and the Sungs, when we find the standard of literary attainment greatly elevated, the graduates arranged in three classes, and officials in nine—a classification which is still retained.

Arriving at the close of the fourth millennium, under the sway of the Mings and the Tsings of the present day, we find the simple trials instituted by Shun expanded into a colossal system, which may well claim to be the growth of four thousand years. It still exhibits the features that were prominent in its earlier stages—the "six arts," the "five studies," and the "three degrees" remaining as records of its progressive development. But the "six arts" are not what they once were; and the admirers of antiquity complain that examinations are sadly superficial as compared with those of the olden time, when competitors were required to ride a race, to shoot at a target, and to sing songs of their own composition to the accompaniment of their own guitars. In these degenerate days examiners are satisfied with odes in praise of music, and essays on the archery and horsemanship of the ancients.

Scholarship is a very different thing now from what it was in those ruder ages, when books were few, and the harp, the bow, and the saddle divided the student's time with the oral instructions of some famous master. Each century has added to the weight of his burden; and to the "heir of all the ages" each passing generation has bequeathed a legacy of toil. Doomed to live among the deposits of a buried world, and contending with millions of competitors, he can hardly hope for success without devoting himself to a life of unremitting study. True, he is not called upon to extend his researches beyond the limits of his own national literature; but that is all but infinite. It costs him at the outset years of labor to get possession of the key that unlocks it; for the learned language is totally distinct from his vernacular dialect, and justly regarded as the most difficult of the languages of man. Then he must commit to memory the whole circle of the recognized classics, and make himself familiar with the best writers of every age of a country which is no less prolific in books than in men. No doubt his course of study is too purely literary and too exclusively Chinese, but it is not superficial. In a popular "Student's Guide" we lately met with a course of reading drawn up for thirty years! We proposed putting it into the hands of a young American residing in China, who had asked advice as to what he should read. "Send it," he replied, "but don't tell my mother."

But it is time to take a closer view of these examinations as they are actually conducted. The candidates for office—those who are acknowledged as such in consequence of sustaining the initial trial—are divided into the three grades of *siu-ts'ai*, *chü-jin*, and *tsin-shi*—"budding geniuses," "promoted scholars," and those who are "ready for office." The trials for the first are held in the chief city of each district or *hien*, a territorial division which corresponds to our county or to an English shire. They are conducted by a chancellor, whose jurisdiction extends over an entire province containing, it may be, sixty or seventy such districts, each of which he is required to visit once a year, and each of which is provided with a resident sub-chancellor, whose duty it is to examine the scholars in the interval, and to have them in readiness on the chancellor's arrival.

About two thousand competitors enter the lists, ranging in age from the precocious youth just entering his teens up to the venerable grandsire of seventy winters. Shut up for a night and a day, each in his narrow cell, they produce each a poem and one or two essays on themes assigned by the chancellor, and then return to their homes to await the bulletin announcing their place in the scale of merit. The chancellor, assisted by his clerks, occupies several days in sifting the heap of manuscripts, from which he picks out some twenty or more that are distinguished by beauty of penmanship and grace of diction. The authors of these are honored with the degree of "Budding Genius," and are entitled to wear the decorations of the lowest grade in the corporation of mandarins.

The successful student wins no purse of gold and obtains no office, but he has gained a prize which he deems a sufficient compensation for years of patient toil. He is the best of a hundred scholars, exempted from liability to corporal punishment, and raised above the vulgar herd. The social consideration to which he is now entitled makes it a grand day for him and his family.

Once in three years these "Budding Geniuses," these picked men of the districts, repair to the provincial capital to engage in competition for the second degree—that of *chü-jin*, or "Promoted Scholar." The number of competitors amounts to ten thousand, more or less, and of these only one in every hundred can be admitted to the coveted degree. The trial is conducted by special examiners sent down from Peking; and this examination takes a wider range than the preceding. No fewer than three sessions of nearly three days each are occupied, instead of the single day for the first degree. Compositions in prose and verse are required, and themes are assigned with a special view to testing the extent of reading and depth of scholarship of the candidates. Penmanship is left out of the account—each production, marked with a cipher, being copied by an official scribe, that the examiners may have no clew to its author and no temptation to render a biassed judgment.

The victor still receives neither office nor emolument; but the honor he achieves is scarcely less than that which was won by the victors in the Olympic games. Again, he is one of a hundred, each of whom was a picked man; and as a result of this second victory he goes forth an acknowledged superior among ten thousand contending scholars. He adorns his cap with the gilded button of a higher grade, erects a pair of lofty flag-staves before the gate of his family residence, and places a tablet over his door to inform those who pass by that this is the abode of a literary prize-man. But our "Promoted Scholar" is not yet a mandarin in the proper sense of the term. The distinction already attained only stimulates his desire for higher honors—honors which bring at last the solid recompense of an income.

In the spring of the following year he proceeds to Peking to seek the next higher degree, attainment of which will prove a passport to office. The contest is still with his peers; that is, with other "Promoted Scholars," who, like himself, have come up from all the provinces of the empire. But the chances are this time more in his favor, as the number of prizes is now tripled; and if the gods are propitious, his fortune is made.

Though ordinarily not very devout, he now shows himself peculiarly solicitous to secure the favor of the divinities. He burns incense and gives alms. If he sees a fish floundering on the hook, he pays its price and restores it to its native element. He picks struggling ants out of the rivulet made by a recent shower, distributes moral tracts, or, better still, rescues chance bits of printed paper from being trodden in the mire of the streets.* If his name appears among the favored few, he not only wins himself a place in the front ranks of the lettered, but he plants his foot securely on the rounds of the official ladder by which, without the prestige of birth or the support of friends, it is possible to rise to a seat in the Grand Council of State or a place in the Imperial Cabinet. All this advancement presents itself in the distant prospect, while the office upon which he im-

---

* The bearing of good works of this kind on the result of the competition is copiously illustrated by collections of anecdotes which are widely circulated.

mediately enters is one of respectability, and it may be of profit. It is generally that of mayor or sub-mayor of a district city, or sub-chancellor in the district examinations — the vacant posts being distributed by lot, and therefore impartially, among those who have proved themselves to be "ready for office."

Before the drawing of lots, however, for the post of a magistrate among the people, our ambitious student has a chance of winning the more distinguished honor of a place in the Imperial Academy. With this view, the two or three hundred survivors of so many contests appear in the palace, where themes are assigned them by the Emperor himself, and the highest honor is paid to the pursuit of letters by the exercises being presided over by his Majesty in person. Penmanship reappears as an element in determining the result, and a score or more of those whose style is the most finished, whose scholarship the ripest, and whose handwriting the most elegant, are drafted into the college of Hanlin, the "forest of pencils," a kind of Imperial Institute the members of which are recognized as standing at the head of the literary profession. These are constituted poets and historians to the Celestial Court, or deputed to act as chancellors and examiners in the several provinces.*

But the diminishing series in this ascending scale has not yet reached its final term. The long succession of contests culminates in the designation by the Emperor of some individual whom he regards as the *chuang-yuen*, or model scholar of the Empire —the bright consummate flower of the season. This is not a common annual like the senior wranglership of Cambridge, nor the product of a private garden like the valedictory orator of our American colleges. It blooms but once in three years, and the whole Empire yields but a single blossom—a blossom that is culled by the hand of Majesty and esteemed among the brightest ornaments of his dominion. Talk of academic honors such as

* *Vide* preceding article for details concerning the Hanlin Yuan.

are bestowed by Western nations in comparison with those which this Oriental Empire heaps on her scholar laureate! Provinces contend for the shining prize, and the town that gives the victor birth becomes noted forever. Swift heralds bear the tidings of his triumph, and the hearts of the people leap at their approach. We have seen them enter a humble cottage, and amidst the flaunting of banners and the blare of trumpets announce to its startled inmates that one of their relations had been crowned by the Emperor as the laureate of the year. And so high was the estimation in which the people held the success of their fellow-townsman that his wife was requested to visit the six gates of the city, and to scatter before each a handful of rice, that the whole population might share in the good-fortune of her household. A popular tale, *La Bleue et la Blanche*, translated from the Chinese by M. Julien, represents a goddess as descending from heaven, that she might give birth to the scholar laureate of the Empire.

All this has, we confess, an air of Oriental display and exaggeration. It suggests rather the dust and sweat of the great national games of antiquity than the mental toil and intellectual triumphs of the modern world. But it is obvious that a competition which excites so profoundly the interest of a whole nation must be productive of very decided results. That it leads to the selection of the best talent for the service of the public we have already seen; but beyond this—its primary object—it exercises a profound influence upon the education of the people and the stability of the government. It is all, in fact, that China has to show in the way of an educational system. She has few colleges and no universities in our Western sense, and no national system of common-schools; yet it may be confidently asserted that China gives to learning a more effective patronage than she could have done if each of her emperors had been an Augustus and every premier a Mæcenas. She says to all her sons, "Prosecute your studies by such means as you may be able to command, whether in public or in private; and, when you are prepared, present yourselves in the examination-hall. The government will judge of your proficiency and reward your attainments."

Nothing can exceed the ardor which this standing offer infuses into the minds of all who have the remotest prospect of sharing in the prizes. They study not merely while they have teachers to incite them to diligence, but continue their studies with unabated zeal long after they have left the schools; they study in solitude and poverty; they study amidst the cares of a family and the turmoil of business; and the shining goal is kept steadily in view until the eye grows dim. Some of the aspirants impose on themselves the task of writing a fresh essay every day; and they do not hesitate to enter the lists as often as the public examinations recur, resolved, if they fail, to continue trying, believing that perseverance has power to command success, and encouraged by the legend of the man who, needing a sewing-needle, made one by grinding a crowbar on a piece of granite.

We have met an old mandarin who related with evident pride how, on gaining the second degree, he had removed with his whole family to Peking, from the distant province of Yunnan, to compete for the third; and how at each triennial contest he had failed, until, after more than twenty years of patient waiting, at the seventh trial, and at the mature age of threescore, he bore off the coveted prize. He had worn his honors for seven years, and was then mayor of the city of Tientsin. In a list now on our table of ninety-nine successful competitors for the second degree, sixteen are over forty years of age, one sixty-two, and one eighty-three. The average age of the whole number is above thirty; and for the third degree the average is of course proportionally higher.

So powerful are the motives addressed to them that the whole body of scholars who once enter the examination-hall are devoted to study as a life-long occupation. We thus have a class of men, numbering in the aggregate some millions, who keep their faculties bright by constant exercise, and whom it would be difficult to parallel in any Western country for readiness with the pen and retentiveness of memory. If these men are not highly educated, it is the fault, not of the competitive system, which proves its power to stimulate them to such prodigious exertions, but of the false standard of intellectual merit established in China. In that country letters are everything and science nothing. Men occupy themselves with words rather than with things; and the powers of acquisition are more cultivated than those of invention.

The type of Chinese education is not that of our modern schools; but when compared with the old curriculum of languages and philosophy it appears by no means contemptible. A single paper, intended for the last day of the examination for the second degree, may serve as a specimen. It covers five subjects—criticism, history, agriculture, military affairs, and finance. There are about twenty questions on each subject, and while they certainly do not deal with it in a scientific manner, it is something in their favor to say that they are such as cannot be answered without an extensive course of reading in Chinese literature. One question under each of the five heads is all that our space will allow us to introduce.

1. "How do the rival schools of Wang and Ching differ in respect to the exposition of the meaning and the criticism of the text of the Book of Changes?"

2. "The great historian Sze-ma-ts'ien prides himself upon having gathered up much material that was neglected by other writers. What are the sources from which he derived his information?"

3. "From the earliest times great attention has been given to the improvement of agriculture. Will you indicate the arrangements adopted for that purpose by the several dynasties?"

4. "The art of war arose under Hwangte, forty-four hundred

years ago. Different dynasties have since that time adopted different regulations in regard to the use of militia or standing armies, the mode of raising supplies for the army, etc. Can you state these briefly?"

5. "Give an account of the circulating medium under different dynasties, and state how the currency of the Sung dynasty corresponded with our use of paper money at the present day."

In another paper, issued on a similar occasion, astronomy takes the place of agriculture; but the questions are confined to such allusions to the subject as are to be met with in the circle of their classical literature, and afford but little scope for the display of scientific attainments. Still, the fact that a place is found for this class of subjects is full of hope. It indicates that the door, if not fully open, is at least sufficiently ajar to admit the introduction of our Western sciences with all their progeny of arts, a band powerful enough to lift the Chinese out of the mists of their mediæval scholasticism, and to bring them into the full light of modern knowledge. If the examiners were scientific men, and if scientific subjects were made sufficiently prominent in these higher examinations, millions of aspiring students would soon become as earnest in the pursuit of modern science as they now are in the study of their ancient classics.* Thus reformed and renovated by the injection of fresh blood into the old arte-

---

* As a sample of the practical bearing which it is possible to give to these examination exercises, we take a few questions from another paper:

"Fire-arms began with the use of rockets in the Chau dynasty (B.C. 1100); in what book do we first meet with the word for cannon? What is the difference in the two classes of engines to which it is applied (applied also to the catapult)? Is the defence of K'aifungfu its first recorded use? Kublai Khan, it is said, obtained cannon of a new kind; from whom did he obtain them? The Sungs had several varieties of small cannon, what were their advantages? When the Mings, in the reign of Yungloh, invaded Cochin-China, they obtained a kind of cannon called the 'weapons of the gods;' can you give an account of their origin?"

ries, this noble institution would rise to the dignity of a great national university—a university not like those of Oxford and Cambridge, which train their own graduates, but—to compare great things with small—like the University of London, promoting the cause of learning by examining candidates and conferring degrees. The University of London admits to its initial examination annually about fourteen hundred candidates, and passes one half. The government examinations of China admit about two million candidates every year, and pass only one or two per cent.

The political bearings of this competitive system are too important to be passed over, and yet too numerous to be treated in detail. Its incidental advantages may be comprehended under three heads.

1. It serves the State as a safety-valve, providing a career for those ambitious spirits which might otherwise foment disturbances or excite revolutions. While in democratic countries the ambitious flatter the people, and in monarchies fawn on the great, in China, instead of resorting to dishonorable arts or to political agitation, they betake themselves to quiet study. They know that their mental calibre will be fairly gauged, and that if they are born to rule, the competitive examinations will open to them a career. The competitive system has not, indeed, proved sufficient to employ all the forces that tend to produce intestine commotion; but it is easy to perceive that without it the shocks must have been more frequent and serious.

2. It operates as a counterpoise to the power of an absolute monarch. Without it the great offices would be filled by hereditary nobles, and the minor offices be farmed out by thousands to imperial favorites. With it a man of talent may raise himself from the humblest ranks to the dignity of viceroy or premier. *Tsiang siang pun wu chung*—"The general and the prime-minister are not born in office"—is a line that every schoolboy is taught to repeat. Rising from the people, the mandarins under-

stand the feelings and wants of the people, though it must be confessed that they are usually avaricious and oppressive in proportion to the length of time it has taken them to reach their elevation. Still, they have the support and sympathy of the people to a greater extent than they could have if they were the creatures of arbitrary power. The system, therefore, introduces a popular element into the government—a check on the prerogative of the Emperor as to the appointment of officers, and serves as a kind of constitution to his subjects, prescribing the conditions on which they shall obtain a share in the administration of the power of the State.

3. It gives the government a hold on the educated gentry, and binds them to the support of existing institutions. It renders the educated classes eminently conservative, because they know that in the event of a revolution civil office would be bestowed, not as the reward of learning, but for political or military services. The *literati*, the most influential portion of the population, are for this reason also the most loyal. It is their support that has upheld the reigning house, though of a foreign race, through these long years of civil commotion, while to the "rebels" it has been a ground of reproach and a source of weakness that they have had but few literary men in their ranks.

In districts where the people have distinguished themselves by zeal in the Imperial cause, the only recompense they crave is a slight addition to the numbers on the competitive prize-list. Such additions the government has made very frequently of late years, in consideration of money supplies. It has also, to relieve its exhausted exchequer, put up for sale the decorations of the literary orders, and issued patents admitting contributors to the higher examinations without passing through the lower grades. But though the government thus debases the coin, it guards itself jealously against the issue of a spurious currency. Seven years ago Peiching, first president of the Examining Board at Peking, was put to death for having fraudulently conferred two or three degrees. The fraud was limited in extent, but the damage it threatened was incalculable. It tended to shake the confidence of the people in the administration of that branch of the government which constituted their only avenue to honors and office. Even the Emperor cannot tamper with it without peril. It is the Chinaman's ballot-box, his grand charter of rights; though the Emperor may lower its demands, in accordance with the wishes of a majority, he could not set it aside without producing a revolution.

Such is the Chinese competitive system, and such are some of its advantages and defects. May it not be feasible to graft something of a similar character on our own republican institutions? More congenial to the spirit of our free government, it might be expected to yield better fruits in this country than in China. In British India it works admirably. In Great Britain, too, the diplomatic and consular services have been placed on a competitive basis; and something of the kind must be done for our own foreign service if we wish our influence abroad to be at all commensurate with our greatness and prosperity at home. When will our government learn that a good consul is worth more than a man-of-war, and that an able minister is of more value than a whole fleet of iron-clads? To secure good consuls and able ministers we must choose them from a body of men who have been picked and trained.

In effecting these reforms, Mr. Jenckes's (of Rhode Island) bill might serve as an entering wedge. It would secure the acknowledgment of the principle—certainly not alarmingly revolutionary—that places should go by merit. But it does not go far enough. "It does not," he says, "touch places which are to be filled with the advice and consent of the Senate. It would not in the least interfere with the scramble for office which is going on at the other end of the Avenue, or which fills with anxious crowds the corridors of the other wing of the Capitol. This measure, it should be remembered, deals only with the inferior officers, whose appointment is made by the President alone, or by the heads of departments."

But what danger is there of infringing on the rights of the Senate? Is there anything that would aid the Senate so much in giving their "advice and consent" as the knowledge that the applicants for confirmation had proved their competence before a Board of Examiners? And would not the knowledge of the same fact lighten the burdens of the President, and relieve him of much of the difficulty which he now experiences in the selection of qualified men? Such an arrangement would not take away the power of executive appointment, but regulate its exercise. Nor would it, if applied to elective offices, interfere with the people's freedom of choice further than to insure that the candidates should be men of suitable qualifications. It may not be easy to prescribe rules for that popular sovereignty which follows only its own sweet will, but it is humiliating to reflect that our "mandarins" are so far from being the most intellectual class of the community.

EDUCATION IN CHINA.*

I. INFLUENCE ON NATIONAL CHARACTER.

THE interest of the inquiry on which we are about to enter is based on the assumption that differences of national character are mainly due to the influence of education. This we conceive

---

* This paper was first published in 1877 by the United States Bureau of Education. The following letter of the late Mr. Avery, United States Minister to China, may serve to explain its origin:

"*To the Commissioner of Education.*

"LEGATION OF THE UNITED STATES,
PEKING, *May* 28, 1875.

"SIR,—Before my departure for China, I received from you a request to secure for use by your Bureau an accurate and full statement of the methods of education in China, and 'the relation of the methods to the failure of their civilization.'

"On my arrival at Peking, bearing your request in mind, I was confirmed in the opinion entertained before, that to no one else could I apply for the information desired with so much propriety as to Dr. W. A. P. Martin, our fellow-countryman, president of the Imperial College for Western Science at Peking, whose long residence in China, scholarly knowledge of Chinese literature, and familiar acquaintance with native methods of education must be well known to you.

"Dr. Martin, at my solicitation, agreed to furnish a paper on the subject you indicated, which I have just received from his hands, and now forward to you through the courtesy of the State Department. I scarcely need add that you will find it alike interesting and valuable. In connection with the subject of Dr. Martin's paper, permit me to call your attention to a despatch written by S. Wells Williams, then chargé d'affaires at this legation, to the State Department, under date of August 26, 1869, numbered 58, and referring to the enormous difficulties of the Chinese language, whether spoken or written, as one of the principal obstacles to the progress of this people.

to be true, except in extreme cases, such as those of the inhabitants of torrid or frigid regions, where everything succumbs to the tyranny of physical forces. In such situations climate shapes education, as, according to Montesquieu, it determines morals and dictates laws. But in milder latitudes the difference of physical surroundings is an almost inappreciable element in the formation of character in comparison with influences of an intellectual and moral kind. Much, for example, is said about the inspiration of mountain scenery—an inspiration felt most sensibly, if not most effectively, by those who see the mountains least frequently; but, as John Foster remarks, the character of a lad brought up at the foot of the Alps is a thousandfold more affected by the companions with whom he associates than by the mountains that rear their heads above his dwelling.

The peculiar character of the Chinese—for they have a character which is one and distinct—is not to be accounted for by their residence in great plains, for half the empire is mountainous. Neither is it to be ascribed to their rice diet, as rice is a luxury in which few of the northern population are able to indulge. Still less is it to be referred to the influence of climate, for they spread over a broad belt in their own country, emigrate in all directions, and flourish in every zone. It is not even explained by the unity and persistency of an original type, for in their earlier career they absorbed and assimilated several other races, while history shows that at different epochs their own character has undergone remarkable changes. The true secret of this phenomenon is the presence of an agency which, under our own eyes, has shown itself sufficiently powerful to transform the turbulent nomadic Manchu into the most Chinese of the in-

---

Dr. Martin touches on this point, but it did not enter into his object to enlarge upon it.

"I am, sir,

"Your obedient servant,

"BENJ. P. AVERY.

"HON. JOHN EATON,
"*Commissioner of Education.*"

habitants of the Middle Kingdom. The general name for that agency, which includes a thousand elements, is education. It is education that has imparted a uniform stamp to the Chinese under every variety of physical condition; just as the successive sheets of paper applied to an engraving bring away, substantially, the same impression, notwithstanding differences in the quality of the material.

In this wide sense we shall not attempt to treat the subject, though it may not be out of place to remark that the Chinese themselves employ a word which answers to education with a similar latitude. They say, for instance, that the education of a child begins before its birth. The women of ancient times, say they, in every movement had regard to its effect on the character of their offspring. This they denominate *kiao*, reminding us of what Goethe tells us in his autobiography of certain antecedents which had their effect in imparting to him

> "That concord of harmonious powers
> Which forms the soul of happiness."

All this, whatever its value, belongs to physical discipline. We shall not go so far back in the history of our typical Chinese, but, confining ourselves strictly to the department of intellectual influences, take him at the time when the young idea first begins to shoot, and trace him through the several stages of his development until he emerges a full-fledged Academician.*

II. HOME EDUCATION.

With us the family is the first school. Not only is it here that we make the most important of our linguistic acquirements, but

* For an account of the Hanlin or Imperial Academy, see the *North American Review* for July, 1874, where much may be found to supplement the present paper. The same periodical (some time in 1870) contains an article by the present writer on Civil-service Competitive Examinations in China. (I leave this note in its original form, though the papers referred to may now be found between the covers of the present volume.)

with parents who are themselves cultivated there is generally a persistent effort to stimulate the mental growth of their offspring, to develop reason, form taste, and invigorate the memory.

In many instances parental vanity applies a spur where the curb ought to be employed, and a sickly precocity is the result; but in general a judicious stimulus addressed to the mind is no detriment to the body, and it is doubtless to the difference of domestic training rather than to race that we are to ascribe the early awaking of the mental powers of European children as compared with those of China. The Chinese have, it is true, their stories of infant precocity—their Barretiers and Chattertons. They tell of Li-muh, who, at the age of seven, was thought worthy of the degree of *tsin-shi*, or the literary doctorate, and of Hie-tsin, the "divine child," who, at the age of ten, composed a volume of poems, still in use as a juvenile text-book. But these are not merely exceptions; they are exceptions of rarer occurrence than among us.

The generality of Chinese children do not get their hands and feet so soon as ours, because, in the first months of their existence, they are tightly swathed and afterwards overloaded with cumbrous garments. The reason for their tardier mental development is quite analogous. European children exhibit more thought at five than Chinese children at twice that age. This is not a partial judgment, nor is the fact to be accounted for by a difference of race; for in mental capacity the Chinese are, in my opinion, not inferior to the "most favored nation." Deprive our nurseries of those speaking pictures that say so much to the infant eye; of infant poems, such as those of Watts and Barbauld; of the sweet music that impresses those poems on the infant mind; more than all, take away those Bible stories and scraps of history which excite a thirst for the books that contain them, and what a check upon mental growth, what a deduction from the happiness of childhood! With us the dawn of knowledge precedes the use of books, as the rays of morning, refracted by the atmosphere and glowing with rosy hues, anticipate the rising of the sun. In China there is no such accommodating medium, no such blushing aurora. The language of the fireside is not the language of the books.

Mothers and nurses are not taught to read; nor are fathers less inclined than with us to leave the work of instruction to be begun by the professional teacher. This they are the more disposed to do, as an ancient maxim, sanctioned by classic authority, prohibits a parent being the instructor of his own children; still some fathers, yielding to better instincts, do take a pride in teaching their infant sons; and some mothers, whose exceptional culture makes them shine like stars in the night of female ignorance, have imparted to their children the first impulse in a literary career.

How many of those who have obtained seats in the literary Olympus were favored with such early advantages it is impossible to ascertain. That the number is considerable, we cannot doubt. We remember hearing of two scholars in Chekiang who were not only taught the mechanical art of writing, but the higher art of composition, by an educated mother, both of them winning the honors of the Academy.

As another instance of the same kind, the Memoirs of the Academy embalm the memory of such a noble mother along with the name of her illustrious son, the Emperor Kienlung, with vermilion pencil, celebrating the talents of the one and the virtues of the other.

Dropping the "meed of a melodious tear" on the grave of an eminent literary servant, Chien-chön-keun, a member of the Hanlin, the Emperor says, "He drew his learning from a hidden source, a virtuous mother imparting to him her classic lore." In the prose obituary prefixed to the verses, his Majesty says, "Chien's mother, Lady Chen, was skilled in ornamental writing. In his boyhood it was she who inspired and directed his studies. He had a painting which represented his mother holding a distaff and at the same time explaining to him the classic page. I admired it, and inscribed on it a complimentary verse." A graceful tribute from an exalted hand, worth more, in the estimation of the Chinese, than all the marble or granite that might be heaped upon her sepulchre.

III. COMMENCEMENT OF SCHOOL LIFE.

In general, however, a Chinese home is not a hot-bed for the development of mind. Nature is left to take her own time, and the child vegetates until he completes his seventh or eighth year. The almanac is then consulted, and a lucky day chosen for inducting the lad into a life of study. Clad in festal robe, with tasselled cap, and looking a mandarin in small, he sets out for the village school, his face beaming with the happy assurance that all the stars are shedding kindly influence, and his friends predicting that he will end his career in the Imperial Academy. On entering the room, he performs two acts of worship: the first is to prostrate himself before a picture of the Great Sage, who is venerated as the fountain of wisdom, but is not supposed to exercise over his votaries anything like a tutelar supervision. The second is to salute with the same forms, and almost equal reverence, the teacher who is to guide his inexperienced feet in the pathway to knowledge. In no country is the office of teacher more revered. Not only is the living instructor saluted with forms of profoundest respect, but the very name of teacher, taken in the abstract, is an object of almost idolatrous homage. On certain occasions it is inscribed on a tablet in connection with the characters for heaven, earth, prince, and parents, as one of the five chief objects of veneration, and worshipped with solemn rites. This is a relic of the primitive period, when books were few and the student dependent for everything on the oral teaching of his sapient master. In those days, in Eastern as well as Western Asia and Greece, schools were peripatetic, or (as Jeremy Taylor says of the Church in his time) *ambulatory.* Disciples were wont to attend their master by day and night, and follow him on his peregrinations from State to State, in order to catch and treasure up his most casual discourses.

As to the pursuit of knowledge, they were at a great disadvantage compared with modern students, whose libraries contain books by the thousand, while their living teachers are counted by the score. Yet the student life of those days was not without its compensating circumstances. Practical morality, the formation of character, was the great object, intellectual discipline being deemed subordinate; and in such a state of society physical culture was, of course, not neglected. The personal character of the teacher made a profound impression on his pupils, inspiring them with ardor in the pursuit of virtue; while the necessity of learning by question and answer excited a spirit of inquiry and favored originality of thought. But now all this is changed, and the names and forms continue without the reality.

A man who never had a dozen thoughts in all his life sits in the seat of the philosophers and receives with solemn ceremony the homage of his disciples. And why not? For every step in the process of teaching is fixed by unalterable usage. So much is this the case that in describing one school I describe all, and in tracing the steps of one student I point out the course of all; for in China there are no new methods or short roads.

In other countries, a teacher, even in the primary course, finds room for tact and originality. In those who dislike study a love of it is to be inspired by making "knowledge pleasant to the taste," and the dull apprehension is to be awakened by striking and apt illustrations; while, to the eager and industrious, "steps to Parnassus" are, if not made easy, at least to be pointed out so clearly that they shall waste no strength in climbing by wrong paths. In China there is nothing of this. The land of uniformity, all processes in arts and letters are as much fixed by universal custom as is the cut of their garments or the mode of wearing their hair. The pupils all tread the path trodden by their ancestors of a thousand years ago, nor has it grown smoother by the attrition of so many feet.

IV. STAGES OF STUDY.

The undergraduate course may be divided into three stages, in each of which there are two leading studies:

In the first, the occupations of the student are committing to memory (not reading) the canonical books and writing an infinitude of diversely formed characters as a manual exercise.

In the second, they are the translation of his text-books (i. e. reading) and lessons in composition.

In the third, they are belles-lettres and the composition of essays.

Nothing could be more dreary than the labors of the first stage. The pupil comes to school, as one of his books tells him, "a rough gem, that requires grinding;" but the process is slow and painful. His books are in a dead language, for in every part of the Empire the style of literary composition is so far removed from that of the vernacular speech that books, when read aloud, are unintelligible even to the ear of the educated, and the sounds of their characters convey absolutely no meaning to the mind of a beginner. Nor, as a general thing, is any effort made to give them life by imparting glimpses of their signification. The whole of this first stage is a dead lift of memory, unalleviated by the exercise of any other faculty. It is something like what we should have in our Western schools if our youth were restricted to the study of Latin as their sole occupation, and required to stow away in their memory the contents of the principal classics before learning a word of their meaning.

The whole of the Four Books and the greater part of the Five Classics are usually gone through in this manner, four or five years being allotted to the cheerless task. During all this time the mind has not been enriched by a single idea. To get words at the tongue's end and characters at the pencil's point is the sole object of this initial discipline. It would seem, indeed, as if the wise ancients who devised it had dreaded nothing so much as early development, and, like prudent horticulturists, resorted to this method for the purpose of heaping snow and ice around the roots of the young plant to guard against its premature blossoming. All the arrangements of the system are admirably adapted to form a safeguard against precocity. Even the stimulus of companionship in study is usually denied, the advantages resulting from the formation of classes being as little appreciated as those of other labor-saving machinery. Each pupil reads and writes alone, the penalty for failure being so many blows with the ferule or kneeling for so many minutes on the rough brick pavement which serves for a floor.

At this period fear is the strongest motive addressed to the mind of the scholar; nor is it easy to say how large a share this stern discipline has in giving him his first lesson in political duty—viz., that of unquestioning submission—and in rendering him cringing and pliant towards official superiors. Those sallies of innocent humor and venial mischief so common in Western schools are rarely witnessed in China.

A practical joke in which the scholars indulged at the expense of their teacher I have seen represented in a picture, but never in real life. The picture, the most graphic I ever saw from a Chinese pencil, adorns the walls of a monastery at the Western Hills, near Peking. It represents a village school, the master asleep in his chair and the pupils playing various pranks, the least of which, if the tyrant should happen to awake, would bring down his terrible baton. But, notwithstanding the danger to which they expose themselves, two of the young unterrified stand behind the throne, threatening to awake the sleeper by tickling his ear with the tail of a scorpion.

So foreign, indeed, is this scene from the habits of Chinese schoolboys that I feel compelled to take it in a mystic rather than a literal signification. The master is reason, the boys are the passions, and the scorpion conscience. If passion gets at the ear of the soul while reason sleeps, the stings of conscience are sure to follow—those

"Pangs that pay joy's spendthrift thrill
With bitter usury."

Thus understood, it conveys a moral alike worthy of Christian or Buddhist ethics.

Severity is accounted the first virtue in a pedagogue; and its opposite is not kindness, but negligence. In family schools, where the teacher is well watched, he is reasonably diligent and sufficiently severe to satisfy the most exacting of his patrons. In others, and particularly in charity-schools, the portrait of Squeers in Nicholas Nickleby would be no caricature. With modifications and improvements in the curriculum, a teacher has nothing to do. His business is to keep the mill going, and the time-honored argument *a posteriori* is the only persuasion he cares to appeal to.

This arctic winter of monotonous toil once passed, a more auspicious season dawns on the youthful understanding. The key of the Cabala which he has been so long and so blindly acquiring is put into his hands. He is initiated in the translation and exposition of those sacred books which he had previously stored away in his memory, as if apprehensive lest another tyrant of Tsin might attempt their destruction. The light, however, is let in but sparingly, as it were, through chinks and rifts in the long dark passage. A simple character here and there is explained, and then, it may be after the lapse of a year or two, the teacher proceeds to the explication of entire sentences. Now for the first time the mind of the student begins to take in the *thoughts* of those he has been taught to regard as the oracles of wisdom. His dormant faculties wake into sudden life, and, as it would seem, unfold the more rapidly in consequence of their protracted hibernation. To him it is like

> "The glorious hour when spring goes forth
> O'er the bleak mountains of the shadowy north,
> And with one radiant glance, one magic breath,
> Wakes all things lovely from the sleep of death."

The value of this exercise can hardly be overestimated. When judiciously employed, it does for the Chinese what translation into and out of the dead languages of the West does for us. It calls into play memory, judgment, taste, and gives him a command of his own vernacular which, it is safe to assert, he would never acquire in any other way. Yet even here I am not able to bestow unqualified commendation. This portion of the course is rendered too easy; as much too easy as the preceding is too difficult. Instead of requiring a lad, dictionary in hand, to quarry out the meaning of his author, the teacher reads the lesson for him, and demands of him nothing more than a faithful reproduction of that which he has received; memory again, sheer memory! Desirable as this method might be for beginners, when continued, as the Chinese do through the whole course, it has the inevitable effect of impairing independence of judgment and fertility of invention—qualities for which Chinese scholars are by no means remarkable, and for the deficiency of which they are, no doubt, indebted to this error of schoolroom discipline.

Simultaneously with translation the student is initiated in the art of composition—an art which, in any language, yields to nothing but practice. In Chinese it is beset with difficulties of a peculiar kind. In the majority of cultivated languages the syntax is governed by rules, while inflections, like mortise and tenon, facilitate the structure of the sentence.

Not so in this most primitive form of human speech. Verbs and nouns are undistinguished by any difference of form, the verb having no voice, mood, or tense, and the noun neither gender, number, nor person. Collocation is everything; it creates the parts of speech and determines the signification of characters. The very simplicity of the linguistic structure thus proves a source of difficulty, preventing the formation of any such systems of grammatical rules as abound in most inflected languages, and throwing the burden of acquisition on the imitative faculty; the problem being, not the erection of a fabric from parts which are adjusted and marked, but the building of an arch with cobble-stones.

If these uniform, unclassified atoms were indifferent to position, the labor of arrangement would be nothing, and style impossible. But most of them appear to be endowed with a kind of mysterious polarity which controls their collocation, and renders them incapable of companionship except with certain characters, the choice of which would seem to be altogether arbitrary. The origin of this peculiarity is not difficult to discover. In this, as in other things among the Chinese, usage has become law. Combinations which were accidental or optional with the model writers of antiquity, and even their errors, have, to their imitative posterity, become the *jus et norma loquendi.* Free to move upon each other when the language was young and in a fluid state, its elements have now become crystallized into invariable forms. To master this pre-established harmony without the aid of rules is the fruit of practice and the labor of years.

The first step in composition is the yoking together of double characters. The second is the reduplication of these binary compounds and the construction of parallels—an idea which runs so completely through the whole of Chinese literature that the mind of the student requires to be imbued with it at the very outset. This is the way he begins: The teacher writes "Wind blows," the pupil adds "Rain falls;" the teacher writes "Rivers are long," the pupil adds "Seas are deep" or "Mountains are high," etc.

From the simple subject and predicate, which in their rude grammar they describe as "dead" and "living" characters, the teacher conducts his pupil to more complex forms, in which qualifying words and phrases are introduced. He gives as a model some such phrase as "The Emperor's grace is vast as heaven and earth," and the lad matches it by "The sovereign's favor is profound as lake and sea." These couplets often contain two propositions in each member, accompanied by all the usual modifying terms; and so exact is the symmetry required by the rules of the art that not only must noun, verb, adjective, and particle respond to each other with scrupulous exactness, but the very tones of the characters are adjusted to each other with the precision of music.

Begun with the first strokes of his untaught pencil, the student, whatever his proficiency, never gets beyond the construction of parallels. When he becomes a member of the Institute or a minister of the Imperial Cabinet, at classic festivals and social entertainments the composition of impromptu couplets, formed on the old model, constitutes a favorite pastime. Reflecting a poetic image from every syllable, or concealing the keen point of a cutting epigram, they afford a fine vehicle for sallies of wit; and poetical contests such as that of Melibœus and Menalcas are in China matters of daily occurrence. If a present is to be given, on the occasion of a marriage, a birthday, or any other remarkable occasion, nothing is deemed so elegant or acceptable as a pair of scrolls inscribed with a complimentary distich.

When the novice is sufficiently exercised in the "parallels" for the idea of symmetry to have become an instinct, he is permitted to advance to other species of composition which afford freer scope for his faculties. Such are the *shotiah*, in which a single thought is expanded in simple language; the *lun*, the formal discussion of a subject more or less extended, and epistles addressed to imaginary persons and adapted to all conceivable circumstances. In these last, the forms of the "complete letter-writer" are copied with too much servility; but in the other two, substance being deemed of more consequence than form, the new-fledged thought is permitted to essay its powers and to expatiate with but little restraint.

In the third stage, composition is the leading object, reading being wholly subsidiary. It takes, for the most part, the artificial form of verse, and of a kind of prose called *wen-chang*, which is, if possible, still more artificial. The reading required embraces mainly rhetorical models and sundry anthologies. History is studied, but only that of China, and that only in compends; not for its lessons of wisdom, but for the sake of the allusions with which it enables a writer to embellish classic essays. The same may be said of other studies; knowledge and mental discipline are at a discount, and style at a premium. The goal of the long course, the flower and fruit of the whole system, is the *wen-chang;* for this alone can insure success in the public examinations for the civil service, in which students begin to adventure soon after entering on the third stage of their preparatory course.

The examinations we reserve for subsequent consideration, and in that connection we shall notice the *wen-chang* more at length. We may, however, remark in passing that to propose such an end as the permanent object of pursuit must of necessity have the effect of rendering education superficial. In our own universities surface is aimed at rather than depth; but what, we may ask, besides an empty glitter would remain if none of our students aspired to anything better than to become popular newspaper-writers? Yet successful essayists and penny-a-liners require as a preparation for their functions a substratum of solid information. They have to exert themselves to keep abreast of an age in which great facts and great thoughts vibrate instantaneously throughout a hemisphere. But the idea of progressive knowledge is alien to the nature of the *wen-chang.*

A juster parallel for the intense and fruitless concentration of energy on this species of composition is the passion for Latin verse which was dominant in our halls of learning until dethroned by the rise of modern science.

V. GRADES OF SCHOOLS.

The division of the undergraduate course into the three stages which we have described gives rise to three classes of schools: the primary, in which little is attended to beyond memoriter recitation and imitative chirography; the middle, in which the canonical books are expounded; and the classical, in which composition is the leading exercise. Not unfrequently all three departments are embraced in one and the same school; and still more frequently the single department professed is so neglected as to render it utterly abortive for any useful purpose. This, as we have elsewhere intimated, is particularly the case with what are called public schools. National schools there are none, with the exception of those at the capital for the education of the Bannermen, originally established on a liberal scale, but now so neglected that they can scarcely be reckoned among existing institutions.

A further exception may be made in favor of schools opened in various places by provincial officers for special purposes; but it is still true that China has nothing approaching to a system of common-schools designed to diffuse among the masses the blessings of a popular education. Indeed, education is systematically left to private enterprise and public charity; the government contenting itself with gathering the choicest fruits and encouraging production by suitable rewards. A government that does this cannot be accused of neglecting the interests of education, though the beneficial influence of such patronage seldom penetrates to the lower strata of society.

Even higher institutions, those that bear the name of colleges, are, for the most part, left to shift for themselves on the same principle. Such colleges differ little from schools of the middle and higher class, except in the number of professors and students; the professors, however numerous, teaching nothing but the Chinese language, and the students, however long they may remain in the institution, studying nothing but the Chinese language. Colleges in the modern sense, as institutions in which the several sciences are taught by men who are specially expert, are, as yet, almost unknown. But there is reason to believe that the government will soon perceive the necessity of supplying its people with the means of a higher, broader culture than they can derive from the grammar and rhetoric of their own language.

In establishing and contributing to the support of schools, the gentry are exceedingly liberal; but they are not always careful to see that their schools are conducted in an efficient manner. In China nothing flourishes without the stimulus of private interest. Accordingly, all who can afford to do so endeavor to employ private instructors for their own families; and where a single family is unable to meet the expense, two or three of the same clan or family name are accustomed to club together for that object.

Efforts for the promotion of education are specially encouraged by enlightened magistrates. Recently, over three hundred new schools were reported as opened in one department of the Province of Canton as the result of official influence, but not at government expense. The Emperor, too, has a way of bringing his influence to bear on this object without drawing a farthing from his exchequer. I shall mention three instances by way of illustration.

Last year, in Shantung, a man of literary standing contributed four acres of ground for the establishment of a village school. The governor recommended him to the notice of the Emperor, and his Majesty conferred on him the titular rank of professor in the *Kwotszekien*, or Confucian College.

Three or four years ago, in the Province of Hupeh, a retired officer of the grade of *Tautai*, or intendant of circuit, contributed twenty thousand taels for the endowment of a college at Wuchang. The Viceroy Li-Han-Chang reporting to the throne this act of munificence, the Chinese Peabody was rewarded by the privilege of wearing a red button instead of a blue one, and inscribing on his card the title of provincial judge.

The third instance is that of a college in Kwei-Lin-Foo, the capital of Quangsi. Falling into decay and ruin during the long years of the Taiping rebellion, the gentry, on the return of peace, raised contributions, repaired the building, and started it again in successful operation. The governor solicits on behalf of these public-spirited citizens some marks of the Imperial approbation; and his Majesty sends them a laudatory inscription written by the elegant pencils of the Hanlin.

But private effort, however stimulated, is utterly inadequate to the wants of the public. In Western countries the enormous exertions of religious societies, prompted as they are by pious zeal enhanced by sectarian rivalry, have always fallen short of the educational necessities of the masses. It is well understood that no system of schools can ever succeed in reaching all classes of the people unless it has its roots in the national revenue.

In China, what with the unavoidable limitation of private effort and the deplorable inefficiency of charity-schools, but a small fraction of the youth have the advantages of the most elementary education brought within their reach.

I do not here speak of the almost total absence of schools for girls, for against these Chinese are principled. The government, having no demand for the services of women in official posts, makes no provision for their education; and popular opinion regards reading and writing as dangerous arts in female hands. If a woman, however, by any chance, emerging from the shaded hemisphere to which social prejudices have consigned her (*si qua fata aspera rumpat*), vindicates for herself a position among the historians, poets, or scholars of the land, she never fails to be greeted with even more than her proper share of public admiration. Such instances induce indulgent fathers now and then to cultivate the talents of a clever daughter, and occasionally neighborhood schools for the benefit of girls are to be met with; but the Chinese people have yet to learn that the best provision they could make for the primary education of their sons would be to educate the mothers, and that the education of the mothers could not fail to improve the intellectual character of their offspring. But even for the more favored sex the facilities for obtaining an education are sadly deficient; only a small percentage of the youth attend school, and, owing to the absurd method which we have described, few of them advance far enough to be initiated into the mysteries of ideography.

On this subject a false impression has gone abroad. We hear it asserted that "education is universal in China; even coolies are taught to read and write." In one sense this is true, but not as we understand the terms "reading and writing." In the alphabetical vernaculars of the West the ability to read and write implies the ability to express one's thoughts by the pen, and to grasp the thoughts of others when so expressed. In Chinese, and especially in the classical or book language, it implies nothing of the sort. A shopkeeper may be able to write the numbers and keep accounts without being able to write anything else; and a lad who has attended school for several years will pronounce the characters of an ordinary book with faultless precision, yet not comprehend the meaning of a single sentence. Of those who can read understandingly (and nothing else ought to be called reading), the proportion is greater in towns than in rural districts. But striking an average, it does not, according to my observation, exceed one in twenty for the male sex and one in ten thousand for the female—rather a humiliating exhibit for a country which has maintained for centuries such a magnificent institution as the Hanlin Academy.

With all due allowance for the want of statistical accuracy where no statistics are obtainable, compare this with the educational statistics of the United States as given in the last census (that of 1870). Taking the country as a whole, the ratio of illiteracy among persons over ten years of age is 1 in 6; taking the Northern States alone, the ratio is 57 to 1000, or about 1 in 18.*

VI. SYSTEM OF EXAMINATIONS.†

To some it may be a matter of surprise that popular education is left to take care of itself in a country where letters are held sacred and their inventor enrolled among the gods; to others it may appear equally strange that mental cultivation is so extensively diffused, considering the cumbrous vehicle employed for the transmission of thought and the enormous difficulty of getting command of it. Both phenomena find their solution in the fact that the government does not value education for its own sake, but regards it as means to an end. The great end is the repose of the State; the instruments for securing it are able officers, and education is the means for preparing them for the discharge of their duties. This done, an adequate supply of disciplined agents once secured, the education of the people ceases to be an object. The repose of the State, one of the ancient philosophers tells us, might be assured by a process the opposite of popular education. "Fill the people's bellies and empty their minds; cause that they neither know nor desire anything, and you have the secret of a tranquil government." Such is the advice of Laukeun, which I am inclined to take as an utterance of Socratic irony rather than Machiavelian malice. So far from subscribing to this sentiment in its literal import, the Chinese government holds its officers responsible for the instruction of its

* Report of the Commissioner of Education, 1871.

† In this section certain words and phrases may remind the reader of the preceding article, but it is far from being a mere repetition.

subjects in all matters of duty; and in Chinese society the idea of instruction as the one thing needful has so wrought itself into the forms of speech as to become a wearisome cant. The red card that invites you to an entertainment solicits "instruction." When a friend meets you he apologizes for having so long absented himself from your "instructions;" and in familiar conversation, simple statements and opinions are often received as "precious instruction" by those who do not by any means accept them. It is more to the point to add that one of the classical books denounces it as the greatest of parental faults to bring up a child without instruction. This relates to the moral rather than to the intellectual side of education. The Chinese government does, nevertheless, encourage purely intellectual culture; and it does so in a most decided and effectual manner—viz., by testing attainments and rewarding exertion. In the magnificence of the scale on which it does this, it is unapproached by any other nation of the earth.

Lord Mahon, in his History of England, speaking of the patronage extended to learning in the period preceding Walpole, observes that "though the sovereign was never an Augustus, the minister was always a Mæcenas. Newton became Master of the Mint; Locke was Commissioner of Appeals; Steele was Commissioner of Stamps; Stepney, Prior, and Gray were employed in lucrative and important embassies; Addison was Secretary of State; Tickell, Secretary in Ireland. Several rich sinecures were bestowed on Congreve and Rowe, on Hughes and Ambrose Philips." And he goes on to show how the illiberality of succeeding reigns was atoned for by popular favor, the diffusion of knowledge enabling the *people* to become the patron of genius and learning.

The Chinese practise none of these three methods. The Emperor, less arbitrary than monarchs of the West, does not feel at liberty to reward an author by official appointments, and his minister has no power to do so. The inefficiency of popular patronage is less to their credit, authors reaping oftentimes much honor and little emolument from their works. But it is something to be able to add that all three are merged in a regulated State patronage, according to which the reward of literary merit is a law of the Empire and a right of the people. This brings us to speak of the examination system; not, indeed, a fresh theme, but one which is not yet exhausted. Though not new to the Occidental public, these examinations are not properly understood, for the opinion has been gaining ground that their value has been overrated, and that they are to be held responsible for all the shortcomings of Chinese intellectual culture. The truth is just the reverse. These shortcomings (I have not attempted to disguise them) are referable to other causes, while for something like two thousand years this system of literary competition has operated as a stimulating and conservative agency, to which are due not only the merits of the national education, such as it is, but its very existence. Nor has its political influence been less deep and beneficial. Essentially political in its aims, it has effected far more in the way of political good than its authors ever ventured to anticipate. By enlarging the liberties of the people it contributes to the strength of the State; and by affording occupation to the restless and aspiring it tends to secure the tranquillity of the public. The safety-valve of society, it provides a vent for that ambition and energy which would otherwise burst forth in civil strife and bloody revolution.

These examinations are of two kinds, which we shall distinguish as pre-official and post-official; the former is the offspring of the latter, which it has outgrown and overshadowed. Their genesis is not difficult to trace; and, paradoxical as it may appear, these literary examinations date back to a period anterior to the rise of literature. The principles that lie at their foundation are found clearly expressed among the received maxims of government under the earliest of the historic dynasties. It was not, however, until the dynasties of the Tang and Sung (618–

1120) that these examinations assumed substantially the form in which we now find them. Coming down from the past, with the accretions of many centuries, they have expanded into a system whose machinery is as complex as its proportions are enormous. Its ramifications extend to every district of the Empire; and it commands the services of district magistrates, prefects, and other civil functionaries up to governors and viceroys. These are all auxiliary to the regular officers of the literary corporation.

In each district there are two resident examiners with the title of professor, whose duty it is to keep a register of all competing students, and to exercise them from time to time in order to stimulate their efforts and keep them in preparation for the higher examinations in which degrees are conferred. In each province there is one chancellor or superintendent of instruction, who holds office for three years, and is required to visit every district and hold the customary examinations within that time, conferring the first degree on a certain percentage of the candidates. There are, moreover, two special examiners for each province, generally members of the Hanlin, deputed from the capital to conduct the great triennial examination and confer the second degree.

The regular degrees are three:

First, *Siu-ts'ai*, or "Budding talent."

Second, *Chu-jin*, or "Deserving of promotion."

Third, *Tsin-shi*, or "Fit for office."

To which may be added as a fourth degree the Hanlin, or member of the "Forest of Pencils." The first of these is sometimes compared to the degree of B.A., conferred by colleges and universities; the second to M.A.; and the third to D.C.L. or LL.D. The last is accurately described by membership in the Imperial Academy; always bearing in mind how much a Chinese academy must differ from a similar institution in the West. But so faint is the analogy which the other degrees bear to the literary degrees of Western lands that the interchange of terms is sure to lead to misconceptions. Chinese degrees represent talent, not knowledge; they are conferred by the State, without the intervention of school or college; they carry with them the privileges of official rank; and they are bestowed on no more than a very small percentage of those who engage in competition. With us, on the contrary, they give no official standing; they attest, where they mean anything, acquirements rather than ability; and the number of those who are "plucked" is usually small in comparison with those who are allowed to "pass." But, after all, the new-fledged bachelor of an Occidental college, his head crammed with the outlines of universal knowledge, answers quite as nearly to the sprightly *siu-ts'ai*,

> "Whose soul proud science never taught to stray
> Far as the solar walk or Milky Way,"

as does a Western general to the chief of an undisciplined horde of so-called soldiers.

The following report of Panszelien, Chancellor of the Province of Shantung, though somewhat vague, will give us an idea of the official duties of the chief examiner and the spirit in which he professes to discharge them:

"Your Majesty's servant," says the chancellor, "has guarded the seal of office with the utmost vigilance. In every instance where frauds were detected he has handed the offender over to the proper authorities for punishment. In re-examining the successful, whenever their handwriting disagreed with that of their previous performances, he has at once expelled them from the hall, without granting a particle of indulgence. He everywhere exhorted the students to aim at the cultivation of a high moral character. In judging of the merit of compositions, he followed reason and the established rules. At the close of each examination he addressed the students face to face, exhorting them not to walk in ways of vanity, nor to concern themselves with things foreign to their vocation, but to uphold the credit of scholarship and to seek to maintain or retrieve the literary reputation of their several districts. Besides these occupations, your servant, in passing from place to place, observed that the snow has everywhere exercised a reviving influence; the young wheat is beginning to shoot up; the people are perfectly quiet and well disposed; the price of provisions is moderate; and those who suffered from the recent floods are gradually returning to their forsaken homes. For literary culture, Hincheu stands pre-eminent, while Tsaocheu is equally so in military matters."

This is the whole report, with the exception of certain stereotyped phrases, employed to open and conclude such documents, and a barren catalogue of places and dates. It contains no statistical facts, no statement of the number of candidates, nor the proportion passed; indeed, no information of any kind, except that conveyed in a chance allusion in the closing sentence.

From this we learn that the chancellor is held responsible for examinations in the military art; and it might be inferred that he reviews the troops and gauges the attainments of the cadets in military history, engineering, tactics, etc.; but nothing of the kind: he sees them draw the bow, hurl the discus, and go through various manœuvres with spear and shield, which have no longer a place in civilized warfare.

The first degree only is conferred by the provincial chancellor, and the happy recipients, fifteen or twenty in each department, or one per cent. of the candidates, are decorated with the insignia of rank and admitted to the ground-floor of the nine-storied pagoda. The trial for the second degree is held in the capital of each province, by special commissioners, once in three years. It consists of three sessions of three days each, making nine days of almost continuous exertion—a strain to the mental and physical powers to which the infirm and aged frequently succumb.

In addition to composition in prose and verse, the candidate is required to show his acquaintance with history (the history of China), philosophy, criticism, and various branches of archæology.

Again one per cent. are decorated; but it is not until the more fortunate among them succeed in passing the metropolitan triennial that the meed of civil office is certainly bestowed. They are not, however, assigned to their respective offices until they have gone through two special examinations within the palace and in the presence of the Emperor. On this occasion the highest on the list is honored with the title of *chuang-yuen*, or "laureate"—a distinction so great that in the last reign it was not thought unbefitting the daughter of a *chuang-yuen* to be raised to the position of consort of the Son of Heaven.

A score of the best are admitted to membership in the Academy, two or three score are attached to it as pupils or probationers, and the rest drafted off to official posts in the capital or in the provinces, the humblest of which is supposed to compensate the occupant for a life of penury and toil.

In conclusion, this noble institution—the civil-service competitive system—appears destined to play a conspicuous part in carrying forward an intellectual movement the incipient stages of which are already visible. It has cherished the national education, such as it is; and if it has compelled the mind of China for ages past to grind in the mill of barren imitation, that is not the fault of the system, but its abuse.

When the growing influence of Western science animates it with a new spirit, as it must do ere long, we shall see a million or more of patient students applying themselves to scientific studies with all the ardor that now characterizes their literary competition.

Six years ago the Viceroy of Fuhkien, now a member of the Imperial Cabinet, proposed the institution of a competition in mathematics. The suggestion was not adopted; but a few days ago it was brought up in a new form, with the addition of the physical sciences, by Li-Hung-Chang, the famous governor of the metropolitan province. When adopted, as it must be, it will place the entire examination system on a new basis, and inaugurate an intellectual revolution whose extent and results it would be difficult to predict.

In remodelling her national education, Japan has begun with her schools, and, however reluctant, China will be compelled to do the same. Thus far her efforts in that direction have been few and feeble, all that she has to show being a couple of schools at Canton and Shanghai, with forty students each; three or four schools in connection with the arsenal at Fuhchow, with an aggregate of three hundred; and in the capital an Imperial College for Western Science, with an attendance of about a hundred.*

The proposed modifications in the civil-service examination system will not only invest each of these schools with a new importance, and give a higher value to every educated youth; it will have the effect of creating for itself a system of schools and colleges on the basis of an existing organization.

In every department and district there is a government school with two or more professors attached. The professors give no instruction, and the students only present themselves at stated times for examination. With the introduction of science these professors will become teachers, and each of these now deserted schools a centre of illumination.

---

* The number of students in this institution is limited by the fact that they are on government pay and training for government service. The faculty of instruction consists of eleven professors, seven foreign and four Chinese.

A printing-office with six presses has lately been erected in connection with the college, with a view to the printing and circulation of scientific works. These are expected to be supplied in part by the professors and students, who are at present largely occupied with the translation of useful books.

APPENDIX.*

"HARTFORD, CONN., *March* 17, 1876.

"DEAR SIR,—Enclosed herewith I beg to hand you a brief report of our Chinese students in this country. I should have written it much earlier had not my time been well taken up by other duties connected with the mission. Should you have any inquires to make about our students, do not hesitate to put them.

"I remain, your obedient servant,

"YUNG WING.†

"Hon. J. EATON,

"*Commissioner of Education, Washington, D. C.*"

"Since the statement of January 7, 1873, respecting the arrival in September, 1872, of the first detachment of Chinese government students in this country was published, we have had three more detachments of thirty students each, who came in succession in the years 1873,'74,'75; thus completing the whole number of one hundred and twenty, as originally determined upon by the Chinese government. These students are located in towns in Connecticut and Massachusetts all along the Connecticut valley.

"The first detachment has been here about three years and a half, up to the 1st of March, 1876; the second detachment has been two years and a half; the third, one year and a half; and the fourth, only four months.

"Most of the first detachment have joined classes in public schools and academies, and are now studying algebra, Greek, and Latin.

"It is expected that about three years from now (March, 1876) they will be able to enter colleges and scientific schools. Those of the second and other detachments are still prosecuting their English studies, such as arithmetic, geography, grammar, and history. A few of them have exhibited decided taste for drawing and sketching. Specimens of these, together with manuscripts of written examinations in all their studies, were sent to Hon. B. G. Northrop for the Centennial Exhibition. These papers may be taken

---

* These documents appended by the Commissioner of Education to the original publication are retained on account of their intrinsic interest.

† Mr. Yung Wing is an alumnus of Yale College, and has received from his Alma Mater the honorary degree of LL.D.

as fair evidences of their progress in the different studies since they have been here.

"Our students, ever since their arrival, have been favored with good health in a remarkable degree. With the exception of one case of death from scarlet fever in 1875, they have, on the whole, enjoyed excellent health. Besides the one who died a year ago, we have dismissed four, thus leaving us only one hundred and fifteen students.

"There have been some material changes in the mission during the past year. Mr. Chin Lan Pin, one of the commissioners, who returned to China more than a year ago, has been succeeded by Ngen Ngoh Liang; Mr. Kwong Ki Chin has taken the place of Mr. Chan Laisun, translator; and Lin Yun Fong, a young tutor in Chinese, has been added to the staff of teachers."

AN OLD UNIVERSITY IN CHINA.*

It is not, perhaps, generally known that Peking contains an ancient university; for, though certain buildings connected with it have been frequently described, the institution itself has been but little noticed. It gives, indeed, so few signs of life that it is not surprising it should be overlooked. And yet few of the institutions of this hoary Empire are invested with a deeper interest, as venerable relics of the past, and, at the same time, as mournful illustrations of the degenerate present.

If a local situation be deemed an essential element of identity, this old university must yield the palm of age to many in Europe, for in its present site it dates, at most, only from the Yuen, or Mongol, dynasty, in the beginning of the fourteenth century. But as an imperial institution, having a fixed organization and definite objects, it carries its history, or at least its pedigree, back to a period far anterior to the founding of the Great Wall.

Among the Regulations of the House of Chow, which flourished a thousand years before the Christian era, we meet with it already in full-blown vigor, and under the identical name which it now bears, that of *Kwotszekien*, or "School for the Sons of the Empire." It was in its glory before the light of science dawned on Greece, and when Pythagoras and Plato were pumping their secrets from the priests of Heliopolis. And it still exists, but it is only an embodiment of "life in death:" its halls are tombs, and its officers living mummies.

In the 13th Book of the *Chowle* (see *Rites de Tcheou, traduc-*

---

* First published in 1871.

tion par Édouard Biot), we find the functions of the heads of the Kwotszekien laid down with a good deal of minuteness.

The presidents were to admonish the Emperor of that which is good and just, and to instruct the Sons of the State in the "three constant virtues" and the "three practical duties"—in other words, to give a course of lectures on moral philosophy. The vice-presidents were to reprove the Emperor for his faults (i. e. to perform the duty of official censors) and to discipline the Sons of the State in sciences and arts—viz., in arithmetic, writing, music, archery, horsemanship, and ritual ceremonies. The titles and offices of the subordinate instructors are not given in detail, but we are able to infer them with a good degree of certainty from what we know of the organization as it now exists.

The old curriculum is religiously adhered to, but greater latitude is given, as we shall have occasion to observe, to the term "Sons of the State." In the days of Chow, this meant the heir-apparent, princes of the blood, and children of the nobility. Under the Tatsing dynasty it signifies men of defective scholarship throughout the provinces, who purchase literary degrees, and more specifically certain indigent students of Peking, who are aided by the imperial bounty.

The Kwotszekien is located in the northeastern angle of the Tartar city, with a temple of Confucius attached, which is one of the finest in the Empire. The main edifice (that of the temple) consists of a single story of imposing height, with a porcelain roof of tent-like curvature. It shelters no object of veneration beyond simple tablets of wood inscribed with the name of the sage and those of his most illustrious disciples. It contains no seats, as all comers are expected to stand or kneel in presence of the Great Teacher. Neither does it boast anything in the way of artistic decoration, nor exhibit any trace of that neatness and taste which we look for in a sacred place. Perhaps its vast area is designedly left to dust and emptiness, in order that nothing may intervene to disturb the mind in the contemplation of a great name which receives the homage of a nation.

Gilded tablets, erected by various emperors—the only ornamental objects that meet the eye—record the praises of Confucius; one pronounces him the "culmination of the sages," another describes him as forming a "trinity with Heaven and Earth," and a third declares that "his holy soul was sent down from heaven." A grove of cedars, the chosen emblem of a fame that never fades, occupies a space in front of the temple, and some of the trees are huge with the growth of centuries.

In an adjacent block or square stands a pavilion known as the "Imperial Lecture-room," because it is incumbent on each occupant of the Dragon throne to go there at least once in his lifetime to hear a discourse on the nature and responsibilities of his office—thus conforming to the letter of the *Chowle*, which makes it the duty of the officers of the university to administer reproof and exhortation to their sovereign,* and doing homage to the university by going in person to receive its instruction.

A canal spanned by marble bridges encircles the pavilion, and arches of glittering porcelain, in excellent repair, adorn the grounds. But neither these nor the pavilion itself constitutes the chief attraction of the place.

Under a long corridor which encloses the entire space may be seen as many as one hundred and eighty-two columns of massive granite, each inscribed with a portion of the canonical books. These are the "Stone Classics"—the entire "Thirteen," which form the staple of a Chinese education, being here enshrined in a material supposed to be imperishable. Among all the universities in the world, the Kwotszekien is unique in the possession of such a library.

This is not, indeed, the only stone library extant—another of

* They still discharge these functions in writing, their memorials frequently appearing in the pages of the *Peking Gazette.*

equal extent being found at Singanfu, the ancient capital of the Tangs. But that, too, was the property of the Kwotszekien ten centuries ago, when Singan was the seat of empire. The "School for the Sons of the Empire" must needs follow the migrations of the court; and that library, costly as it was, being too heavy for transportation, it was thought best to supply its place by the new edition which we have been describing.

The use of this heavy literature is a matter for speculation, a question almost as difficult of solution as the design of the pyramids. Was it intended to supply the world with a standard text—a safe channel through which the streams of wisdom might be transmitted pure and undefiled? Or were their sacred books engraved on stone to secure them from any modern madman, who might take it into his head to emulate the Tyrant of Tsin, the burner of the books and builder of the Great Wall? If the former was the object, it was useless, as paper editions, well executed and carefully preserved, would have answered the purpose equally well. If the latter, it was absurd, as granite, though fire-proof, is not indestructible; and long before these columns were erected, the discovery of the art of printing had forever placed the depositories of wisdom beyond the reach of the barbarian's torch. It is characteristic of the Chinese to ask for no better reason than ancient custom. Their forefathers engraved these classics on stone, and they must do the same. But whatever may have been the original design, the true light in which to regard these curious books is that of an impressive tribute to the sources of their civilization.

I may mention here that the Rev. Dr. Williamson, on a visit to Singanfu, saw many persons engaged in taking "rubbings" from the stone classics of that city; and he informs us that complete copies were sold at a very high rate. The popularity of the Singan tablets is accounted for by the flavor of antiquity which they possess, and especially by the style of the engraving, which is much admired—or, more properly, the calligraphy which it reproduces. Those of Peking are not at all patronized by the printers, and yet if textual accuracy were the object, they ought, as a later edition, to be more highly prized than the others. A native cicerone whom I once questioned as to the object of these stones replied, with a naïveté quite refreshing, that they were "set up for the amusement of visitors"—an answer which I should have set to the credit of his ready wit, if he had not proceeded to inform me that neither students nor editors ever came to consult the text, and that "rubbings" are never taken.

In front of the temple stands a forest of columns of scarcely inferior interest. They are three hundred and twenty in number, and contain the university roll of honor, a complete list of all who since the founding of the institution have attained to the dignity of the doctorate. Allow to each an average of two hundred names, and we have an army of doctors sixty thousand strong! (By the doctorate I mean the third or highest degree.) All these received their investiture at the Kwotszekien, and, throwing themselves at the feet of its president, enrolled themselves among the "Sons of the Empire." They were not, however—at least the most of them were not—in any proper sense alumni of the Kwotszekien, having pursued their studies in private, and won their honors by public competition in the halls of the Civil-service Examining Board.

This granite register goes back for nearly six hundred years; but while intended to stimulate ambition and gratify pride, it reads to the new graduate a lesson of humility—showing him how remorselessly time consigns all human honors to oblivion. The columns are quite exposed, and those that are more than a century old are so defaced by the weather as to be no longer legible.

If in the matter of conferring degrees the Kwotszekien "beats the world," it must be remembered that it enjoys the monopoly of the Empire—so far as the doctorate is concerned.

Besides these departments, intended mainly to commemorate

the past, there is an immense area occupied by lecture-rooms, examination-halls, and lodging-apartments. But the visitor is liable to imagine that these, too, are consecrated to a monumental use—so rarely is a student or a professor to be seen among them. Ordinarily they are as desolate as the halls of Baalbec or Palmyra. In fact, this great school for the "Sons of the Empire" has long ceased to be a seat of instruction, and degenerated into a mere appendage of the civil-service competitive examinations, on which it hangs as a dead weight, corrupting and debasing instead of advancing the standard of national education.

By an old law, made for the purpose of enhancing the importance of this institution, the possession of a scholarship carries with it the privilege of wearing decorations which belong to the first degree, and of entering the lists to compete for the second. This naturally caused such scholarships to be eagerly sought for, and eventually had the effect of bringing them into market as available stock on which to raise funds for government use. A price was placed on them, and like the papal indulgences, they were vended throughout the Empire.

Never so high as to be beyond the reach of aspiring poverty, their price has now descended to such a figure as to convert these honors into objects of contempt. In Peking it is twenty-three taels (about thirty dollars), but in the provinces they can be had for half that sum. Not long ago one of the censors expostulated with his Majesty on the subject of these sales. He expressed in strong language his disgust at the idea of clodhoppers and muleteers appearing with the insignia of literary rank, and denounced in no measured terms the cheap sale of ranks and offices generally. Still—and the fact is not a little curious—it was not the principle of selling which he condemned, but that reckless degradation of prices which had the effect of spoiling the market.

It is not our purpose to take up the lamentation of this patriotic censor, or to show how the opening of title and office brokeries lowers the credit and saps the influence of the government. And yet this entire traffic has a close relation to the subject in hand; for, whatever rank or title may be the object of purchase, a university scholarship must of necessity be purchased along with it, as the root on which it is grafted. Accordingly the flood-gates of this fountain of honors are kept wide open, and a very deluge of diplomas issues from them. A year or two ago a hundred thousand were sent into the provinces at one time!

The scholars of this old institution accordingly outnumber those of Oxford or Paris in their palmiest days. But there are thousands of her adopted children who have never seen the walls of Peking, and thousands more within the precincts of the capital who have never entered her gates.

Those who are too impatient to wait the slow results of competition in their native districts are accustomed to seek at the university the requisite qualifications for competing for the higher degrees. These qualifications are not difficult of attainment—the payment of a trifling fee and submission to a formal examination being all that is required.

For a few weeks previous to the great triennial examinations, the lodging-houses of the university are filled with students who are "cramming" for the occasion. At other times they present the aspect of a deserted village.

On the accession of the Manchu Tartars two centuries ago (1644), eight large schools or colleges were established for the benefit of the eight tribes or banners into which the Tartars of Peking are divided. They were projected on a liberal scale, and affiliated to the university, their special object being to promote among the rude invaders a knowledge of Chinese letters and civilization. Each was provided with a staff of five professors, and had an attendance of one hundred and five pupils, who were encouraged by a monthly stipend and regarded as in training for the public service. The central luminary and its satellites presented at that time a brilliant and imposing spectacle.

At present, however, the system is practically abandoned, the college buildings have fallen to ruin, and not one of them is open for the instruction of youth. Nothing remains as a reminiscence of the past but a sham examination, which is held from time to time to enable the professors and students to draw their pay. Some ten years ago an effort was made to resuscitate these government schools by requiring attendance *once in three days*, but such an outcry was raised against it that it soon fell through. Those who cared to learn could learn better at home, and those who did not care for learning would choose to dispense with their pensions rather than take the trouble of attending so frequently. So the students remain at home, and the professors enjoy their sinecures, having no serious duty to perform, excepting the worship of Confucius. The presidents of the university are even designated by a title which signifies libation-pourers, indicating that this empty ceremony is regarded as their highest function. Twice a month (viz., at the new and full moon) all the professors are required to assemble in official robes, and perform nine prostrations on the flag-stones, at a respectful distance, in front of the temple.

But even this duty a pliable conscience enables them to alleviate by performing it by proxy, one member only of each college appearing for the rest, and after the ceremony inscribing the names of his colleagues in a ledger called the "Record of Diligence," in evidence that they were all present.

But negligent and perfunctory as they are, they are not much to be blamed; they do as much as they are paid for. Two *taels per month* (three dollars), together with two suits of clothes and two bushels of rice per annum, and a fur-jacket once in three years—these are their emoluments as fixed by law. Scant as the money allowance originally was, it is still further reduced by being paid in depreciated currency, and actually amounts to less than one dollar per month. The requisition for government rice is disposed of at a similar discount, the hungry professor being obliged to sell it to a broker instead of drawing directly from the imperial storehouses. As for the clothing, there is room to suspect that it has warmed other shoulders before coming into his possession.

These professorships, however, possess a value independent of salary. The empty title carries with it a certain social distinction; and the completion of a three years' term of nominal service renders a professor eligible to the post of district magistrate. These places, therefore, do not go a-begging, though their incumbents sometimes do.

In order to form a just idea of the Kwotszekien, we must study its constitution. This will acquaint us with the design of its founders, and show us what it was in its prime, at the beginning of the present dynasty, or, for that matter, at the beginning of any other dynasty that has ruled China for the last three thousand years. We find it in the *Tatsing hweitien*, the collected statutes of the reigning dynasty; and it looks so well on paper that we cannot refrain from admiring the wisdom and liberality of the ancient worthies who planned it, however poorly its present state answers to their original conception. We find our respect for the Chinese increasing as we recede from the present; and in China, among the dust and decay of her antiquated and effete institutions, one may be excused for catching the common infection, and becoming a worshipper of antiquity.

Its officers, according to this authority, consist of a rector, who is selected from among the chief ministers of the State; two presidents and three vice-presidents, who have the grade and title of *tajen*, or "great men," and, together with the rector, constitute the governing body; two *poh-she*, or directors of instruction; two proctors; two secretaries; and one librarian: these are general officers. Then come the officers of the several colleges.

There are six colleges for Chinese students, bearing the names of the "Hall for the Pursuit of Wisdom," the "Hall of the Sincere Heart," "Hall of True Virtue," "Hall of Noble Aspirations," "Hall of Broad Acquirements," and the "Hall for the Guidance of Nature." Each of these has two regular professors, and I know not how many assistants. There are eight colleges for the Manchu Tartars, as above mentioned, each with five professors. And, lastly, there is a school for the Russian language, and a school for mathematics and astronomy, each with one professor. To these we add six clerks and translators, and we have a total of seventy-one persons, constituting what we may call the corporation of the university.

As to the curriculum of studies, its literature was never expected to go beyond the thirteen classics engraved on the stones which adorn its halls; while its arts and sciences were all comprehended in the familiar "Six," which from the days of Chow, if not from those of Yaou and Shun, have formed the trivium and quadrivium of the Chinese people.

It would be doing injustice to the ancients to accuse them of limiting the scientific studies of the Kwotszekien by their narrow formulæ. The truth is, that, little as the ancients accomplished in this line, their modern disciples have not attempted to emulate or overtake them. In the University of Grand Cairo, it is said, no science that is more recent than the twelfth century is allowed to be taught. In that of China, the "School for the Sons of the Empire," no science whatever is pretended to be taught.

This is not, however, owing to any restriction in the constitution or charter, as its terms afford sufficient scope for expansion if the officers of the university had possessed the disposition or the capacity to avail themselves of such liberty. It is there said, for example, "As to practical arts, such as the art of war, astronomy, engraving, music, law, and the like, let the professors lead their students to the original sources and point out the defects and the merits of each author."

Is there any ground to hope that this ancient school, once an ornament and a blessing to the Empire, may be renovated, remodelled, and adapted to the altered circumstances of the age? The prospect, we think, is not encouraging. A traveller, on entering the city of Peking, is struck by the vast extent and skilful masonry of its sewers; but he is not less astonished at their present dilapidated condition, reeking with filth and breeding pestilence, instead of ministering to the health of the city. When these *cloacæ* are restored, and lively streams of mountain water are made to course through all their veins and arteries, then, and not till then, may this old university be reconstructed and perform a part in the renovation of the Empire.

Creation is sometimes easier than reformation. It was a conviction of this fact that led the more enlightened among the Chinese ministers some years ago to favor the establishment of a new institution for the cultivation of foreign science, rather than attempt to introduce it through any of the existing channels, such as the Kwotszekien, Astronomical College, or Board of Works.

Their undertaking met with strenuous opposition from a party of bigoted conservatives, headed by Wojin, a member of the privy council, and tutor to his Majesty. Through his influence mainly, the educated classes were induced to stand aloof, professing that they would be better employed in teaching the Western barbarians than in learning from them. Wojin scouted the idea that in so vast an Empire there could be any want of natives who would be found qualified to give instruction in all the branches proposed to be studied.

The Emperor took him at his word, and told him to come forward with his men; and he might have *carte-blanche* for the establishment of a rival school. He declined the trial in the form in which it was proposed; but he now has the opportunity of making the experiment on a much more extensive scale.

This hater of foreigners and vaunter of native science is now

Rector of the Kwotszekien—the "School for the Sons of the Empire." Let us see what he will make of it. Under his care will it become a fountain of light, or will it continue to be what it now is, a wholesale manufactory of spurious mandarins?*

---

* Wojin died not long after his appointment to this office, and at the present hour (1879) the old university continues to be just what it was eight years ago.

THE SAN KIAO, OR THREE RELIGIONS OF CHINA.*

The religious experience of the Chinese is worthy of attentive study. Detached at an early period from the parent stock, and for thousands of years holding but little intercourse with other branches of the human family, we are able to ascertain with a good degree of precision those ideas which constituted their original inheritance, and to trace in history the development or corruption of their primitive beliefs. Midway in their long career, importing from India an exotic system, and more recently coming in contact with Mahometanism and Christianity, we are enabled to observe the manner in which their indigenous creeds have been affected or modified by foreign elements.

In their long experience each of the leading systems has been fairly tested. The arena has been large enough, and the duration of the experiment long enough, to admit of each system working out its full results; and these experiments are of the greater value, because they have been wrought out in the midst of a highly organized society, and in connection with a high degree of intellectual culture.

In their views and practices, the Chinese of to-day are polytheistic and idolatrous. The evidence of this strikes the attention of the voyager on every hand. In the sanpan that carries him to the shore, he discovers a small shrine which contains an image of the river-god, the god of wealth, or Kwanyin (the goddess of mercy). His eye is charmed by the picturesqueness of pagodas perched on mountain-crags, and monasteries nestling in

* This paper first appeared in the *New-Englander* quarterly review, April, 1869.

sequestered dells; and, on entering even a small town, he is surprised at the extent, if not the magnificence, of temples erected to Cheng-hwang, the "city defender," and Confucius, the patron of letters. Heaps of gilt paper are consumed in the streets, accompanied by volleys of fire-crackers. Bonzes, modulating their voices by the sound of a wooden rattle, fill the air with their melancholy chant; and processions wind through narrow lanes, bearing on their shoulders a silver effigy of the "dragon king," the god of rain.

These temples, images, and symbols, he is informed, all belong to *San kiao* (three religions). All three are equally idolatrous, and he inquires in vain for any influential native sect, which, more enlightened or philosophical than the rest, raises a protest against the prevailing superstition. Yet, on acquiring the language and studying the popular superstitions in their myriad fantastic shapes, he begins to discover traces of a religious sentiment, deep and real, which is not connected with any of the objects of popular worship—a veneration for Tien, or Heaven, and a belief that in the visible heavens there resides some vague power who provides for the wants of men, and rewards them according to their deeds.

Personified as Lautienye—not Heavenly Father, as it expresses the Christian's conception of combined tenderness and majesty, but literally "Old Father Heaven," much as we say "Old Father Time"—or designated by a hundred other appellations, this august but unknown Being, though universally acknowledged, is invoked or worshipped only to a very limited extent. Some, at the close of the year, present a thank-offering to the Great Power who has controlled the course of its events; others burn a stick of incense every evening under the open sky; and in the marriage ceremony all classes bow down before Tien as the first of the five objects of veneration.*

* The other four are the earth, the prince, parents, and teachers.

When taxed with ingratitude in neglecting to honor that Being on whom they depend for existence, the Chinese uniformly reply, "It is not ingratitude, but reverence, that prevents our worship. He is too great for us to worship. None but the Emperor is worthy to lay an offering on the altar of Heaven." In conformity with this sentiment, the Emperor, as the high-priest and mediator of his people, celebrates in Peking the worship of Heaven with imposing ceremonies.

Within the gates of the southern division of the capital, and surrounded by a sacred grove so extensive that the silence of its deep shades is never broken by the noises of the busy world, stands the Temple of Heaven. It consists of a single tower, whose tiling of resplendent azure is intended to represent the form and color of the aerial vault. It contains no image, and the solemn rites are not performed within the tower; but, on a marble altar which stands before it, a bullock is offered once a year as a burnt-sacrifice, while the master of the Empire prostrates himself in adoration of the Spirit of the Universe.*

This is the high-place of Chinese devotion; and the thoughtful visitor feels that he ought to tread its courts with unsandalled feet.† For no vulgar idolatry has entered here: this mountain-top still stands above the waves of corruption, and on this solitary altar there still rests a faint ray of the primeval faith. The tablet which represents the invisible Deity is inscribed with the name of Shangte, the Supreme Ruler; and as we contemplate the Majesty of the Empire prostrate before it while the smoke ascends from his burning sacrifice, our thoughts are irresistibly

* Another tower of similar structure but larger dimensions stands in a separate enclosure as a kind of vestibule to the more sacred place. It is called 祈年殿, and here it is that the Emperor prays for "fruitful seasons."

† Dr. Legge, the distinguished translator of the Chinese Classics, visiting Peking some years after this was written, actually "put his shoes from off his feet" before ascending the steps of the great altar.

carried back to the time when the King of Salem officiated as "Priest of the Most High God."

The writings and the institutions of the Chinese are not, like those of the Hindoos and the Hebrews, pervaded with the idea of God. It is, nevertheless, expressed in their ancient books with so much clearness as to make us wonder and lament that it has left so faint an impression on the national mind.

In their books of History it is recorded that music was invented for the praise of Shangte. Rival claimants for the throne appeal to the judgment of Shangte. He is the arbiter of nations, and, while actuated by benevolence, is yet capable of being provoked to wrath by the iniquities of men. In the Book of Changes he is represented as restoring life to torpid nature on the return of spring. In the Book of Rites it is said that the ancients "prayed for grain to Shangte," and presented in offering a bullock, which must be without blemish, and stall-fed for three months before the day of sacrifice. In the Book of Odes, mostly composed from eight hundred to a thousand years before the Christian era, and containing fragments of still higher antiquity, Shangte is represented as seated on a lofty throne, while the spirits of the good "walk up and down on his right and left."

In none of these writings is Shangte clothed in the human form or debased by human passion like the Zeus of the Greek. There is in them even less of anthropomorphism than we find in the representations of Jehovah in the Hebrew Scriptures. The nearest approach to exhibiting him in the human form is the ascription to Shangte of a "huge footprint," probably an impression on some mass of rock. But how far the conception of the Supreme Ruler is removed from gross materialism may be inferred from that line in one of the ancient odes, *Shangte wu sheng wu hiu*—"God has no voice or odor," i. e. he is imperceptible by the senses. And the philosopher Chuhe says, in his Commentary on the Ancient Classics, that "Shangte is *le*,"

i. e. a principle of nature. Educated Chinese, on embracing Christianity, assert that the Shangte of their fathers was identical with the Tienchu, the Lord of Heaven, whom they are taught to worship.*

There is therefore no need of an extended argument, even if our space would admit of it, to establish the fact that the early Chinese were by no means destitute of the knowledge of God. They did not, indeed, know him as the Creator, but they recognized him as supreme in providence, and without beginning or end.

Whence came this conception? Was it the mature result of ages of speculation, or was it brought down from remote antiquity on the stream of patriarchal tradition? The latter, we think, is the only probable hypothesis. In the earlier books of the Chinese there is no trace of speculative inquiry. They raise no question as to the nature of Shangte, or the grounds of their faith in such a being, but in their first pages allude to him as already well known, and speak of burnt-offerings made to him on mountain-tops as an established rite. Indeed, the idea of Shangte, when it first meets us, is not in the process of development, but already in the first stages of decay. The beginnings of that idolatry by which it was subsequently almost obliterated are distinctly traceable. The heavenly bodies, the spirits of the hills and rivers, and even the spirits of deceased men, were admitted to a share in the divine honors of Shangte. The religious sentiment was frittered away by being directed to a multiplicity of objects, and the popular mind seemed to take refuge among the creatures of its own fancy, as Adam did amidst the trees of the Garden, from the terrible idea of a holy God. A debasing superstition became universal. Such was the state of things prior to the rise of the Three Religions.

---

* Paul Seu, a member of the Hanlin Academy, and cabinet minister under the Ming dynasty, makes this assertion in an eloquent apology addressed to the throne in behalf of his new faith and its teachers.

In order to understand the mutual relations of these three systems—in other words, to understand the religious aspects of China at the present day—it will be necessary to give separate attention to the rise and progress of each. We begin with Confucianism.

There are two classes of great men who leave their mark on the condition of their species—those who change the course of history without any far-reaching purpose, much as a falling cliff changes the direction of a stream; and those, again, who, like skilful engineers, excavate a channel for the thought of future generations. Pre-eminent among the latter stands the name of Confucius. Honored during his lifetime to such a degree that the princes of several states lamented his decease like that of a father, his influence has deepened with time and extended with the swelling multitudes of his people. Buddhism and Tauism both give signs of decay, but the influence and the memory of Confucius continue as green as the cypresses that shade his tomb. After the lapse of three-and-twenty centuries, he has a temple in every city, and an effigy in every schoolroom. He is venerated as the fountain of wisdom by all the votaries of letters, and worshipped by the mandarins of the realm as the author of their civil polity. The estimation in which his teachings continue to be held is well exhibited in the reply which the people of Shantung, his native province, gave to a missionary who, some thirty years ago, offered them Christian books: "We have seen your books," said they, "and neither desire nor approve of them. In the instructions of our Sage we have sufficient, and they are superior to any foreign doctrines that you can bring us."

Born B.C. 551, and endowed with uncommon talents, Confucius was far from relying on the fertility of his own genius. "Reading without thought is fruitless, and thought without reading dangerous," is a maxim which he taught his disciples, and one which he had doubtless followed in the formation of his own mind. China already possessed accumulated treasures of literature and history. With these materials he stored his memory, and by the aid of reflection digested them into a system for the use of posterity.

Filled with enthusiasm by the study of the ancients, and mourning over the degeneracy of his own times, he entered at an early age on the vocation of reformer. He at first sought to effect his objects by obtaining civil office and setting an example of good government, as well as by giving instruction to those who became his disciples. At the age of fifty-five he was advanced to the premiership of his native State; and in a few months the improvement in the public morals was manifest. Valuables might be exposed in the street without being stolen, and shepherds abandoned the practice of filling their sheep with water before leading them to market.

The circumstance that led him to renounce political life is worth recording. The little kingdom of Lu grew apace in wealth and prosperity; and the princes of rival states, in order to prevent its acquiring an ascendency in the politics of the Empire, felt it necessary to counteract the influence of the wise legislator. Resorting to a stratagem similar to that which Louis XIV. employed with Charles II., they sent to the Prince of Lu, instead of brave generals or astute statesmen, a band of beautiful girls who were skilled in music and dancing. The prince, young and amorous, was caught in the snare, and, giving the rein to pleasure, abandoned all the schemes of reform with which he had been inspired by the counsels of the Sage. Disappointed and disgusted, Confucius retired into private life.

Thwarted, as he had often been, by royal pride and official jealousy, he henceforth endeavored to attain his ends by a less direct but more certain method. He devoted himself more than ever to the instruction of youth. His fame attracted young men of promise from all the surrounding principalities. No fewer than three thousand received his instructions, among whom five hundred became distinguished mandarins, and seventy-two of them are enrolled on the list of the sages of the Empire. Through these and the books which he edited subsequently to this period, there can be no doubt that he exerted a greater influence on the destinies of the Empire than he could have done had he been seated on the Imperial throne. He won for himself the title of *Su Wang*, "the unsceptred monarch," whose intellectual sway is acknowledged by all ages.

Confucius understood the power of proverbs, and, incorporating into his system such as met his approval, he cast his own teachings in the same mould. His speeches are laconic and oracular, and he has transmitted to posterity a body of political ethics expressed in formulæ so brief and comprehensive that it may easily be retained in the weakest memory. Thus, *kuin chieng*, *fu tsz*, *fu fu*, *hiungte*, *pung yiu*, are ten syllables which every boy in China has at his tongue's end. They contain the entire framework of the social fabric—the "five relations" of sovereign and subject, parent and child, husband and wife, brother and brother, friend and friend, which, according to the Chinese, comprehend the whole duty of man as a social being. The five cardinal virtues—benevolence, justice, order, prudence, and fidelity—so essential to the well-being of society, Confucius inculcated in the five syllables *jen è lé che sin*.

The following sentences, taken from his miscellaneous discourses, may serve as illustrations of both the style and the matter of his teaching:

"Good government consists in making the prince a prince, the subject a subject, the parent a parent, and the child a child."

"Beware of doing to another what you would not that others should do to you."

"He that is not offended at being misunderstood is a superior man."

"Have no friend who is inferior to yourself in virtue."

"Be not afraid to correct a fault. He that knows the right and fears to do it is not a brave man."

"If you guide the people by laws, and enforce the laws by punishment, they will lose the sense of shame and seek to evade them; but if you guide them by a virtuous example, and diffuse among them a love of order, they will be ashamed to transgress."

"To know what we know, and to know what we do not know, is knowledge."

"We know not life, how can we know death?"

"The filial son is one who gives his parents no anxiety but for his health."

Filial piety, Confucius taught, is not merely a domestic virtue, but diffuses its influence through all the actions of life. A son who disgraces his parents in any way is unfilial; one who maltreats a brother or a relative, forgetful of the bonds of a common parentage, is unfilial. This powerful motive is thus rendered expansive in its application, like piety to God in the Christian system, for which, indeed, it serves as a partial substitute. It is beautifully elaborated in the *Hiao king*, the most popular of the Thirteen Classics.

Virtue, Confucius taught with Aristotle, is the mean between two vices, and this theory is developed by his grandson in the *Chungyung*, the sublimest of the sacred books.

The secret of good government, he taught, consists in the cultivation of personal virtue on the part of rulers; and the connection between private morals and national politics is well set forth in the *Ta hio*, or Great Study.

This brief tractate is the only formal composition, with the exception of an outline of history, which the Great Sage put forth as the product of his own pen. "I am an editor, and not an author," is the modest account which he gives of himself, and it is mainly to his labors in this department that China is indebted for her knowledge of antecedent antiquity.

The spirit in which he discharged this double duty to the past and future may be inferred from the impressive ceremony with which he concluded his great task. Assembling his disciples, he led them to the summit of a neighboring hill, where sacrifices were usually offered. Here he erected an altar, and placing on it an edition of the sacred books which he had just completed, the gray-haired philosopher, now seventy years of age, fell on his knees, devoutly returned thanks for having had life and strength granted him to accomplish that laborious undertaking, at the same time imploring that the benefit his countrymen would receive from it might not be small. "Chinese pictures," says Pauthier, "represent the Sage in the attitude of supplication, and a beam of light or a rainbow descending on the sacred volumes, while his disciples stand around him in admiring wonder." *

Thales expired about the time Confucius drew his infant breath, and Pythagoras was his contemporary; but the only names among the Greeks which admit of comparison with that of Confucius are Socrates and Aristotle, the former of whom revolutionized the philosophy of Greece, and the latter ruled the dialectics of mediæval Europe. Without the discursive eloquence of the one or the logical acumen of the other, Confucius surpassed them both in practical wisdom, and exceeds them immeasurably in the depth, extent, and permanence of his influence.

It is not surprising that when missionaries attempt to direct their attention to the Saviour, the Chinese point to Confucius and challenge comparison; nor that they should sometimes fail to be satisfied with the arguments employed to establish the superiority of Jesus Christ. But the thoughtful Christian who has studied the canonical books of China can hardly return to the perusal of the New Testament without a deeper conviction of its divine authority. In the Confucian classics he detects

* Since reading this passage in Pauthier, I have myself seen this picture in a native pictorial biography of Confucius.

none of that impurity which defiles the pages of Greek and Roman authors, and none of that monstrous mythology which constitutes so large a portion of the sacred books of the Hindoos, but he discovers defects enough to make him turn with gratitude to the revelations of the "Teacher sent from God."

Disgusted at the superstitions of the vulgar, and desirous of guarding his followers against similar excesses, Confucius led them into the opposite extreme of scepticism. He ignored, if he did not deny, those cardinal doctrines of all religion, the immortality of the soul, and the personal existence of God, both of which were currently received in his day. In place of *Shangte* (Supreme Ruler), the name under which the God of Nature had been worshipped in earlier ages, he made use of the vague appellation *T'ien* (Heaven); thus opening the way, on the one hand, for that atheism with which their modern philosophy is so deeply infected, and, on the other, for that idolatry which nothing but the doctrine of a personal God can effectually counteract. When his pupils proposed inquiries respecting a future state, he either discouraged them or answered ambiguously, and thus deprived his own precepts of the support they might have derived from the sanctions of a coming retribution. Thus in a remarkable discourse reported in the *Kia-yu*—a collection the authority of which is not, however, above suspicion—he says, "If I should say the soul survives the body, I fear the filial would neglect their living parents in their zeal to serve their deceased ancestors. If, on the contrary, I should say the soul does not survive, I fear lest the unfilial should throw away the bodies of their parents and leave them unburied."

We may add that, while his writings abound in the praises of virtue, not a line can be found inculcating the pursuit of truth. Expediency, not truth, is the goal of his system. Contrast with this the Gospel of Christ, which pronounces him the only freeman whom the "truth makes free," and promises to his followers "the Spirit of Truth" as his richest legacy.

The style of Confucius was an ipse-dixit dogmatism, and it has left its impress on the unreasoning habit of the Chinese mind. Jesus Christ appealed to evidence and challenged inquiry, and this characteristic of our religion has shown itself in the mental development of Christian nations. Nor is the contrast less striking in another point. *Illius dicta, hujus facta laudantur*, to borrow the words of Tully in comparing Cato with Socrates. Confucius selected disciples who should be the depositaries of his teachings; Christ chose apostles who should be witnesses of his actions. Confucius died lamenting that the edifice he had labored so long to erect was crumbling to ruin. Christ's death was the crowning act of his life; and his last words, "It is finished."

It was a philosophy, not a religion, that Confucius aimed to propagate. "Our Master," say his disciples, "spake little concerning the gods." He preferred to confine his teachings to the more tangible realities of human life; but so far from setting himself to reform the vulgar superstition, he conformed to its silly ceremonies and enjoined the same course on his disciples. "Treat the gods with respect," he said to them, but, he added, in terms which leave no ambiguity in the meaning of the precept, "keep them at a distance," or, rather, "keep out of their way." A cold sneer was not sufficient to wither or eradicate the existing idolatry, and the teachings of Confucius gave authority and prevalence to many idolatrous usages which were only partially current before his day.

Confucianism now stands forth as the leading religion of the Empire. Its objects of worship are of three classes—the powers of nature, ancestors, and heroes. Originally recognizing the existence of a Supreme personal Deity, it has degenerated into a pantheistic medley, and renders worship to an impersonal *anima mundi* under the leading forms of visible nature. Besides the concrete universe, separate honors are paid to the sun, moon, and stars, mountains, rivers, and lakes.

Of all their religious observances, the worship of ancestors is that which the Chinese regard as the most sacred. As Æneas obtained the name of "Pius" in honor of his filial devotion, so the Chinese idea of piety rises no higher. The Emperor, according to the Confucian school, may worship the Spirit of the Universe, but for his subjects it is sufficient that each present offerings to the spirits of his own ancestors. These rites are performed either at the family tombs or in the family temple, where wooden tablets, inscribed with their names, are preserved as sacred to the memory of the deceased, and worshipped precisely in the same manner as the popular idols.

The class of deified heroes comprehends illustrious sages, eminent sovereigns, faithful statesmen, valiant warriors, filial sons, and public benefactors—Confucius himself occupying the first place, and constituting, as the Chinese say, "one of a trinity with Heaven and Earth."

Like Confucianism, Tauism is indigenous to China, and, coeval with the former in its origin, it was also coheir to the mixed inheritance of good and evil contained in the more ancient creeds. The Tauists derive their name from *tau*, reason, and call themselves Rationalists; but, with a marvellous show of profundity, nothing can be more irrational than their doctrine and practice. Their founder, Li-erl, appears to have possessed a great mind, and to have caught glimpses of several sublime truths; but he has been sadly misrepresented by his degenerate followers. He lived in the sixth century B.C., and was contemporary with, but older than, Confucius. So great was the fame of his wisdom that the latter philosopher sought his instructions; but, differing from him in mental mould as widely as Aristotle did from Plato, he could not relish the boldness of his speculations or the vague obscurity of his style. He never repeated his visit, though he always spoke of him with respect and even with admiration.

Lautsz, the "old Master," is the appellation by which the

great Tauist is commonly known, and it was probably given him during his lifetime to distinguish him from his younger rival. The rendering of "old child" is no more to be received than the fiction of eighty years' gestation invented to account for it.

Lautsz bequeathed his doctrines to posterity in "five thousand words," which compose the *Tau teh king*, the Rule of Reason and Virtue. In expression, this work is extremely sententious; and in the form of its composition, semi-poetical. It abounds in acute apothegms, and some of its passages rise to the character of sublimity; but so incoherent are its contents that it is impossible for any literal interpretation to form them into a system. Its inconsistencies, however, readily yield to that universal solvent—the hypothesis of a mystical meaning underlying the letter of the text. The following passage appears to embody some obscure but lofty conceptions of the True God:

"That which is invisible is called *ye*.
That which is inaudible is called *he*.
That which is impalpable is called *wei*.
These three are inscrutable, and blended in one.
The first is not the brighter; nor the last the darker.
It is interminable, ineffable, and existed when there was nothing.
A shape without shape, a form without form.
A confounding mystery!
Go back, you cannot discover its beginning.
Go forward, you cannot find its end.
Take the ancient Reason to govern the present,
And you will know the origin of old.
This is the first principle of *Tau*."

Some European scholars discover here a notion of the Trinity, and, combining the syllables *ye*, *he*, and *wei*—for which process, however, they are unable to assign any very good reason—they obtain *yehewei*, which they accept as a distorted representation of the name Jehovah. Lautsz is said to have travelled in countries to the west of China, where it is supposed he may have met with Jews, and learned from them the name and nature of the Supreme Being. Whatever truth there may be in these conjectures, it is certain that some native commentators recognize in the passage a description of Shangte, the God of the Chinese patriarchs; and the three syllables of which the name is composed are admitted to have no assignable meaning in the Chinese language.

Here we find a connection between the degenerate philosophy of after-ages and the pure fountain of primeval truth. In fact, this very Shangte, though they have debased the name by bestowing it on a whole class of their *dii superiores*, is still enthroned on the summit of the Tauist Olympus, with ascriptions more expressive of his absolute divinity than any to be met with in the canonical books of the Confucian school. At the head of their Theogony stands the triad of the *San tsing*, the "Three Pure" ones; the first of whom is styled "The mysterious sovereign who has no superior;" "The self-existent source and beginning;" the "Honored one of Heaven."

He is said to have created the "three worlds;" to have produced men and gods; to have set the stars in motion, and caused the planets to revolve. But, alas! this catalogue of sublime titles and divine attributes is the epitaph of a buried faith. The Tauists persuaded themselves that this August Being, wrapped in the solitude of his own perfections, had delegated the government of the universe to a subordinate, whom they style *Yuhwang* Shangte. The former has dwindled into an inoperative idea, the latter is recognized as the actual God; and this deity, who plays mayor of the palace to a *roi fainéant*, is regarded as the apotheosis of a mortal by the name of Chang, an ancestor of the present hierarch of the Tauist religion. It is painful, after discoursing to them of the attributes of the True God, to hear the people exclaim, "That is our Yuhwang Shangte."

In its philosophy, this school is radically and thoroughly materialistic. The soul itself they regard as a material substance, though of a more refined quality than the body it inhabits. Liable to dissolution, together with the body, it may be rendered capable of surviving the wreck by undergoing a previous discipline; and even the body is capable of becoming invulnerable by the stroke of death, so that the etherealized form will, instead of being laid in the grave, be wafted away to the abodes of the genii. It is scarcely possible to represent the extent to which this idea fired the minds of the Chinese for ages after its promulgation, or to estimate the magnitude of its consequences. The prospect of a corporeal immortality had for them attractions far stronger than a shadowy existence in the land of spirits; and they sought it with an eagerness amounting to frenzy. The elixir of life became the grand object of pursuit, and alchemy, with its foolish failures and grand achievements, sprang directly from the religion of Tau.*

The leading principle of Tauism, of which their dogma concerning the human soul is only a particular application, is that every species of matter possesses a soul—a subtile essence endowed with individual conscious life. Freed from their grosser elements, these become the genii that preside over the various departments of nature. Some wander at will through the realms of space, endowed with a protean facility of transformation; others, more pure and ethereal, rise to the regions of the stars, and take their places in the firmament. Thus the five principal planets are called by the names of the "five elements" from which they are believed to have originated, and over which they are regarded as presiding. The stars are divinities, and their motions control the destinies of men and things—a notion which has done much to inspire the zeal of the Chinese for recording the phenomena of the heavens.

---

* See Essay on Alchemy in this volume.

A theogony like this is rich in the elements of poetry; and most of the machinery in Chinese works of imagination is, in fact, derived from this source. The *Liauchai*, for example, a collection of marvellous tales which, in their general character, may be compared to the Metamorphoses of Ovid, is largely founded on the Tauist mythology.

In accordance with the materialistic character of the Tauist sect, nearly all the gods whom the Chinese regard as presiding over their material interests originated with this school. The god of rain, the god of fire, the god of medicine, the god of agriculture, and the *lares*, or kitchen gods, are among the principal of this class.

A system which supplies deities answering to the leading wants and desires of mankind cannot be uninfluential; but, in addition to the strong motives that attract worshippers to their temples, the Tauist priesthood possess two independent sources of influence. They hold the monopoly of geomancy, a superstitious art which professes to select on scientific principles those localities that are most propitious for building and burial; and they have succeeded in persuading the people that they alone are able to secure them from annoyance by evil spirits. The philosophy of Tau has thus not only given birth to a religion, but degenerated into a system of magical imposture, presided over by an arch-magician who lives in almost imperial state,* and sways the sceptre over the spirits of the invisible world as the Emperor does over the living population of the Empire.

As a religion, Buddhism seems to enjoy more of the popular favor than Tauism; though the former professes to draw men away from the world and its vanities, while the latter proffers the blessings of health, wealth, and long life.

* This is not quite true of the present High-priest, who is so reduced in circumstances that he sometimes leaves his residence in the Lunghu mountains to raise money in wealthier regions.

It is rarely that we find a Buddhist temple of any considerable reputation that is not situated in a locality distinguished for some feature of its natural scenery. One situated in the midst of a dusty plain, not far from the gates of Tientsin, seemed to us, when we first visited it, to present a striking exception to the general rule. Subsequently, however, a brilliant mirage, which we frequently saw as we approached the temple, furnished us at once with the explanation of its location and its name. It is called the temple of the "Sea of Light;" and its founders, no doubt, placed it there in order that the deceptive mirage, which is always visible in bright sunny weather, might serve its contemplative inmates as a memento of the chief tenet of their philosophy—that all things are unreal, and human life itself a shifting phantasmagoria of empty shadows.

Sequestered valleys enclosed by mountain-peaks, and elevated far above the world which they profess to despise, are favorite seats for the monastic communities of Buddhism. But it is no yearning after God that leads them to court retirement; nor is it the adoration of nature's Author that prompts them to place their shrines in the midst of his sublimest works. To them the universe is a vacuum, and emptiness the highest object of contemplation.

They are a strange paradox—religious atheists! Acknowledging no First Cause or Conscious Ruling Power, they hold that the human soul revolves perpetually in the urn of fate, liable to endless ills, and enjoying no real good. As it cannot cease to be, its only resource against this state of interminable misery is the extinction of consciousness—a remedy which lies within itself, and which they endeavor to attain by ascetic exercises.

Their daily prayers consist of endless repetitions, which are not expected to be heard by the unconscious deity to whom they are addressed, but are confessedly designed merely to exert a reflex influence on the worshipper—i. e. to occupy the mind with empty sounds and withdraw it from thought and feeling.

Tama, one of their saints, is said thus to have sat motionless for nine years with his face to the wall; not engaged, as a German would conjecture, in "thinking the wall," but occupied with the more difficult task of thinking nothing at all.

Those in whom the discipline is completest are believed to have entered the Nirvana—not an Elysium of conscious enjoyment, but a negative state of exemption from pain. Such is the condition of all the Buddhas, who, though the name is taken to signify supreme intelligence, are reduced to an empty abstraction in a state which is described as *pu sheng pu mie*, "neither life nor death;" and such is the aspiration of all their votaries. Melancholy spectacle! Men of acute minds, bewildered in the maze of their own speculations, and seeking to attain perfection by stripping themselves of the highest attributes of humanity!

As a philosophy, Buddhism resembles Stoicism in deriving its leading motive from the fear of evil. But while the latter encased itself in panoply, and, standing in martial attitude, defied the world to spoil the treasures laid up in its bosom, the former seeks security by emptying the soul of its susceptibilities and leaving nothing that is capable of being harmed or lost—i. e. treating the soul as Epictetus is said to have done his dwelling-house, in order that he might not be annoyed by the visits of thieves. It dries up the sources of life, wraps the soul in the cerements of the grave, and aims to convert a living being into a spiritual mummy which shall survive all changes without being affected by them.

This is the spirit and these the principles of esoteric Buddhism as enunciated by those members of the inner circle whose wan cheeks and sunken, rayless eyes indicate that they are far advanced in the process of self-annihilation. In their external manifestations they vary with different schools and countries, the lamas of Tartary and the sarmanas of Ceylon appearing to have little in common.

To adapt itself to the comprehension of the masses, Buddhism has personified its abstract conceptions and converted them into divinities; while, to pave the way for its easier introduction, it readily embraces the gods and heroes of each country in its comprehensive pantheon.

In China the Nirvana was found to be too subtle an idea for popular contemplation, and, in order to furnish the people with a more attractive object of worship, the Buddhists brought forward a Goddess of Mercy, whose highest merit was that, having reached the verge of Nirvana, she declined to enter, preferring to remain where she could hear the cries and succor the calamities of those who were struggling with the manifold evils of a world of change. From this circumstance she is called the Tsz'-pei Kwan-yin, the "merciful goddess who hears the prayers" of men.

This winning attribute meets a want of humanity, and makes her a favorite among the votaries of the faith. While the Three Buddhas hold a more prominent position in the temple, she occupies the first place in the hearts of their worshippers. Temples of a secondary class are often devoted especially to her; and in the greater ones she almost always finds a shrine or corner where she is represented with a thousand hands ready to succor human suffering, or holding in her arms a beautiful infant, and ready to confer the blessing of offspring on her faithful worshippers—in this last attitude resembling the favorite object of popular worship in papal countries.

In the Sea-light Monastery above referred to, she appears in a large side hall, habited in a cloak, her head encircled by an inscription in gilded characters which proclaims her as the "goddess whose favor protects the *second birth*." This language seems to express a Christian thought; but in reality nothing could be more intensely pagan. It relates to the transmigration of souls, which is the fundamental doctrine of the system; and informs the visitor that this is the divinity to whom he is to look for protection in passing through the successive changes of his future existence. Within the mazes of that mighty labyrinth, there is room for every condition of life on earth, and for purgatories and paradises innumerable besides. Beyond these the common Buddhist never looks. To earn by works of merit—which play an important part in the modified system—the reversion of a comfortable mandarinate, or a place in the "Paradise of the Western Sky," bounds his aspirations. And to escape from having their souls triturated in a spiritual mortar, or ground between spiritual millstones in Hades; or avoid the doom of dwelling in the body of a brute on earth, constitutes with the ignorant the strongest motive to deter them from vice—those and a thousand other penalties being set forth by pictures and rude casts to impress the minds of such as are unable to read.

Buddhism was little known in China prior to the year A.D. 66. At that time the Emperor Mingte of the Han dynasty is said to have had a remarkable dream that led to its introduction. He had seen, he said to his courtiers, a man of gold, holding in his hand a bow and two arrows. They, recognizing in these objects the elements of Foh—the name of Buddha as it is written in the Chinese language—and calling to mind a saying ascribed to Confucius, "that the Holy One is in the West," expounded the dream as an intimation that the Buddhist religion ought to be introduced from India. The embassy thus sent to the West by Imperial command, in quest of a foreign religion, was, it is thought, incited by some indistinct rumor of the appearance of our Saviour in Judea; and it is interesting to speculate as to what the condition of China might have been if the ambassadors, instead of stopping in India, had proceeded to Palestine. As it is, the success of Buddhism demonstrates the possibility of a foreign faith taking root in the soil of China.

The San Kiao, or Three Religions, have now passed in revision. We have viewed them, however, owing to the limits of our space, only in outline, neither allowing ourselves, on the one hand, to follow out those superstitious practices which attach themselves to the several schools like the moss and ivy that festoon the boughs of aged trees, nor, on the other, to enter into a minute investigation of those systems of philosophy in which they have their root. The fact that each takes its rise in a school of philosophy is significant of the tendencies of human thought.

The Confucian philosophy in its prominent characteristics was ethical, occupying itself mainly with social relations and civil duties, shunning studiously all questions that enter into ontological subtleties or partake of the marvellous and the supernatural.

The philosophy of Tau as developed by the followers of Lautsze, if not in the form in which it was left by their master, may be characterized as physical. For the individual it prescribed a physical discipline; and, without any conception of true science, it was filled with the idea of inexhaustible resources, hidden in the elements of material nature.

The Buddhist philosophy was pre-eminently metaphysical. Originating with a people who, far more than the Chinese, are addicted to abstruse speculations, it occupied itself with subtle inquiries into the nature and faculties of the human mind, the veracity of its perceptions, and the grounds of our delusive faith in the independent existence of an external world.

These three philosophies, differing thus widely in their essential character—one being thoroughly material, another purely ideal, and the third repudiating all such questions and holding itself neutral and indifferent—yet exhibit some remarkable points of agreement. They agree in the original omission or negation of religious ideas; and they coincide no less remarkably in evolving each, from its negative basis, a system of religion; and in contributing each its quota to the popular idolatry.

Confucius "seldom spoke of the divinities," and taught his disciples to "keep them at a distance;" and yet the forms of respect which he enjoined for deceased ancestors led to their virtual deification, and promoted, if it did not originate, the national hero-worship. Like the modern apostle of positivism, professing to occupy himself wholly with positive ideas—like him, he was unable to satisfy the cravings of his spiritual nature without having recourse to a religion of humanity.

The Buddhist creed denies alike the reality of the material world and the existence of an overruling mind; yet it has peopled an ideal universe with a race of ideal gods, all of whom are entities in the belief of the vulgar.

The Tauist creed acknowledges no such category as that of spirit in contradistinction from matter; yet it swarms heaven and earth with tutelar spirits whom the people regard as divine.

We see here a process directly the reverse of that which certain atheistic writers of modern Europe assert to be the natural progress of the human mind. According to them, men set out with the belief of many gods, whom they at length reduce to unity, and finally supersede by recognizing the laws of nature as independent of a personal administrator. The history of China is fatal to this theory. The worship of one God is the oldest form of Chinese religion, and idolatry is an innovation. Even now new idols are constantly taking their place in the national pantheon; and so strong is the tendency in this direction that in every case where philosophy has laid the foundation, idolatry has come in to complete the structure.

It is incorrect to assert that any one of the San Kiao is a State religion to the exclusion of the others, though the Confucian is sometimes so regarded on account of its greater influence with the ruling classes and its marked prominence in connection with State ceremonials. Not only are they all recognized and tolerated, but they all share the Imperial patronage. The shrines of each of the Three Religions are often erected by Imperial munificence, and their priests and sacred rites provided for at the Imperial expense with impartial liberality.

Not only do they coexist without conflict in the Empire, but they exercise a joint sway over almost every mind in its immense population. It is impossible to apportion the people among these several creeds. They are all Confucians, all Buddhists, all Tauists. They all reverence Confucius and worship their ancestors—all participate in the "feast of hungry ghosts," and employ the Buddhist burial-service; and all resort to the magical devices of the Tauists to protect themselves against the assaults of evil spirits, or secure "good luck" in business. They celebrate their marriages according to the Confucian rites; in building their houses, and in cases of alarming illness, they ask the advice of a Tauist; and at death they commit their souls to the keeping of the Buddhists. The people assert, and with truth, that these religions, originally three, have become one; and they are accustomed to symbolize this unity by erecting *San kiao tang* temples of the Three Religions, in which Lautsze and Buddha appear on the right and left of Confucius as completing the triad of sages. This arrangement, however, gives great offence to some of the more zealous disciples of the latter; and a few years ago a memorial was presented to the Emperor, praying him to destroy the *San kiao tang*, which stood near the tomb of their great teacher, who has "no equal but Heaven."

This feeling is only a faint echo of a determined opposition which for ages withstood the advance of the rival systems, and which has now been overcome to such an extent that they hold a co-ordinate place in the popular mind, and receive nearly equal honors at the hand of the government.

The effects of this coalition may be traced in their literature as well as in the manners and customs of the people. Of this, one example will suffice, though we might go on, if space permitted, to show how freely the later works of each school appropriate the phraseology of the others, and to point out the extent to which the general language of the country has been enriched by a vocabulary of religious terms, chiefly of Buddhist origin, all of which are incorporated in the Imperial Dictionary and pass as current coin in the halls of the literary tribunal.

In the collection of Tales above referred to, there is a story which owes its humor to the bizarre intermixture of elements from each of the Three Religions.

A young nobleman, riding out, hawk in hand, is thrown from his horse and taken up for dead. On being conveyed to his house, he opens his eyes and gradually recovers his bodily strength; but to the grief of his family, he is hopelessly insane. He fancies himself a Buddhist priest, repels the caresses of the ladies of his harem, and insists on being conveyed to a distant province, where he affirms he has passed his life in a monastery. On arriving he proves himself to be the abbot; and the mystery of his transfiguration is at once solved.

The young nobleman had led a dissolute life, and his flimsy soul, unable to sustain the shock of death, was at once dissipated. The soul of a priest who had just expired happened to be floating by, and, led by that desire to inhabit a body which some say impelled the devils to enter the herd of swine, it took possession of the still warm corpse.

The young nobleman was a Confucian of the modern type. The idea of the soul changing its earthy tenement is Buddhistic. And that which rendered the metamorphosis possible, without waiting for another birth, was the Tauist doctrine that the soul is dissolved with the body, unless it be purified and concentrated by vigorous discipline.

It is curious to inquire on what principles this reconciliation has been effected. Have the three creeds mingled together like gases in the atmosphere, each contributing some ingredient to the composition of a vital fluid; or blended like the rays of the spectrum, each imparting its own hue, and all concurring in the production of light? Alas! it is not a healthy atmosphere that supplies the breath of the new-born soul in China; no pure or steady light cheers its opening eyes. Yet each of these systems meets a want; and the whole, taken together, supplies the cravings of nature as well perhaps as any creed not derived from a divine revelation.

The Three Religions are not, as the natives thoughtlessly assume, identical in signification and differing only in their mode of expression. As we have already seen, it is hardly possible to conceive of three creeds more totally distinct or radically antagonistic; and yet, to a certain extent, they are supplementary. And to this it is that they owe their union and their permanence.

Confucius gave his people an elaborate theory of their social organization and civil polity; but when they looked abroad on nature with its unsolved problems, they were unable to confine their thoughts within the limits of his cautious positivism. They were fascinated by mystery, and felt that in nature there were elements of the supernatural which they could not ignore, even if they did not understand them. Hence the rise of Tauism, captivating the imagination by its hierarchy of spirits and personified powers, and meeting, in some degree, the longing for a future life by maintaining, though under hard conditions, the possible achievement of a corporeal immortality.

With the momentous question of existence suspended on this bare possibility, Buddhism came to them like an evangel of hope, assuring every man of an inalienable interest in a life to come. It gave them a better psychology of the human mind than they had before possessed; afforded a plausible explanation of the inequalities in the condition of men; and, by the theory of metempsychosis, seemed to reveal the link that connects man with the lower animals, on the one hand, and with the gods, on the other. No wonder it excited the popular mind to a pitch of enthusiasm, and provoked the adherents of the other creeds to virulent opposition.

Tauism, as opposed to it, became more decidedly material, and Confucianism more positively atheistic. The disciples of the latter especially assailed it with acrimonious controversy—denying, though they had hitherto been silent on such questions, the personality of God and the future life of the human soul.

Now, however, the effervescence of passions has died away—the antagonistic elements have long since neutralized each other, and the three creeds have subsided into a stable equilibrium, or rather become compacted into a firm conglomerate. The ethical, the physical, and the metaphysical live together in harmony. The school that denies the existence of matter, that which occupies itself wholly with the properties of matter, and that, again, which denounces the subtleties of both have ceased their controversies. One deriving its motive from the fear of death, another actuated by a dread of the evils attendant on human life, and the third absorbed in the present and indifferent alike to hope or fear, all are accepted with equal faith by an unreasoning populace. Without perceiving their points of discrepancy, or understanding the manner in which they supplement each other, they accept each as answering to certain cravings of their inward nature, and blend them all in a huge heterogeneous and incongruous creed.

It would be interesting to inquire, had we sufficient space, what have been the intellectual and moral influences of these several systems, separate and combined. They have, it is true, given rise to various forms of degrading superstition, and, supporting instead of destroying each other, they bind the mind of the nation in threefold fetters; still, we are inclined to think that each has served a useful purpose in the long education of the Chinese people. But, in the providence of God, the time has now come when they are offered a better faith—one which is in every part consistent with itself and adequate to satisfy all their spiritual necessities. Will they receive it? The habit of receiving such contradictory systems has rendered their minds almost incapable of weighing evidence; and they never ask concerning a religion "is it true?" but "is it good?" Christianity, however, with its exclusive and peremptory claims, has already begun to arouse their attention; and when the spirit of inquiry is once thoroughly awakened, the San Kiao, or Three Creeds, will not long sustain the ordeal.

NOTE.—As the reader may be at a loss to reconcile some of the statements in the foregoing article, it may not be amiss to remind him that each of the Three Systems appears under a twofold aspect—first as an esoteric philosophy, and afterwards as a popular religion. Thus a chief object of the discipline enjoined by the founder of Buddhism was the extinction of individual consciousness; yet the Chinese embraced it as their best assurance of a future life. What the philosopher was anxious to cast away, the populace were eager to possess.

REMARKS ON THE ETHICAL PHILOSOPHY OF THE CHINESE.*

Widely as the Chinese have departed from the meagre outline of a religious system left them by Confucius, they have generally adhered to his moral teachings. Developed by his followers, received by the suffrages of the whole people, and enforced by the sanctions of the Three Religions, the principles which he inculcated may be said to have moulded the social life of one third of the human family. These are nowhere to be found digested into a scientific form, but diffused through the mingled masses of physics and metaphysics which compose the *Sing-li Ta-tseuen*, or sparkling in the detached apothegms of "The Sages." Happily for our convenience we have them brought to a focus in the chart a translation of which is given below.

We shall confine ourselves to the task of explaining this important document, as the best method of exhibiting the system in its practical influence; though an independent view would afford freer scope for developing its principles.

This chart is anonymous; but the want of a name detracts nothing from its value. The author has no merit beyond the idea of presenting the subject in a tabular view, and the pictorial taste with which he has executed the design. Of the ethical system so exhibited he originated nothing; and the popularity of his work is due mainly to the fact that it is regarded

---

* Read before the American Oriental Society in 1861; published in the *Princeton Review*, 1862.

as a faithful synopsis of the Confucian morals. In this view it is highly esteemed by the Sien-sengs of Ningpo, a city which ranks among the foremost in the Chinese Empire in point of literary culture.*

The half-illuminated sphere prefixed to the chart has scarcely more connection with its subject-matter than the royal coat-of-arms stamped on the title-page of some editions has with the contents of King James's Bible. It represents the mundane egg, or mass of chaotic matter, containing *Yin* and *Yang*, the seminal principles from whose action and reaction all things were evolved. *Woo-keih* produced *Tai-keih; Tai-keih* produced *Yin* and *Yang;* and these dual principles generated all things. This is the lucid cosmogony of the Chinese; and it adds little to its clearness to render the above terms, as they are usually translated, by the "great extreme," the "male and female powers," etc.

The primitive signification of *Yang* and *Yin* is *light* and *darkness*, a meaning exhibited in the shading of the diagram. *Tai-keih* may be rendered the Great Finite, and *Woo-keih*, the Indefinite or Infinite. We have, then, the following statement as the starting-point of their philosophy and history:

The Infinite produced the Finite (the conditioned), and the Finite evolved light and darkness. The passage, thus given, is rational. It admits a creative power anterior to chaos, makes the production of light one of the earliest of creative acts, and, with at least poetical truth, ascribes the generation of all things to the action of light and darkness, or the succession of days and seasons. It is so far consonant with the Genesis of the Christian Scriptures. Whether it was ever so understood, it is impossible to affirm; though it is certain that no such meaning is attached to it at the present day.

The dual principles of the Chinese, as explained by themselves, are not light and darkness; neither are they, like those

* The chart was obtained at Ningpo.

of the ancient Persians, the antagonistic powers of good and evil. The creation and preservation of the universe are ascribed to them; and yet they are not regarded as deities, but as unconscious impersonal agents. Popúlarly they are understood, in a phallic sense, as the energies of the universal sexual system; and philosophically as certain forces, positive and negative, to which, automatic and uncontrolled by any intelligence, are referable all the changes in the universe. They are the pillars of a materialistic atheism.

Part I. is an epitome of the *Tahio*, the first of the four chief canonical books of the Chinese, and the most admired production of their great philosopher.*

Voluminous as an editor, piously embalming the relics of antiquity, Confucius occupies but a small space as an author; a slender compend of history and this little tract of a few hundred words being the only original works which emanated from his own pen. The latter, the title of which signifies the "Great Study," is prized so highly for the elegance of its style and the depth of its wisdom that it may often be seen inscribed in letters of gold, and suspended as an ornamental tableau in the mansions of the rich. It treats of the Practice of Virtue and the Art of Government; and in the following table these two subjects are arranged in parallel columns. In the first we have the lineaments of a perfect character superscribed by the word *Sheng*, a "Holy Sage," the name which the Chinese give to their ideal. In the other we have a catalogue of the social virtues as they spread in widening circles through the family, the neighborhood, the State, and the world. These are ranged under *Wang*, the "Emperor," whose duty it is to cherish them in his subjects, the force of example being his chief instrument, and the cultivation of personal virtue his first obligation.

* The doctrines of Confucius are well exhibited in an article by the Rev. J. K. Wight, in the *Princeton Review* for April, 1858.

A CHART OF CHINESE ETHICS,

IN FOUR PARTS.

PART I.—CHART OF THE GREAT STUDY.

This contains the True Tradition of the Holy Sages. Whoever obtains this doctrine may live in prosperity and die in peace. I have accordingly condensed it into a chart, to be hung on the right of your easy-chair, to aid your study of virtue, just as the ancients made use of inscriptions on their girdles and wash-basins.

Heaven having given existence to man, the doctrine of the Great Study succeeded, and established order in society.

Restricted in its sphere, it produces the perfection of individual excellence—a Holy Sage.	With free scope for its exercise, it makes a Reformer of the World—a True King.
His aim is,	His aim is,
PERSONAL VIRTUE.	SOCIAL IMPROVEMENT.
The means to its attainment are—	The means to its attainment are—

From the Son of Heaven down to the private man, every one must begin with the Cultivation of Personal Virtue.

1. Propriety of Conduct.
- Fidelity and Truth.
- Suavity and Respect.
- Dignity of Carriage.
- Precision of Words and Actions.

2. Right Feeling.
- Avoiding Prejudice.
- Restraining the Passions.
- Cherishing Good Impulses.
- Adhering to the Just Mean.

3. Sincerity of Purpose.
- Self-examination.
- Scrutiny of Secret Motives.
- Religious Reverence.
- Fear of Self-deception.

4. Intelligence of Mind.
- Rejection of Error.
- Comprehension of the Truth.
- Quickness of Moral Perception.
- Insight into Providence.
- Study of the Laws of Nature.
- Study of the Constitution of Man.
- Study of the Records of History.

1. The Discipline of the Family.
- Filial Piety.
- Fraternal Love.
- Conjugal Fidelity.
- Care in Choice of Associates.
- Strictness in Intercourse of the Sexes.
- Attention to Established Rules.
- Instruction to Children.
- Caution against Partiality.
- Harmony with Neighbors.
- Regard for Frugality.

2. The Government of the Empire.
- Science of Government.
- Power of Combination.
- Reverence for Heaven and Ancestors.
- Discrimination in Choice of Agents.
- Love for the People.
- Zeal for Education.
- Strictness in Executing the Laws.

3. The Subjugation (*lit.* Pacification) of the World.
- Wisdom in Conducting War.
- Righteousness in Rewards and Punishments.
- Liberality in Admitting the Expression of Sentiment.
- Frugality in Expenditures.
- Skill in Legislation.

The Great Study stops only at Perfection.

PART II.—A CHART OF THE HEART.—The Chart of the Great Study will acquaint you with the principles of virtue; but as the keeping of the heart is a matter of great difficulty, I accordingly subjoin this chart of it.

*

The Wisdom Heart is minute and subtle (i. e. the germ of virtue is small and feeble).

The Human Heart is in constant jeopardy (i. e. beset with dangers and prone to evil).

Point of Divergence between *Shun* and *Cheh.*†

The Wisdom Heart. Influence of Primordial Harmony.

1. Obeys Heaven.

(*a*) In Propriety of Conduct.

By { Regulating the External Actions, and Moderating the Internal Passions.

(*b*) In the Exercise of Charity.

By { Conquering the Malevolent Affections, and Governing the Desires and Aversions.

2. Restrains Self.

(*a*) In Subduing the Lusts.

By { Repressing Self-love, and Curbing Animal Appetite.

(*b*) In Guarding against the Dangers of Solitude.

By { Not Injuring one's Body, Soul, Nature, or Life; Not Forgetting the Reverential Exercise of Self-control.

He who pursues this course will daily rise in illumination, and finally become a saint or sage. Propitious stars will shine on him, and happiness attend his footsteps.

The Human Heart. Influence of Gross Matter.

1. Indulges Self.

(*a*) In Habits of Indolence.

Leading to { Gluttony and Drunkenness. Idleness and Waste of Time.

(*b*) In Carnal Lusts.

Leading to { Shameless Excesses. Abominable Immoralities.

(*c*) In Avarice.

Leading to { Filthy Lucre. Violent Extortion.

2. Dismisses Conscience.

(*a*) In Yielding to Impulse.

For { Sensual Pleasure. Anger, Strife, etc.

(*b*) In Treachery.

Involving { Flattery and Deceit.

(*c*) In Hypocrisy.

Involving { Dissimulation and Falsehood.

He who follows this course, daily drifts into deeper corruption, and finally becomes a beast or monster. Evil stars glare on him, and calamity overtakes him.

* Sin, the Chinese character for heart.

† The best and worst characters mentioned in history.

Part III.—A Chart of Moral Excellence.—The two roads of virtue and vice are clearly treated in the above chart, but as the virtues are not easy to practise, I add a chart of moral excellence.

Momentarily keep it in mind.

BENEVOLENCE.

Public Spirit.—Give all their dues, and let not self set up an opposing interest; but find your own good in the common weal.

Charity.—Do not to others what you would not have done to you.
Remember not old injuries, and treat men according to their several capacity.

Filial Piety.—Gratify the wishes of your parents, and worship your ancestors;
Carry out their purposes, and reflect honor on their name.

Mercy.—Treat all children with kindness, not your own only.
Pity the widow and fatherless, and give succor to brute animals.

Magnanimity.—A great soul can bear an offence without resenting it.
He mingles with men on easy terms, and affects no superiority.
Kindness must be repaid, but not injury.
Rather suffer a wrong than do one.

Tremblingly hold it fast.

JUSTICE.

Manliness.—If you fail in anything, seek help in yourself.
Stand to your post, and let not vague desires draw you from it.

Fraternity.—Respect your elder, and be kind to your younger brothers.
Reverence age, and give precedence to years.

Courage.—When you see the right, do it; when you know your fault, correct it.
If rich, be not insolent; nor cringing if poor.

Integrity.—Hold it fast; change not for custom.
Be content with simple fare; and when you see gain, ask, Is it just?

Modesty.—Let the men be continent, the women chaste.
Abhor evil, and fear falling.

WISDOM.

Knowledge of Man.—Detect false pretences; cleave to the virtuous, and avoid the vicious. Let not floating rumors move you to dislike a good man.

Knowledge of Nature.—Be erudite, inquisitive, thoughtful, discriminating; investigating heaven and earth, the past and present.

Knowledge of Fate.—Practise virtue, take care of yourself, do your duty; and let good or ill fortune come as it may.

Use of the Eyes and Ears.—Keep the distant in clear view, and have an open ear for good counsel. Read no immoral books, hearken not to flattering words.

POLITENESS.

Respect.—Proceeding from an inward feeling.
It manifests itself in apparel and demeanor.

Caution.—Treasures the fruits of observation, hides the bad, and publishes the good.
It preserves conjugal harmony, and maintains decorum in the intercourse of the sexes.

Humility.—When rich, feels poor; when full, feels empty.
Makes no boast of abilities, nor prides itself on place or reputation.

Deference.—Declines much, and takes little;
And is only solicitous to find a lower place than others.

GOOD FAITH.

Simplicity.—In word and deed, in and out, one and the same.
In study or action, uniform from beginning to end.

Truth.—The words of the inner chambers should bear repeating in the palace.
Your private life should be such that heaven and earth might witness it.

Sincerity of Purpose.—Complete your engagements.
And be faithful in behalf of others.

Honesty of Intention.—So live that your heart will not condemn you, the people dislike you, your family shame you, or your friends reproach you.

Part IV.—A Chart for Self-Examination.—The virtues may be copied from the chart of moral excellence, but lest vices should creep in unawares, I conclude with a formula for self-examination.

If you have faults, correct them.

OFFENCES AGAINST BENEVOLENCE.

Cruelty.—Inflicting misery on family relatives,
And finding pleasure in giving pain to man or beast.

Envy.—Jealous of the advantages of others, obstructing their promotion.
Offended at the superiority of others, indulging in detraction.

Malice.—Playing wicked pranks, and forgetting favors.
Delighting to hear of others' faults, and taking pleasure in publishing them.

Selfishness.—Consulting its own interest, and
Seeking its own advantage.

Treachery.—Inveigling others into evil, and
Involving them in calamity for its own ends.

Petulance.—With spirit so contracted as not to endure an accidental touch.

If none, redouble your zeal in the pursuit of virtue.

OFFENCES AGAINST JUSTICE.

Cupidity.—Never satisfied, but always longing.
Indulging the senses, coveting fame, and pursuing gain.

Flattery.—With artificial smiles and simulated voice.
Playing the sycophant in hope of power.

Parsimony.—Neither succoring the needy nor rewarding the deserving.
Concealing wealth, and affecting poverty.

Indecision.—Indolently procrastinating, and shifting with custom.
Drifting with the current, and bending before power.

Discontent.—Uneasy in its condition, and destitute of self-satisfaction.
In everything it murmurs against Heaven, and finds fault with man.

Perversity.—Capricious in choices and aversions, not seeking the right.
Following inclination, and regarding neither good nor evil.

OFFENCES AGAINST WISDOM.

Depravity.—Neither caring for right and wrong,
Nor distinguishing good from evil.

Levity.—Leading to inconsiderate words and actions.

Shallowness.—Prying and meddlesome.
Mistaking slight praise or blame for glory or shame.
Interpreting slight favor or opposition as love or hatred.

Obstinacy.—Holding to its own opinions, and refusing to be convinced.

Narrowness.—Content with a humble circle of familiar thoughts, and
Unwilling to extend the view, or enlarge the sphere of knowledge.

OFFENCES AGAINST POLITENESS.

Pride.—Using wealth and power for self-magnification.
Employing talents and learning to eclipse others.

Arrogance.—Immodest in language, disrespectful to the aged.
Perverse in action, and heedless of advice.

Carelessness.—In affairs negligent of details.
In disposition harsh, in manners blunt.

Ostentation.—In all things tending to excess.
In general aiming to outshine others.

OFFENCES AGAINST GOOD FAITH.

Superficiality.—Without solid virtues, seeking an empty reputation.
Making a fair show, but hasty and insincere in friendship.

Insincerity.—With heart and life at variance,
Coveting the name of virtue.

Deceit.—In words false, in actions dishonest.

Intrigue.—Scheming, calculating,
Plotting and shifting.

The passage which is here analyzed, and which constitutes the foundation of the whole treatise, is the following:

"Those ancient princes who desired to promote the practice of virtue throughout the world first took care to govern their own states. In order to govern their states, they first regulated their own families. In order to regulate their families, they first practised virtue in their own persons. In order to the practice of personal virtue, they first cultivated right feeling. In order to insure right feeling, they first had regard to the correctness of their purposes. In order to secure correctness of purpose, they extended their intelligence. This intelligence is to be obtained by inquiring into the nature of things."

This diminishing series is beautiful. However widely the branches may extend, the quality of their fruit is determined by the common root. Virtue in the State depends on virtue in the family, that of the family on that of the individual; and individual virtue depends not only on right feelings and proper motives, but, as a last condition, on right knowledge. Nor is there anything in which Confucius more strikingly exhibits the clearness of his perceptions than in indicating the direction in which this indispensable intelligence is to be sought—viz., in the nature of things; in understanding the relations which the individual sustains to society and the universe. The knowledge of these is truth, conformity to them is virtue; and moral obligations, Confucius appears, with Dr. Samuel Clarke, to have derived from a perception of these relations, and a sense of inherent fitness in the nature of things. Just at this point we have a notable hiatus. The editor tells us the chapter on the Study of "Nature" is wanting; and Chinese scholars have never ceased to deplore its loss.

But whatever of value to the student of virtue it may have contained, it certainly did not contain the "beginning of wisdom." For skilfully as Confucius had woven the chain of human relationships, he failed to connect the last link with heaven

—to point out the highest class of our relations. Not only, therefore, is one grand division of our duties a blank in his system, but it is destitute of that higher light and those stronger motives which are necessary to stimulate to the performance of the most familiar offices.

The young mandarin who said to a member of one of our recent embassies, in answer to a question as to his object in life, that "he was desirous of performing all his duties to God and man," was not speaking in the language of the Confucian school. He had discovered a new world in our moral relations which was unknown to the ancient philosopher.

The principal relations of the individual to society are copiously illustrated in this and the other classics. They are five—the *governmental*, *parental*, *conjugal*, *fraternal*, and that of *friendship*. The first is the comprehensive subject of the treatise; and in the second column of the chart all the others are placed subordinate to it. Though not expressly named, they are implied in the statement of the first four relative duties—*filial piety*, *fraternal love*, *conjugal fidelity*, and *choice of associates*. The last comprehends the principles which regulate general intercourse. Conjugal *fidelity*, in the sense of chastity, is made obligatory only on the female. *Fraternal* duty requires a rigid subordination, according to the gradation of age, which is aided by a peculiarity of language; each elder brother being called *hiung*, and each younger *te;* no common designation, like that of "brother," placing them on equal footing. This arrangement in the family Confucius pronounces a discipline, in which respect is taught for superiors in civil life; and filial piety, he adds, is a sentiment which a son who has imbibed it at home will carry into the service of his prince.

Nothing, in fact, is more characteristic of Chinese society than the scope given to filial piety. Intensified into a religious sentiment by the worship which he renders to his ancestors, it leads the dutiful son to live and act in all situations with reference to his parents. He seeks reputation for the sake of reflecting honor upon them, and dreads disgrace chiefly through fear of bringing reproach on their name. An unkindness to a relative is a sin against them, in forgetting the ties of a common ancestry; and even a violation of the law derives its turpitude from exposing the parents of the offender to suffer with him, in person or in reputation.

It is thus analogous in the universality of its application to the incentive which the Christian derives from his relation to the "Father of spirits;" and if inferior in its efficacy, it is yet far more efficacious than any which a pagan religion is capable of supplying. Its various bearings are beautifully traced by Confucius in a discourse which constitutes one of the favorite text-books in the schools of China.

It is not the book that teaches it, but the art of governing thus founded on the practice of virtue, that is emphatically denominated the "Great Study;" and this designation, expressing, as it does, the judgment of one from whose authority there is no appeal, has contributed to give ethics a decided preponderance among the studies of the Chinese.

Other sciences, in their estimation, may be interesting as sources of intellectual diversion or useful in a subordinate degree, as promotive of material prosperity; but this is *the science*, whose knowledge is wisdom, whose practice is virtue, and whose result is happiness. In the literary examinations, the grand object of which is the selection of men who are qualified for the service of the government, an acquaintance with subjects of this kind contributes more to official promotion than all other intellectual acquirements; and when the aspirant for honors has reached the summit of the scale, and become a member of the Privy Council or Premier of the Empire, he receives no higher appellation than that of *Tahio shë*—a Doctor of the Great Study, an adept in the art of government.

The Chinese Empire has never realized the Utopia of Confucius; but his maxims have influenced its policy to such an extent that in the arrangements of the government a marked preference is given to moral over material interests. Indeed, it would be hard to overestimate the influence which has been exerted by this little schedule of political ethics, occupying, as it has, so prominent a place in the Chinese mind for four-and-twenty centuries—teaching the people to regard the Empire as a vast family, and the Emperor to rule by moral influence, making the goal of his ambition not the wealth, but the virtue, of his subjects. It is certain that the doctrines which it embodies have been largely efficient in rendering China what she is, the most ancient and the most populous of existing nations.

Part II. is chiefly interesting for the views it presents of the condition of human nature. It is not, as its title would seem to indicate, a map of the moral faculties; but simply a delineation of the two ways which invite the footsteps of every human pilgrim. On the one hand are traced the virtues that conduct to happiness; on the other the vices that lead to misery. Over the former is written *Tao-sin*, "Wisdom Heart," and over the latter, *Jin-sin*, "Human Heart," as descriptive of the dispositions from which they respectively proceed.

These terms, with the two sentences of the chart in which they occur, originated in the *Shu-king*, one of the oldest of the sacred books, and are there ascribed to the Emperor Shun, who filled the throne about B.C. 2100. Quaint and ill-defined, they have been retained in use through this long period as a simple expression for an obvious truth, recording as the result of a nation's experience that "to err is human." They contain no nice distinction as to the extent to which our nature is infected with evil; but intimate that its general condition is such that the word *human* may fairly be placed in antithesis to wisdom and virtue.

Yet the prevailing view of human nature maintained by Chinese ethical writers is that of its radical goodness. Though less ancient than the other, this latter is by no means a modern opinion; and it is not a little remarkable that some of those questions which agitated the Christian Church in the *fifth century* were discussed in China nearly a thousand years before. They were not broached by Confucius. His genius was not inquisitive; he was rather an architect seeking to construct a noble edifice, than a chemist testing his materials by minute analysis. And if none are philosophers but those who follow the clew of truth through the mazes of psychological and metaphysical speculation, then he has no right to the title;* but if one who loves wisdom, perceiving it by intuition and recommending it with authority, be a philosopher, there are few on the roll of time who deserve a higher position.

The next age, however, was characterized by a spirit of investigation which was due to his influence only as the intellectual impulse which he communicated set it to thinking. The moral quality of human nature became a principal subject of discussion; and every position admitted by the subject was successively occupied by some leading mind. Tsz-sze, the grandson of the Sage, advanced a theory which implied the goodness of human nature; but Mencius, his disciple (B.C. 317), was the first who distinctly enunciated the doctrine. Kaoutsze, one of his contemporaries, maintained that nature is destitute of any moral tendency, and wholly passive under the plastic hand of education. A discussion arose between them, a fragment of which, preserved in the works of Mencius, will serve to exhibit their mode of disputation as well as the position of the parties.

Nature, said Kaoutsze, is a stick of timber, and goodness is the vessel that is carved out of it.

---

* "Perhaps the subtile genius of Greece was in part withheld from indulging study in ethical controversy by the influence of Socrates, who was much more a teacher of virtue than even a searcher after truth."—Sir J. Mackintosh, *Progress of Ethical Philosophy.*

The bowl, replied Mencius, is not a natural product of the timber; but the tree requires to be destroyed in order to produce it. Is it necessary to destroy man's nature in order to make him good?

Then, said Kaoutsze, varying his illustration, human nature may be compared to a stream of water. Open a sluice to the east, and it flows to the east; open one to the west, it flows to the westward. Equally indifferent is human nature with regard to good and evil.

Water, rejoined Mencius, is indifferent as to the east or the west; but has it no choice between up and down? Now human nature inclines to good, as water does to run downward; and the evil it does is the effect of interference, just as water may be forced to run up hill. Man, he repeats, with rhetoric slightly at variance with his philosophy, inclines to virtue, as water does to flow downward, or as the wild beast does to seek the forest.

A few years later, Seuntsze, an acute and powerful writer, took the ground that human nature is evil. The influence of education he extolled in even higher terms than Kaoutsze, maintaining that whatever good it produces, it achieves by a triumph over nature which is taught to yield obedience to the dictates of prudence: that virtue is the slow result of teaching, and vice the spontaneous fruit of neglected nature.

Yang-tsze, about the commencement of the Christian era, endeavored to combine these opposite views; each contained important truth, but neither of them the whole truth. While human nature possessed benevolent affections and a conscience approving of good, it had also perverse desires and a will that chose the evil. It was therefore both bad and good; and the character of each individual took its complexion, as virtuous or vicious, according to the class of qualities most cultivated.

In the great controversy, Mencius gained the day. The two authors last named were placed on the *Index Expurgatorius* of the literary tribunal; and the advocate of human nature was promoted to the second place among the oracles of the Empire for having added a new doctrine or developed a latent one in the Confucian system. This tenet is expressed in the first line of the *San-tsze-king*, an elementary book, which is committed to memory by every schoolboy in China—*Jin che ts'u, sin pen shan*—"Man commences life with a virtuous nature." But notwithstanding this addition to the national creed, the ancient aphorism of *Shun* is still held in esteem; and a genuine Confucian, in drawing a genealogical tree of the vices, still places the root of evil in the *human* heart.

To remove this contradiction, Chuhe, the authorized expositor of the classics, devised a theory somewhat similar to Plato's account of the origin of evil. It evidently partakes of the three principal systems above referred to; professing, according to the first, to vindicate the original goodness of human nature, yet admitting, with another, that it contains some elements of evil—and thus virtually symbolizing with the third, which represents it as of a mixed character. "The bright principle of virtue," he says in his notes on the *Taiho*, "man derives from his heavenly origin; and his pure spirit, when undarkened, comprehends all truth, and is adequate to every occasion. But it is obstructed by the physical constitution and beclouded by the animal (lit. *jin-yuh*, the *human*) desires, so that it becomes obscure."

The source of virtue, as indicated in the chart, is *Taiho*—"primordial harmony;" and vice is ascribed to the influence of *Wu-hing*—"gross matter." The moral character is determined by the prevailing influence, and mankind are accordingly divided into three classes, which are thus described in a popular formula: Men of the first class are good without teaching; those of the second may be made good by teaching; and the last will continue bad in spite of teaching.

The received doctrine in relation to human nature does not oppose such a serious obstacle as might at first be imagined to the reception of Christianity, though there is reason to fear that it may tinge the complexion of Christian theology. The candid and thoughtful will recognize in the Bible a complete view of a subject which their various theories had only presented in detached fragments. In the state of primitive purity, it gives them a heaven-imparted nature in its original perfection; in the supremacy of conscience, it admits a fact on which they rely as the main support of their doctrine; in the corruption of nature, introduced by sin, it gives them a class of facts to which their consciousness abundantly testifies; and in its plan for the restoration of the moral ruin, it excites hope and satisfies reason.

The doctrine of human goodness, though supported by a partial view of facts, seems rather to have been suggested by views of expediency. Mencius denounced the tenets of Kaoutsze as pernicious to the cause of morality, and he no doubt considered that to convince men that they are endowed with a virtuous nature is the most effectual method of encouraging them to the practice of virtue. In the absence of revelation, there is nothing better. But while faith in ourselves is a strong motive, faith in God is a stronger one; and while the view that man is endowed with a noble nature, which he only needs to develop according to its own generous instincts, is sublime, there is yet one which is more sublime—viz., that while fallen man is striving for the recovery of his divine original, he must work with fear and trembling, because it is God that worketh in him.*

Part III., the Chart of Moral Excellence (as I have called it, or, more literally, of that which is to be *striven after* and *held to*), presents us with goodness in all its forms known to the Chinese. It is chiefly remarkable for its grouping, the entire domain be-

* The writer acknowledges a hint or two on this branch of the subject from an able paper of the Rev. Griffith John, in the *Journal of the North China Branch of the Royal Asiatic Society* for September, 1860, which, however, did not come to hand until this article had assumed its present form and been read on a public occasion.

ing divided into five families, each ranged under a parent virtue. The Greeks and Romans reckoned four cardinal virtues; but a difference in the mode of division implies no incompleteness in the treatment of the subject. The Chinese do not, because they count only twelve hours in the day instead of twenty-four, pretermit any portion of time; neither, when they number twenty-eight signs in the zodiac, instead of twelve, do they assign an undue length to the starry girdle of the heavens. The classification is altogether arbitrary; and Cicero makes four virtues cover the whole ground which the Chinese moralist refers to five.

But while, in a formal treatise, definition and explanation may supply the defects of nomenclature or arrangement, the terms of a general class, like that of the cardinal virtues, are not without effect on the popular mind. In this respect the Chinese have the advantage. Theirs are *Jin*, *E*, *Che*, *Sin*, *Le*—Benevolence, Justice, Wisdom, Good Faith, Politeness.* Those of Plato and Tully are Justice, Prudence, Fortitude, and Temperance. In comparing these, Prudence and Wisdom may be taken as identical, though the former appears to be rather more circumscribed in its sphere and tinged with the idea of self-interest. Temperance and Politeness, as explained in the respective systems, are also identical—the Latin term contemplating man as an individual, and the Chinese regarding him as a member of society. The former, Cicero defines as *τὸ πρέπον*, and a sense of propriety or love of order is precisely the meaning which the Chinese give to the latter. In the European code, the prominence given to Fortitude is characteristic of a martial people, among whom, at an earlier period, under the name of *ἀρετή*, it usurped the entire realm of virtue. In the progress of society, it was compelled to

* Though *politeness* is the common acceptation of the term as expressing a regard for propriety and order in social intercourse, in Chinese ethics it has a wider and higher signification. It is precisely what Malebranche makes the basis of his moral system and denominates "the love of universal order."

yield the throne to Justice and accept the place of a vassal, both Greek and Latin moralists asserting that no degree of courage which is not exerted in a righteous cause is worthy of a better appellation than that of audacity. They erred, therefore, in giving it the position of a cardinal virtue, and the Chinese have exhibited more discrimination by placing it in the retinue of Justice. They describe it by two words, *Chih* and *Yung*. Connected with the former, and explaining its idea, we read the precept, "When you fail, seek help in yourself; stand firm to your post, and let no vague desires draw you from it." Appended to the latter we have the injunction, "When you see the right, do it; when you know a fault, correct it. Neither yield to excess, if rich, nor swerve from right, if poor." What a noble conception of moral courage, of true fortitude!

Benevolence and good faith, which are quite subordinate in the heathen systems of the West, in that of China are each promoted to the leadership of a grand division. In fact, the whole tone of the Chinese morals, as exhibited in the names and order of their cardinal virtues, is quite consonant with the spirit of Christianity.* Benevolence leads the way in prompting to positive efforts for the good of others; justice follows, to regulate its actions and restrain its antagonistic qualities; wisdom sheds

---

* Cicero thus argues that there could be no occasion for the exercise of any virtue in a state of perfect blessedness, taking up the cardinal virtues *seriatim:* "Si nobis, cum ex hac vita migraremus, in beatorum insulis, ut fabulæ ferunt, immortale ævum degere liceret, quid opus esset eloquentia, cum judicia nulla fierent? aut *ipsis* etiam *virtutibus?* Nec enim *fortitudine* indigeremus, nullo proposito aut labore aut periculo; *nec justitia*, cum esset nihil quod appeteretur alieni; nec *temperantia*, quæ regeret eas quæ nullæ essent libidines; ne *prudentia* quidem egeremus, nullo proposito delectu bonorum et malorum. Una igitur essemus beati cognitione rerum et scientia." He has failed to conceive, as Sir J. Mackintosh well suggests, that there would still be room for the exercise of love—of benevolence. The Chinese, educated to regard benevolence as the prime virtue of life, would naturally give it the first place in his ideal of the future state.

her light over both; good faith imparts the stability necessary to success; politeness, or a sense of propriety, by bringing the whole conduct into harmony with the fitness of things, completes the radiant circle; and he whose character is adorned with all these qualities may be safely pronounced *totus teres atque rotundus.*

The theory of moral sentiments early engaged the attention of Chinese philosophers, and particularly the inquiry as to the origin and nature of our benevolent affections. Some, like Locke and Paley, regarded them as wholly artificial—the work of education. Others, like Hobbes and Mandeville, represented them as spontaneous and natural, but still no more than varied phases of that one ubiquitous Proteus—self-love. Mencius, with Bishop Butler, views them as disinterested and original. To establish this, he resorts to his favorite mode of reasoning, and supposes the case of a spectator moved by the misfortune of a child falling into a well. Hobbes would have described the pity of the beholder as the fruit of self-love acting through the imagination—the "fiction of future calamity to himself." Mencius says his efforts to rescue the child would be incited, not by a desire to secure the friendship of its parents or the praise of his neighbors, nor even to relieve himself from the pain occasioned by the cries of the child, but by a spontaneous feeling which pities distress and seeks to alleviate it.

The man who thus vindicates our nature from the charge of selfishness in its best affections sometimes expatiates on their social utility. He does so, however, only to repress utilitarianism of a more sordid type. When the Prince of Liang inquired what he had brought to enrich his kingdom, "Nothing," he replied, "but benevolence and justice;" and he then proceeded to show, with eloquent earnestness, how the pursuit of wealth would tend to anarchy, while that of virtue would insure happiness and peace. An earlier writer, Meh-tsze,* made the

* See an interesting paper on the writings of Meh-tsze, by the Rev. J. Ed-

principle of benevolence the root of all the virtues; and in advocating the duty of *equal* and *universal love*, he seems to have anticipated the fundamental maxim of Jonathan Edwards that virtue consists in *love* to *being* as such, and in *proportion to the amount of being.* This led him to utter the noble sentiment that he would "submit his body to be crushed to atoms if by so doing he could benefit mankind."

The doctrine of Meh-tsze is rejected by the moralists of the established school as heretical, on the ground of its inconsistency with the exercise in due degree of the relative affections, such as filial piety, fraternal love, etc. They adopted a more cautious criterion of virtue—that of the moderate exercise of all the natural faculties. *Virtus est medium vitiorum et utrinque reductum* is with them a familiar maxim. One of the Four Books, the *Chung Yung*, is founded on it. But instead of treating the subject with the inductive accuracy with which it is elaborated by Aristotle in his Nicomachean Ethics, the author kindles with the idea of absolute perfection, and indites a sublime rhapsody on the character of him who holds on his way, undeviating and unimpeded, between a twofold phalanx of opposing vices.

Part IV. is the counterpart of the preceding, and is interesting mainly on account of the use for which it is designed. The whole chart is practical, and is intended, the author tells us, to be suspended in the chamber of the student as a constant monitor. The terms in which he states this contain an allusion to a sentiment engraved by one of the ancient emperors on his wash-basin: "Let my heart be daily cleansed and renewed, and be kept clean and new forever." This part of his work has for its special object to aid the reader in detecting the moral impurities that may have attached themselves to his character, and carrying forward a process of daily and constant improvement.

---

kins, in the *Journal of the North China Branch of the Royal Asiatic Society* for May, 1859.

To some it may be a matter of surprise to find this exercise at all in vogue in a country where a divine religion has not imparted the highest degree of earnestness in the pursuit of virtue. The number who practise it is not large; but even in pagan China, the thorny path of self-knowledge exhibits "here and there a traveller."

Tsang-fu-tsze, an eminent disciple of Confucius, and the Xenophon of his Memorabilia, thus describes his own practice: "I every day examine myself on three points. In exertions on behalf of others, have I been unfaithful? In intercourse with others, have I been untrue? The instruction I have heard, have I made my own?"

An example so revered could not remain without imitators. Whether any of them has surpassed the model is doubtful; but his "three points" they have multiplied into the bristling array displayed in the chart, which they daily press in to their bosoms, as some papal ascetics were wont to do their jagged belts. Some of them, in order to secure greater fidelity in this unpleasant duty, are accustomed to perform it in the family temple, where they imagine their hearts laid bare to the view of their ancestors, and derive encouragement from their supposed approval. The practice is a beautiful one, but it indicates a want. It shows that human virtue is conscious of her weakness; and in climbing the roughest steeps feels compelled to lean on the arm of religion.

In a few cases this impressive form of domestic piety may prove efficacious; but the benefit is due to a figment of the imagination similar to that which Epictetus recommends when he suggests that the student of virtue shall conceive himself to be living in the presence of Socrates. If fancy is thus operative, how much more effectual must faith be—that faith which rises into knowledge and makes one realize that he is acting under the eye of ever-present Deity!

It is one of the glories of Christianity that by diffusing this sentiment she has made virtue not an occasional visitor to our earth, but brought her down to dwell familiarly with men. What otherwise would have been only the severe discipline of a few philosophers she has made the daily habit of myriads.* How many persons in how many lands now close each day of life by comparing every item of their conduct with a far more perfect "chart for self-examination" than our author has furnished? †

Next to the knowledge of right and wrong Confucius placed "sincerity of purpose" in pursuing the right as an essential in the practice of virtue; but as he expressed only the vaguest notions of a Supreme Being, and enjoined for popular observance no higher form of religion than the worship of the ancestral manes, a sense of responsibility, and, by consequence, "sincerity of purpose," are sadly deficient among his disciples. Some of the more earnest, on meeting with a religion which reveals to them a heart-searching God, a sin-atoning Saviour, a soul-sanctifying Spirit, and an immortality of bliss, have joyfully embraced it, confessing that they find therein motives and supports of which their own system is wholly destitute.

GENERAL INFERENCES.

On this sheet (the chart above translated) we have a projection of the national mind. It indicates the high grade in the scale of civilization attained by the people among whom it originated, exhibiting all the elements of an elaborate socialism. Political ethics are skilfully connected with private morals; and the virtues and vices are marshalled in a vast array, which required an advanced state of society for their development.

* "Religion," says Sir James Mackintosh, speaking of Plato, "had not then, besides her own discoveries, brought down the most awful and the most beautiful forms of moral truth to the humblest station in human society."

† There are many evening hymns in which the review of the day is beautifully and touchingly expressed, but in none perhaps better than in that of Gellert commencing "*Ein tag ist wieder hin.*"

The accuracy with which these various traits of character are noted implies the same thing; and the correctness of the moral judgments here recorded infers something more than culture—it discloses a grand fact of our nature, that, whatever may be thought of innate ideas, it contains inherent principles which produce the same fruits in all climates.

These tables indicate, at the same time, that the Chinese have made less proficiency in the study of mind than in that of morals. This is evident from some confusion (more observable in the original than in the translation) of faculties, sentiments, and actions. The system is, on the whole, pretty well arranged; but there are errors and omissions enough to show that their ethics, like their physics, are merely the records of phenomena which they observe *ab extra* without investigating their causes and relations. While they expatiate on the virtues, they make but little inquiry into the nature of virtue; while insisting on various duties, they never discuss the ground of obligation; and while duties are copiously expounded, not a word is said on the subject of rights.

The combined influence of an idolatrous religion and a despotic government, under which there can be no such motto as *Dieu et mon droit*, may account for this latter deficiency. But similar *lacunæ* are traceable in so many directions that we are compelled to seek their explanation in a subjective cause—in some peculiarity of the Chinese mind.

They have, for instance, no system of psychology, and the only rude attempt at the formation of one consists in an enumeration of the organs of perception. These they express as *wu-kwan*, the "five senses." But what are they? The eyes, ears, nose, mouth; and not the skin or nerves, but the heart—the sense of touch, which alone possesses the power of waking us from the Brahma dream of a universe floating in our own brain, and convincing us of the objective reality of an external world, being utterly ignored; to say nothing of the absurdity of classing the "heart"—the intellect (for so they intend the word) —with those passive media of intelligence.

This elementary effort dates from the celebrated Mencius; and perhaps for that very reason the mind of the moderns has not advanced beyond it, as one of their pious emperors abdicated the throne rather than be guilty of reigning longer than his grandfather.

Another instance of philosophical classification equally ancient, equally authoritative, and equally absurd, is that of the five elements. They are given as *kin*, *muh*, *shwuy*, *ho*, *tu*— i. e. metal, wood, water, fire, and earth. Now, not to force this into a disparaging contrast with the results of our recent science, which recognizes nothing as an element but an ultimate form of matter, we may fairly compare it with the popular division of "four elements."

The principle of classification being the enumeration of the leading forms of inorganic matter which enter into the composition of organic bodies, the Chinese have violated it by introducing wood into the category; and they evince an obtuseness of observation utterly inconsistent with the possession of philosophic talent in not perceiving the important part which atmospheric air performs in the formation of other bodies. The extent to which they adhere to the quintal enumeration or classification by "fives" illustrates, in a rather ludicrous manner, the same want of discrimination. Thus, while in mind they have the five senses, and in matter the five elements, in morals they reckon five virtues, in society five relations, in astronomy five planets, in ethnology five races, in optics five colors, in music five notes, in the culinary art five tastes; and, not to extend the catalogue, they divide the horizon into *five quarters*.

These instances evince a want of analytical power; and the deficiency is still further displayed in the absence of any analysis of the sounds of their language until they were brought acquainted with the alphabetical Sanscrit; the non-existence, to the present day, of any inquiry into the forms of speech which might be called a grammar, or of any investigation of the processes of reasoning corresponding with our logic; and the fact that while they have soared into the attenuated atmosphere of ontological speculation, they have left all the regions of physical and abstract science almost as trackless as the arctic snows.

It would be superfluous to vindicate the Chinese from the charge of mental inferiority in the presence of that immense social and political organization which has held together so many millions of people for so many thousands of years, and especially of arts, now dropping their golden fruits into the lap of our own civilization, whose roots can be traced to the soil of that ancient empire. But a strange defect must be admitted in the national mind. We think, however, that it is more in its development than in its constitution, and may be accounted for by the influence of education.

If we include in that term all the influences that affect the mind, the first place is due to language; and a language whose primary idea is the representation of the objects of sense, and which is so imperfect a vehicle of abstract thought that it is incapable of expressing by single words such ideas as space, quality, relation, etc., must have seriously obstructed the exercise of the intellect in that direction. A servile reverence for antiquity which makes it sacrilege to alter the crude systems of the ancients increased the difficulty; and the government brought it to the last degree of aggravation by admitting, in the public-service examinations, a very limited number of authors, with their expositors, to whose opinions conformity is encouraged by honors, and from whom dissent is punished by disgrace.

These fetters can only be stricken off by the hand of Christianity; and we are not extravagant in predicting that a stupendous intellectual revolution will attend its progress. Revealing an omnipresent God as Lord of the Conscience, it will add a new hemisphere to the world of morals; stimulating inquiry in the spirit of the precept "Prove all things, hold fast that which is good," it will subvert the blind principle of deference; and perhaps its grandest achievement in the work of mental emancipation may be the superseding of the ancient ideographic language by providing a medium better adapted to the purposes of a Christian civilization. It would only be a repetition of historic triumphs if some of the vernacular dialects, raised from the depths where they now lie in neglect, and shaped by the forces which heave them to the surface, should be made, under the influence of Christianity, to teem with the rich productions of a new literature, philosophy, and science.

N. B.—These charts are here appended in the original language for the benefit of students of Chinese.

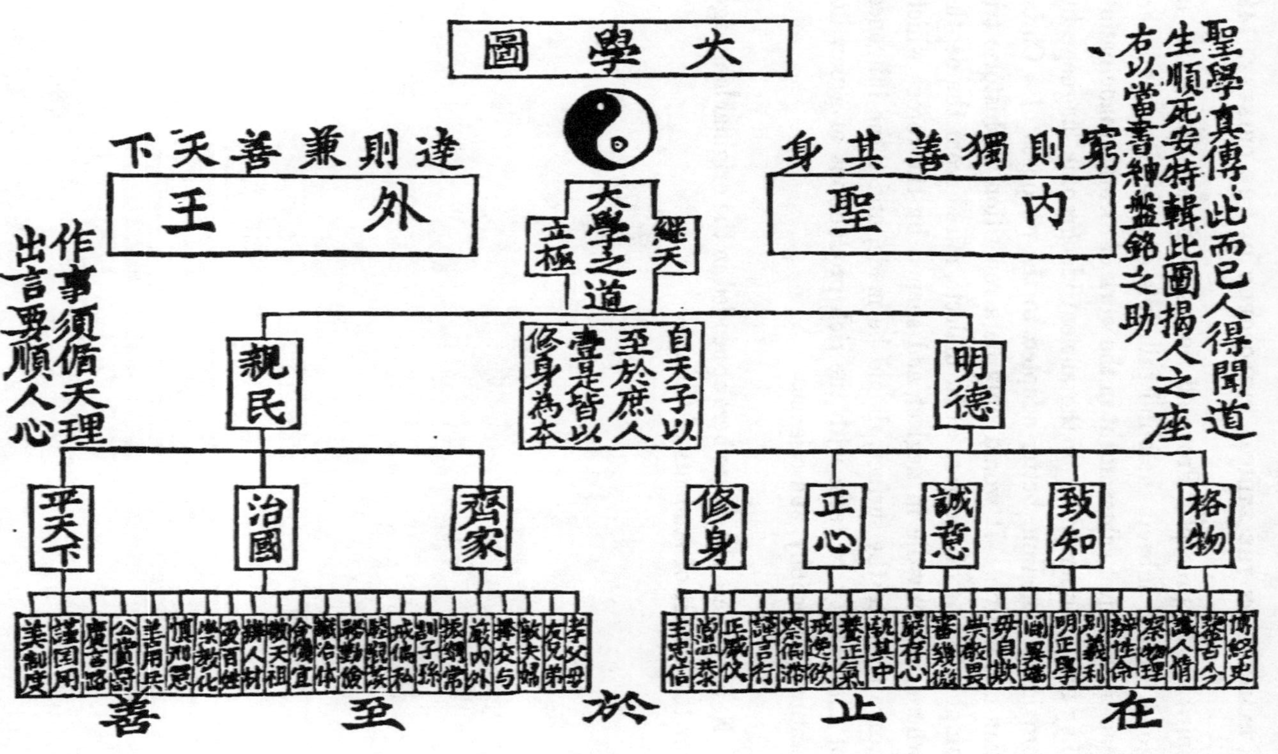
大學圖
窮則獨善其身
達則兼善天下
內聖
外王
大學之道
繼天立極
自天子以至於庶人壹是皆以修身為本
明德
親民
格物
致知
誠意
正心
修身
齊家
治國
平天下
作事須循天理
出言要順人心
聖學真傳此而已人得聞道
生順死安特輯此圖揭人之座
右以當書紳盤銘之助
在止於至善

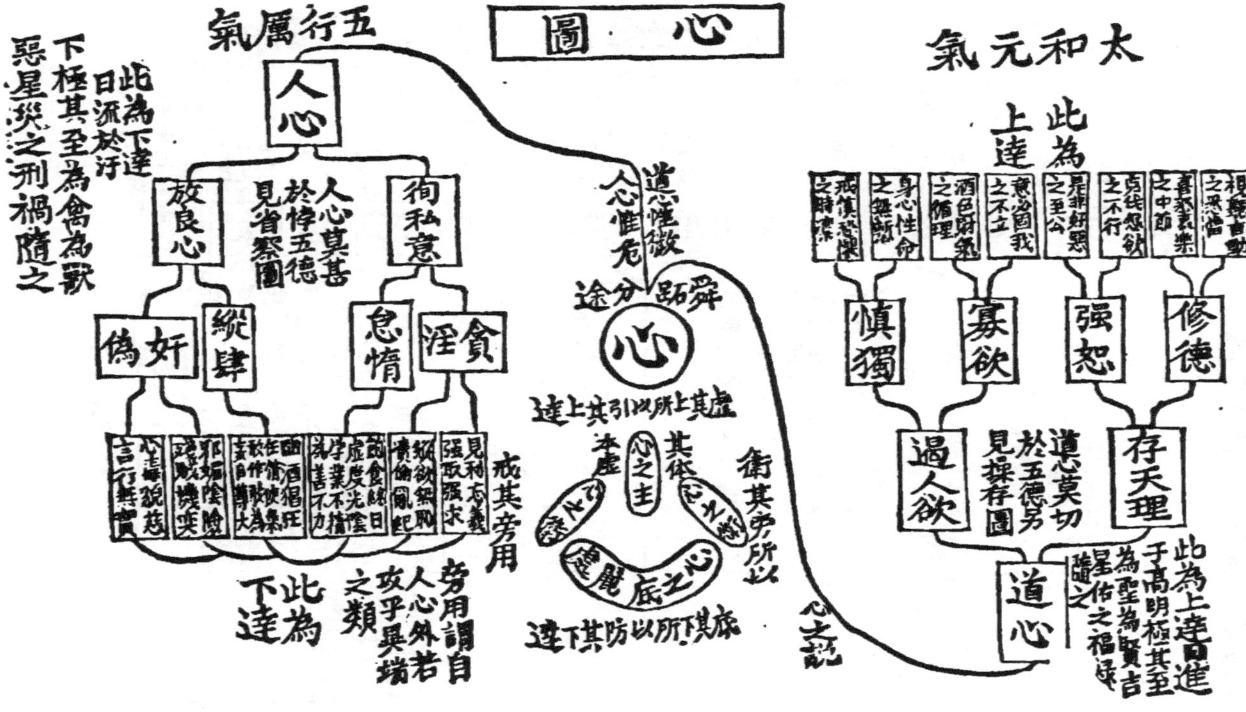

心圖

閱大學圖自知正心矣然難收易放者心也故再輯心圖

太和元氣

此為上達

視聽言動之必禮 | 喜怒哀樂之中節 | 克伐怨欲之不行 | 是非好惡之至公 | 意必固我之不立 | 酒色財氣之循理 | 身心性命之無斷 | 戒慎恐懼之時凛

修德　強恕　寡欲　慎獨

存天理　遏人欲

道心莫切於五德另見操存圖

道心

此為上達日進于高明極其至為聖為賢吉星佑之福祿隨之

道心惟微　人心惟危

舜跖分途

心

虛其上所以引其上達

其体心之主本虛

心之旁　心之旁

衛其旁所以

心之底麗虛

實其下所以防其下達

心之說

五行屬氣

人心

放良心　徇私意

人心莫甚於悖五德見省察圖

偽奸　縱肆　怠惰　貪淫

戒其旁用

旁用謂自人心外若攻乎異端之類

此為下達

此為下達日流於汙下極其至為禽為獸惡星災之刑禍隨之

造次克念　操存圖　戰兢自持

閱心圖既彰彰於善惡之分途矣然
循恐心得之難存也故繼以操存

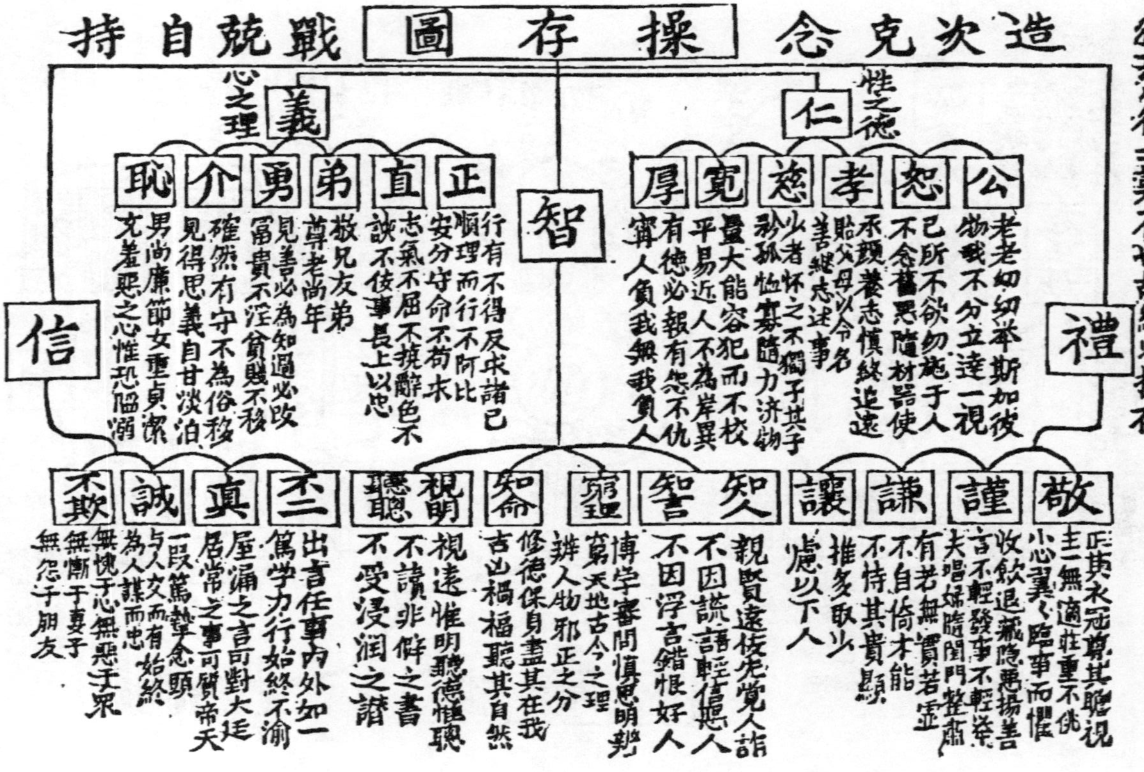

仁（性之德）

- **公**：老老幼幼舉斯加彼　物我不分立達一視
- **恕**：己所不欲勿施于人　不念舊惡隨材器使
- **孝**：承顔養志慎終追遠　貽父母以令名　善繼志述事
- **慈**：少者懷之不獨子其子　矜孤恤寡賑力濟物
- **寬**：量大能容犯而不校　平易近人不為崖異
- **厚**：有德必報有怨不仇　寧人負我無我負人

義（心之理）

- **正**：行有不得反求諸己　順理而行不阿比　安分守命不苟求
- **直**：志氣不屈不挠辭色不　諛不佞事長上以忠
- **弟**：敬兄友弟　尊老尚年
- **勇**：見善必為知過必改　富貴不淫貧賤不移
- **介**：確然有守不為俗移　見得思義自甘淡泊
- **恥**：男尚廉節女重貞潔　充羞惡之心惟恐陷溺

智

禮

- **敬**：正其衣冠尊其瞻視　主一無適莊重不佻　小心翼翼臨事而懼
- **謹**：收歛退藏隱惡揚善　言不輕發事不輕爲　夫唱婦隨閨門整肅
- **謙**：有若無實若虛　不自倚才能　不恃其貴顯
- **讓**：推多取少　慮以下人

智

- **知人**：親賢遠佞先覺人詐　不因譭譽輕信惡人
- **知言**：不因浮言錯恨好人
- **窮理**：博学審問慎思明辨　窮天地古今之理　辨人物邪正之分
- **知命**：修德保身盡其在我　吉凶禍福聽其自然
- **視明聽聰**：視遠惟明聽德惟聰　不讀非僻之書　不受浸潤之譖

信

- **恒**：出言任事內外如一　篤学力行始終不渝
- **真**：屋漏之言可對大廷　居常之事可質帝天　一段篤摯念頭
- **誠**：與人交而有始終　為人謀而忠
- **不欺**：無愧于心無惡于衆　無慚于妻子　無怨于朋友

省察圖

有則改之 無則加勉

問操存圖則心德可常存矣然猶恐非幾之易萌也故復繼以省察

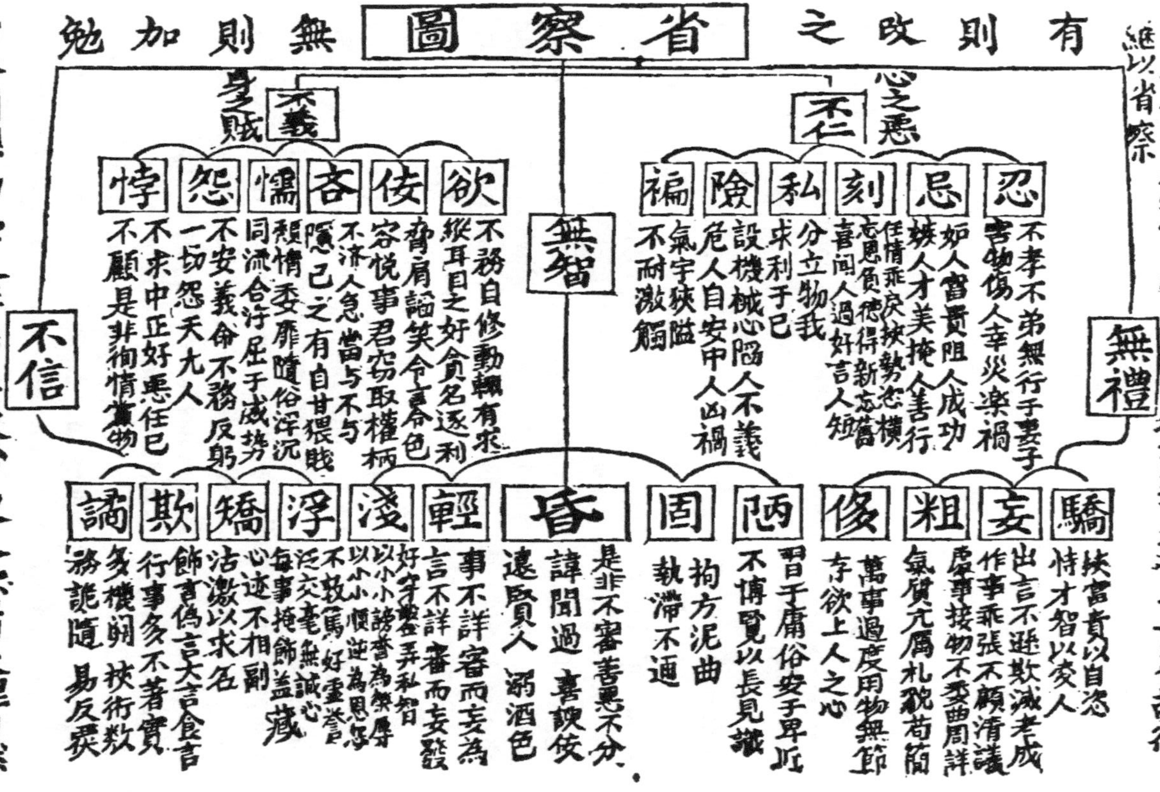

- **不仁**（心之惡）
  - 忍：不孝不弟無行于妻子 害物傷人幸災樂禍
  - 忌：妒人富貴阻人成功 嫉人才美掩人善行
  - 刻：任情乖戾挾勢恣横 忘恩負德得新忘舊 喜聞人過好言人短
  - 私：分立物我 求利于己
  - 險：設機械心陷人不義 危人自安中人凶禍
  - 褊：氣宇狹隘 不耐激觸
- **不義**（身之賊）
  - 欲：不務自修動輒有求 縱耳目之好貪名逐利
  - 佞：脅肩諂笑令言令色 容悅事君竊取權柄
  - 吝：不濟人急當与不与 隱己之有自甘猥賤
  - 懦：頹惰委靡隨俗浮沉 同流合汙屈于威勢
  - 怨：不安義命不務反躬 一切怨天尤人
  - 悖：不求中正好惡任己 不顧是非徇情害物
- **無智**
- **無禮**
  - 驕：挾富貴以自恣 恃才智以交人
  - 妄：出言不遜欺滅老成 作事乖張不顧清議
  - 粗：處事接物不委曲周詳 氣質亢厲礼貌苟簡
  - 侈：萬事過度用物無節 存欲上人之心
  - 陋：習于庸俗安于卑近 不博覽以長見識
- **不信**
  - 固：拘方泥曲 執滯不通
  - 昏：是非不審善惡不分 諱聞過 喜諛佞 遠賢人 溺酒色
  - 輕：事不詳審而妄為 言不詳審而妄發
  - 淺：好守聲名弄私智 以小小謗訾為榮辱 以小小順逆為恩怨 不敦篤好虛譽
  - 浮：泛交毫無誠心 每事掩飾蓋藏
  - 矯：心迹不相副 沽激以求名
  - 欺：飾言僞言大言食言 行事多不著實
  - 譎：多機阱 挾術數 務詭隨 易反覆

右各圖總勸學人時時收放心遏人欲循天理自然入道古來聖賢莫不由此而進有志上達者慎勿忽之

ISIS AND OSIRIS, OR ORIENTAL DUALISM.*

A PHILOSOPHICAL theory is always to be found at the root of a religion. It is accordingly only by a comparative study of their religions that we can hope to arrive at the fundamental conceptions of mankind as to the system of the universe. Ramifying into an infinity of forms, these conceptions are capable of being reduced to a few simple elements; some religions starting from a triad of powers, others from a duality, etc. These terms do not, in all cases, mean the same thing; indeed, the analogy is often limited to a mere numerical correspondence, as we shall see when we come to compare the dualism of China with that of Persia. As an introduction to the subject, I avail myself of an ancient treatise on the religion of the Egyptians.

The superstitions of classical antiquity have been transmitted to us through a thousand channels; but two writers only have given us anything like a philosophical view of the religion of the ancients. These are Cicero and Plutarch. Deeply serious and profoundly erudite, both exercised the mature vigor of their powers on the all-absorbing question of man's relation to the supernatural. The Roman has left us the results of his inquiries in the *Quæstiones Tusculanæ*, and especially in his treatise *De Natura Deorum*. The Greek, besides numerous other works, has embodied his theology in a disquisition concerning Isis and Osiris, or the religion of the Egyptians. The former is well known, but the latter is comparatively rare; and we accordingly propose to give it a cursory review with reference to its bearing

---

* From the *Chinese Recorder*, September, 1867.

on certain systems current in Oriental countries at the present day. The edition we make use of is that of Gustav Parthey, Berlin, 1850. We are not aware that this treatise has ever appeared in an English dress.

Plutarch's philosophy is not profound. It never essays the sublime flights of Plato or the searching analysis of Aristotle; neither is it recommended by originality of thought or grace of diction. Its chief characteristic is a certain comprehensiveness of view, based on a wide induction of particulars. And in this consists its value; for the reader, however he may dissent from the reasoning of the author, will not fail to thank him for the variety of curious information which he has collected. A Neoplatonist brought up at the feet of Ammonius, he learned from his preceptor to apply that universal solvent, not unknown in more modern times, which renders the terms of all religious creeds mutually convertible. The secret of his process is found in the one word "allegory;" and in applying it he always treats with reverence the most insignificant and even discrepant details, looking on them all as cerements of mummied truth. His exordium well expresses the spirit of his undertaking, and touches in our bosoms a chord of melancholy sympathy.

"O Clea!" he exclaims, addressing a learned lady who was a votary of the Egyptian goddess—"O Clea! as it becomes those who are endowed with reason to look to the gods for every good, especially should we, in entering on an inquiry concerning themselves, seek to be guided by them as far as it is possible for the mind of man to penetrate. . . . For neither silver nor gold, nor thunders and lightnings, but wisdom and knowledge, constitute the felicity of the Divine Being. If these attributes were withdrawn, his immortal existence would no longer be a *life*, but merely a sterile *duration*. The search for truth is therefore a striving after the divine—a holier work than any ceremonial purifications or cloistered devotion."

From such a beginning we would expect his track to brighten

at every step; but it is painful to read the conclusion which he arrives at after a survey of the whole field. The search for truth is not always successful. Briefly setting forth his own system, he says (p. 78), "The beginnings of all things are not to be placed, with Democritus and Epicurus, in certain inanimate corpuscles; nor are we to suppose, with the Stoics, that there is but one mind [λόγος], or providence [πρόνοια], which made all things out of primordial matter destitute of quality [i. e. imparted to matter its properties], and which now presides over the affairs of the universe. For it is impossible that there should be anything evil if God were the cause of all, or anything good if God were the cause of nothing." This dictum, while it shows that Plutarch was stumbling at that immemorial snare of philosophers, the origin of evil, also shows how far he falls in grasp of intellect behind the sublime optimism of the great founder of his school. He goes on, "The most ancient doctrine, whose origin is unknown, in which a faith firm and inextinguishable everywhere prevails, expressed not in words, but in rites and sacrifices, is that the universe is not moved as an automaton, without any mind or governor; neither is there merely a single Logos, who rules and guides it as with rudder or rein. But all things proceed from a twofold origin—from two antagonistic powers, of whom one would lead in the right way, but the other opposes and frustrates his purposes, so that life is a mingled cup, and the world (at least so much of it as lies beneath the moon) a mingled scene of good and ill. For if nothing exists without a cause, and good cannot be the cause of evil, it follows that both good and evil must be derived from independent sources." "This," he adds, "is the opinion of the wisest as well as the most numerous portion of mankind," and he startles us by the assertion in another place that it was avowed by Plato himself towards the close of his life. "In the book on Legislation," he says, "Plato, divesting his language of enigmatical symbols and calling things by their right names, declares that the world is moved not by one soul, but perhaps by many, by two at the least—one beneficent, the other of the opposite character."

This doctrine Plutarch finds inculcated in the religion of Egypt—a religion neither lucid nor profound, but one which he tells us was regarded with reverence by such men as Solon, Thales, Plato, and Pythagoras. In reciting the myth by which it is veiled, he admonishes his fair pupil that when she hears of the gods wandering from place to place, and being torn limb from limb, she is not to imagine that anything of the kind ever occurred; for the Egyptians were wont to express their ideas in figurative forms, and to conceal them under shadowy symbols. Having illustrated this by examples, he proceeds to relate the legend of Isis and Osiris.

Those beneficent deities, united in happy wedlock, were assailed by the spite of the malignant Typhon. By a stratagem, this evil being succeeded in inducing Osiris to lie down in a chest or coffin, when, nailing it fast, he committed it to the waters of the Nile to carry out to sea. Isis, in disconsolate widowhood, wanders far and wide in quest of her husband's remains. Being received by the King of Byblus, and employed as a domestic, she seeks to requite his kindness, while nursing an infant prince, by subjecting the child to a process of annealing, with a view to rendering it immortal. The Queen, terrified at the fiery ordeal, cries out and breaks the spell. Here, by a happy accident, she recovers the body of her spouse; but not long after, Typhon, their implacable enemy, finding her off her guard, tears it in pieces, scattering the limbs in distant regions.

In this it is easy to recognize the story of Ceres and Proserpine, which, however, in point of poetic taste, is a great improvement on the Egyptian original. It is easy, too, to see how the wild fancy of a superstitious and unlettered age might give birth to a thousand such fables; but it is not so easy to conceive how any truth, physical or moral, can be grafted on such a stock. Plutarch, however, discovers in it a world of meaning, and recites its minutest details—not a few savoring of grossness and obscenity—because the Egyptian hierophants had thought fit to make it the vehicle of their mystic lore. It is edifying to observe how he labors to extract from it a rational theory of the universe.

Setting out with two principles, he suddenly finds himself encumbered with three, which are required to correspond with the three leading characters in the myth—not to speak of many others which have a subordinate place in the legend, and each of which, in the exposition, must be represented by some force, power, or principle. Instead of representing the simple antithesis of good and evil, he makes Typhon stand alone (though the story gives him a wife) for the energy of evil; and subdivides the beneficent power into two parts, assigning a portion of its functions to each of the favorite deities. But before he reaches this result, he flounders through a quicksand of conflicting interpretations, repudiating some and adopting others with as much discrimination as the Roman pantheon exercised in admitting the gods of the Gentiles. In following his uncertain steps, we are compelled to condense many pages into few.

Some, he says, make this myth or saga a traditionary history of the ancient kings; and some make it a personification of the Nile fructifying the soil of Egypt, and of the sea in turn swallowing up the river. But the wiser priests do not limit the interpretation so narrowly. According to them, Osiris is not merely the Nile, but the principle of moisture (water), and Typhon the antagonistic principle of drought or fire. Others look on Typhon as the sun, and on Osiris as the moon; and others still understand by Typhon the shadow of the earth which envelops the moon during an eclipse. The Egyptians also exhibit Osiris in human form, clothed with a robe of flame, and representing the sun as an embodiment of the beneficent power. Some plainly call the sun Osiris, and maintain that Isis was no other than the moon, hence her statue is crowned with horns. They represent Osiris by an eye and a sceptre, and Typhon by a hippopotamus. Manetho makes Typhon iron, and Horus loadstone —Horus, the son, taking the place of the dead Osiris, and his transforming influence over the hearts of men being compared to that of a magnet, which imparts its own properties to the metal which it attracts.

After comparing these deities to the cabalistic numbers of the Pythagoreans, and to the sides of a triangle, Plutarch offers an explanation of his own. In the human soul, Osiris is the understanding, and Typhon the passions. In nature, Osiris is the masculine energy, and Isis the female. Again, Osiris is the beginning, Isis the continuation, and Horus, their child, the completion. In a word, disorder is Typhon, while order and beauty are the work of Isis—the image of the unseen Osiris.

From this view, it is obvious that not much can be made of the myth—either by the "best-instructed interpreters," whose expositions are directly opposed to each other, or by Plutarch himself, whose own opinions are self-contradictory. Indeed, the learned author betrays his incapacity for the work he has undertaken, *tantas componere lites*, by his performances in the way of etymology.

He says, e.g., "Isis is not a barbarian word, but common alike to the Greek and Egyptian languages. It is derived at once from two words—*ἐπιστήμη*, understanding, and *κίνησις*, motion; just as *θεός* comes from two words—*θεατόν*, the visible [from being invisible?], and *θέων*, hastening, the swift." The derivation, too, of Osiris from the two Greek words *ὅσιος* and *ἱερός*, while with equal confidence he points out an Egyptian origin, is another specimen which we select from many of that kind of reasoning. It is not surprising that one who carries dualism into etymology after this fashion should be able to find two coordinate powers at the root of all things!

Dualism, we have seen, was the goal at which Plutarch aimed in his laborious investigation of the Egyptian mysteries. The veneration in which Egypt was held, as in some sense the fatherland of Grecian culture—its high antiquity, and, above all, the currency which the religions of Egypt had obtained in the Roman Empire, were circumstances conspiring to stimulate research and give importance to doctrines supported by Egyptian testimony. But Plutarch was not content to rest his doctrine on the sole authority of the Egyptians. He found evidence of its prevalence in countries far remote from the banks of the Nile, and boldly asserts that dualism is at once the most ancient and the most widely disseminated of all creeds. This assertion he endeavors to make good by citing analogies in the religious philosophy of various nations. He first appeals to the Persians.

Zoroaster, he says, calls the beneficent deity Oromasdes, and the malignant one Ahrimanius. The former is symbolized by light, the latter by darkness. They are engaged in perpetual conflict; yet a time is looked for when Ahrimanius shall be overcome, and all mankind lead a life of happiness, dwelling together in harmony, and speaking one language. At that time they will no longer stand in need of food, and their bodies no longer cast a shadow.

The Chaldeans held the same doctrine, as Plutarch infers from the fact of their regarding the planets as deities, and distinguishing them into three classes—beneficent, malignant, and indifferent.

Among the Greeks, he says, the same belief is everywhere apparent—good being referred to the domain of Olympian Jove, and evil to that of Hades; while Harmonia is represented as the offspring of Mars and Venus, the happy result from a conflict of opposing principles.

It is unnecessary to follow our author as he traces the dualistic idea in its various manifestations in the countries referred to; indeed, its existence there might have been presumed, independent of demonstration. With the advantage of a more extended view of the world's history, and a wider acquaintance with human beliefs, we are able to add considerably to his catalogue of evidences, and to show that, in a vague sense, he is not far wrong in predicating universality for a certain kind of dualism; though we shall not admit so readily the other claim which he makes on its behalf—that of primogeniture among the religious tenets of the human race. We recognize it in the worship of Baal and Astarte among the nations adjacent to Palestine. We discover it among the wild superstitions of Northern Europe, and may trace it even in the crude theology of the aboriginal Americans. It is more interesting, however, to note the form it takes among those great nations of Southern and Eastern Asia which stand forth as living monuments of antiquity—the sole survivors of an extinct world.

In theory the Hindoos acknowledge a triad, but practically they divide their devotions between two antagonistic deities. Forgetting their slumbering Brahma, whose work of creation is finished, and who no longer interferes with the course of nature, they are only anxious to engage the protection of Vishnu, the Preserver, or to appease the wrath of Siva, the Destroyer. Nor is it unworthy of remark that as the *phallos* of Osiris was worshipped in Egypt, so the *lingam* of Siva is reverenced in India as the symbol of reproductive energy, which only finds scope for its exercise in consequence of decay and death.

In China dualism appears under a peculiar form. There are not here two deities competing for the popular favor; but we find here two classes, called 神 and 鬼, answering very nearly to a distinction current among the Greeks, who, as Plutarch tells us, designated the good deities by *θεός*, and the evil ones by *δαίμων*. They have, I admit, other distinctions than those of moral qualities; but these are uppermost in the popular idea. As we rise, however, from the credulity of vulgar superstition to the subtle region of philosophic speculation, these divinities become divested of their personality and fade into mere forces—

manifestations of the *Yin*, 陰, and the *Yang*, 陽. In these last terms we have the true basis of Chinese dualism. As they are used to express the distinctions of sex, they are often called the male and female principles; and it is undeniable that in the mind of a native a sexual idea is attached to each, while the two together are looked upon as containing the seminal elements of the universe.

Evidence, however, is not wanting to show that this conception had no place in the minds of those who originated the Chinese language. The characters speak for themselves, and furnish us with a perfect mirror of the original idea—signifying respectively "*the luminous*" and "*the dark.*" In this sense they are applied to the sun and moon, the latter being called *T'ai Yin*—not as dark in itself, but as presiding over the realm of darkness. Light was recognized as an active agent in the production of physical changes; and darkness, not less important to the well-being of the material world, was not discovered to be a mere negation, but elevated to the dignity of a co-ordinate principle. The two together are made the foundation of a cosmogony which in the function assigned to light bears some analogy to our Scripture account of the order of creation; and the resemblance is still further increased by a faint conception of something anterior to *Yang*, and even prior to chaos. The common statement given in Chinese histories * may be freely

---

* Chinese histories, like Knickerbocker's History of New York, almost always begin with the creation of the world. Speculative writers following Chow-tsze give this cosmogony a slight variation by omitting the word "produced." "First the indefinite and then the definite [or conditioned]. It moved, and there was light [or *Yang*]; it rested, and there was darkness [or *Yin*]." They make it a mere sequence, and deny causation. Chu-fu-tsze says the "first five terms of the series are so complete that nothing can be added to them or taken from them." It is curious to see light connected with motion. Did the ancient Chinese anticipate the undulatory theory, and the whole modern doctrine of thermo-dynamics? The physical

rendered in the following form: "The indefinite, or 無極, produced the finite or definite, 太極, the elements of nature as yet in a chaotic state. This chaos evolved the principle of *Yang*, or light. The *Yang* produced *Yin*, i. e. darkness followed in the way of alternation; and the *Yin* and the *Yang* together produced all things from the alternations of day and night, and the succession of the seasons." Commencing with this simple idea, the *Yin* and the *Yang* have been gradually metamorphosed into mysterious entities, the foundation of a universal sexual system, and incessantly active in every department of nature—at once the fountain of the deepest philosophy and the aliment of the grossest superstition.*

A comparison of the various phases under which the dualistic idea manifests itself in different countries would, we believe, tend to elucidate some obscure points in the religious history of the human race.

It is customary with a certain school to represent religion as altogether the fruit of an intellectual process. It had its birth, say they, in ignorance, is modified by every stage in the progress of knowledge, and expires when the light of philosophy reaches

---

theory which refers everything to the *Yin* and *Yang* originates in the *Yih-king*, the oldest of their sacred books. If *tai-ki* is matter, then they undoubtedly anticipated the dual bases of modern physics, matter and motion.

* The orthodox view of *kwe* and *shen* is to be found in a passage of the *Chung-yung*. "The Master said vast are the virtues of the *kwe-shen!*" On this dictum of Confucius, Ch'eng-tsze remarks, "The *kwe-shen* are the forces of nature." Chang-tsze calls them "properties of the dual principle *Yin-yang*." Chu-fu-tsze adds, "*Kwe* are the spirits of the *Yin*, and *shen* the spirits of the *Yang*"—the term "spirits" (*ling*) being so vague as to make room at once for the negations of atheism, and for all the divinities of polytheism. In a discourse quoted in the *Sing-li ta-tsuen*, Chu-fu-tsze tries to vindicate his masters, the two Ch'engs, from the suspicion of denying the existence of spiritual beings, i. e. of gods. "They by no means intended," he says, "to assert that there are no such things as spirits, but that there are none such as the vulgar believe in."

its noonday. The fetich gives place to a personification of the powers of nature, and this poetic pantheon is in turn superseded by the high idea of unity in nature, expressed by monotheism.

This theory has the merit of verisimilitude. It indicates what might be the process if man were left to make his own religion; but it has the misfortune to be at variance with facts. A wide survey of the history of civilized nations (and the history of others is beyond reach) shows that the actual process undergone by the human mind in its religious development is precisely opposite to that which this theory supposes; in a word, that man was not left to construct his own creed, but that his blundering logic has always been active in its attempts to corrupt and obscure a divine original. The connection subsisting between the religious systems of ancient and distant countries presents many a problem difficult of solution. Indeed, their mythologies and religious rites are generally so distinct as to admit the hypothesis of an independent origin; but the simplicity of their earliest beliefs exhibits an unmistakable resemblance suggestive of a common source.

China, India, Egypt, and Greece all agree in the monotheistic type of their early religion. The Orphic hymns, long before the advent of the popular divinities, celebrated the *Pantheos*, the Universal God. The odes compiled by Confucius testify to the early worship of *Shangte*, the Supreme Ruler. The Vedas speak of "one unknown true Being, all-present, all-powerful; the Creator, Preserver, and Destroyer of the universe." And in Egypt, as late as the time of Plutarch, there were still vestiges of a monotheistic worship. "The other Egyptians," he says, "all made offerings at the tombs of the sacred beasts; but the inhabitants of the Thebaïd stood alone in making no such offerings, not regarding as a god anything that can die, and acknowledging no god but one whom they call Kneph, who had no birth, and can have no death." Abraham, in his wanderings, found the God of his fathers known and honored in Salem, in Gerar, and in Memphis; while at a later day, Jethro in Midian, and Balaam in Mesopotamia, were witnesses that the knowledge of Jehovah was not yet extinct in those countries. The first step in the corruption of this great traditional truth was probably the substitution of two co-ordinate powers instead of the original ONE.* These were not always conceived from the same point of view; but the human mind, longing for something like an explanation of the mysteries of nature, generally seized on two leading forces or principles, and deified them as the foundation of a crude theory of the universe. The Persians, struck with the existence of moral disorder, explained it by the conflict of Oromasdes and Ahrimanius. The Hindoos, impressed by the vicissitudes of our mortal state, personified their ideas in a Preserver and a Destroyer; and the Chinese, attracted by the most striking of all physical phenomena, pitched on light and darkness as the basis of a physical theory.

---

* A species of dualism may be discovered in the sentiments, if not the doctrines, of the Christian world. Indeed, few persons are aware to what extent Christianity has been affected by the dualism of Persia; for the truths of revelation, distilling like rain-drops pure from heaven, take their color from the channels through which they pass. It is thus that Satan comes to appear in the New Testament as a kind of rival deity, a personification of the power of evil; and all Christendom, with but few exceptions, has taken the personification for a person and assigned to Satan the divine attributes of omnipresence and omniscience, if no others. Now to believe that Satan is forever whispering at the ear of every mortal of the many millions born into this world, as he was at the ear of Eve; and that he literally marshals his armies for battle against the Lord of Hosts, is to mistake the language of poetry for that of philosophy. It deepens the gloom of a world which is already dark enough, and weakens the moral sense by detracting from the feeling of responsibility. It places the soul on its guard rather against a person than a thing—against Satan instead of sin. One may reject this relic of magianism without denying the existence of evil spirits any more than he does that of good ones. On this subject see Bushnell's Nature and the Supernatural; see also the Epistle of St. James, i. 14.

Among all the systems that have passed in review, there seems to be no family-tie or well-established relationship. In fact, the analogies subsisting between them appear to reduce themselves to the two ideas of duality and antithesis. A closer connection, at first view, seems to exist between the Chinese and Persian systems; but their points of resemblance are accidental, and their differences essential. They agree in taking light and darkness for symbols; but the Persian makes them symbols of a moral idea, the Chinese of physical agents. The former regards them as persons; the latter never ascribes to them any attribute of personal existence, but assigns them different values under different circumstances, as the x and y of an indeterminate problem—making them at one time mere terms of distinction, at another the elements of the sexual system, and again the active and passive agencies that pervade all nature.

We are safe in concluding that these several systems sprang up independently in each nation, as the fruit of their earliest efforts in the way of speculative thought. But how little that speculative thought was able to accomplish for the religious enlightenment of mankind, we have melancholy evidence in the fact that each of these dual systems, at a very early period, began to put forth the many branches of the polytheistic upas. In Persia, Plutarch says, each of the principal deities gave birth to half a dozen gods, who took part in their conflict. In Egypt and India, a numerous family of deities connect themselves with the leading characters; and in China the two classes of *Shin* and *Kwei* take their rise from *Yin* and *Yang*. Thus, superstition takes up a philosophic idea, and perverts it to her own purposes; and human philosophy, without light from on high, is unable to oppose any barrier beyond the erection of an altar to the "unknown God," inscribed with some such mournful confession as that which Plutarch gives us from a temple of Isis—"I am all that is, or was, or shall be; and my veil no mortal hand has ever withdrawn."

ALCHEMY IN CHINA.*

"The search itself rewards the pains;
So though the chymist his great secret miss,
For neither it in art nor nature is,
Yet things well worth his toil he gains,
And does his charge and labor pay,
With good unsought experiments by the way."—COWLEY.

ONE in their etymological origin, the words Alchemy and Chemistry describe different stages in the progress of the same science. The former represents it in its infancy, nursed on the bosom of superstition; its field of vision limited to special objects, and vainly striving to accomplish the impossible. The latter presents it in its maturity, when, emancipated from puerile fancies, it claims the realm of nature for its domain, and the laws of matter as its proper study.

In its earlier stage it acknowledged no other aim than the pursuit of the philosopher's stone and the elixir of life. In its more advanced state it renounces them both, yet it secures substantial advantages of scarcely inferior magnitude, alleviating disease and prolonging life by the improvements it has introduced into the practice of medicine; while by the mastery it gives us over the elements of nature it surpasses the most sanguine expectations of its early votaries.†

* Read before the American Oriental Society, October, 1868; revised and published in the *China Review*, January, 1879.

† The eminent chemist Dr. J. W. Draper, of New York, in a recent lecture on evolution, gives ancient alchemists the credit of being the first to seize the grand idea of evolution in its widest extent, as "a progress from the imperfect to the more perfect, including lifeless as well as living nature,

Those early votaries, whether they lived and labored in the West or East, should not be forgotten. They were the intrepid divers who explored the bottom of the stream, and laid the foundation for those magnificent arches on which modern science has erected her easy thoroughfare. Like coral insects, "building better than they knew," they toiled upward in the midst of darkness, guided only by a faint glimmer of the light, but without any conception of the extent and richness of the new world of knowledge that was destined to spring from their ill-directed labors. Heirs of the world's experience, and themselves daring experimenters, we need not be surprised to find them in possession of a large mass of empirical information.*

The old Arabian Geber, as early as the eighth century, was acquainted with the preparation of sulphuric acid and aqua regia,† and gave an elaborate description of the more useful metals.

In the twelfth century, Albertus Magnus understood the cupellation of gold and silver, and their purification by means of lead, as also the preparation of caustic potassa, ceruse, and minium.

---

in an unceasing progression in which all things take part towards a higher and nobler state." "In this slow development," he adds, "nature has no need to hasten—she has eternity to work in; it is for us to ascertain the favoring conditions, and, by imitating or increasing them, to accelerate the work." These views are prominent in the writings of all the leading alchemists of China.

* Cowley expresses this idea in the verses prefixed to this essay, which, it must be confessed, contain more truth than poetry. Humboldt (Cosmos, vol. ii.) speaks of Albertus Magnus as "an independent observer in the domain of analytical chemistry;" and adds, "It is true that his hopes were directed to the transmutation of metals, but in his attempts to fulfil this object he not only improved the practical manipulation of ores, but also enlarged the insight of men into the general mode of action of the chemical forces of nature."

† "Chemistry," says A. von Humboldt, "first begins when men have learned to employ mineral acids and powerful solvents."

In the thirteenth, Roger Bacon described with accuracy the properties of saltpetre, giving the recipe for gunpowder, and approaching very nearly to the explanation of the functions of air in combustion.

In the same century, Raymond Lully described the process of obtaining the essential oils; and, a little later, Basil Valentine obtained copper from blue vitriol by the use of iron; and discovered antimony, sulphuric ether, and fulminating gold. Isaac de Hollandais fabricated gems and described the process. Brandt, while analyzing a human body in quest of the philosopher's stone, stumbled on the discovery of phosphorus.

In the early part of the sixteenth century, Paracelsus did much to overthrow the inert methods of the Galenists, and gained a great and well-deserved reputation by introducing the use of mineral medicines, i. e. of chemical compounds.* This last-named individual, though among its more modern professors, may be taken as the very best type of the so-called science of alchemy, whether in its wisdom or its folly, in the absurdity of its pretensions or in the solid value of its actual achievements. His name, Philippus Aureolus Theophrastus Bombastes Paracelsus von Hohenheim, is synonymous with charlatan; and his fate sadly illustrates the history of his profession, which one of his fellow-laborers describes as "beginning in deceit, progressing with toil, and ending in beggary." His life was terminated, like those of so many professed adepts, by imbibing a draught of his own elixir.† Nor was Paracelsus the last victim of this bewitching

* "With the rise of the Spagyrists and Paracelsus, who taught that the true use of chemistry is not to make gold, but medicines, we seem to perceive the first attempt at a rational pursuit of the study" (review of article "Chemistry" in the *Encyclopædia Britannica; Nature*, January, 1877).

† Of martyrs of science of this description, no country can show a longer catalogue than China. It may be found *in extenso* in native polemics against the Tauist religion, or scattered through the pages of the national histories. It will be sufficient here to refer to the Emperors Mutsung and Wutsung,

delusion. In 1784, Dr. Price, an English physician, after having made gold in the presence of several persons, and presented some of the precious product to George III., on being examined by a scientific commission, committed suicide to escape the shame of exposure.

In the last century, Dr. Semler, a well-known theologian of Germany, also tried the fascinating experiment. A trusty servant, to save him from disappointment, stealthily dropped a little gold-leaf into his wonder-working mixture, and the professor was, of course, successful. When the experiment was repeated, the same servant or some member of his family, to save expense, substituted tambac for gold-leaf. The result was an ignominious failure; and but for conscience, fortified by religious principle, together with the fact that he was more of a dupe than a deceiver, Semler, too, would have hanged or poisoned himself as a refuge from disgrace. To these cases, found in most of the current books,* may be added the name of Dr. Barnard, "the diamond-maker of Sacramento," who, with his feet on the auriferous dust of California, sacrificed his life a few years ago in the vain attempt to manufacture something more precious than gold. Charging a hollow sphere with the costly ingredients, which, on the application of fire, were to crystallize into diamonds, he was blown into the air by a premature explosion, and died without revealing the secret of which he believed himself to be the sole depositary.† This suggests the possibility that

---

of the Tang dynasty, both of whom are said to have shortened their lives by drinking a pretended elixir of immortality.

* Of these one of the most entertaining and instructive is *L'Alchimie et les Alchimistes*, by Louis Figuier.

† His melancholy history was given at length under the title of "The Diamond-maker of Sacramento," some years ago, in the *Overland Monthly*, a spirited magazine of San Francisco, successively edited by the poet Bret Harte, and the Hon. B. P. Avery, late U. S. Minister at Peking. Against the possibility of procuring by artificial means transparent crystals of pure car-

the race of alchemists may not yet be altogether extinct, even among us. In Westphalia, an association of alchemists existed under the name of *Societas Hermetica* as late as the year 1819; and in Canada the papers tell us of a man who recently (1877) committed suicide for the avowed purpose of testing the virtues of a restorative elixir which he professed to have invented.*

In China, the hermetic art still flourishes in full vigor. The Abbé Huc, in his History of Christianity in China, relates an amusing incident illustrating the ardor with which these persevering Orientals still continue to pursue the golden phantom. When the missionaries established themselves in Chau-ch'ing, in Canton province, a company of educated natives possessed of considerable means were busily engaged in seeking to solve the problem of ages. A servant of the missionaries hinted to them that those learned Europeans were already in possession of it. Believing his assertion, they began to load him with favors to induce him to obtain the secret, for their advantage. They gave him fine clothes, and furnished him with money to hire handsome apartments and purchase a beautiful wife; while he, on his part, was in no haste to fulfil his engagement. He was only waiting for the Western sphinxes to open their lips. But the

---

bon, science does not undertake to pronounce; and more than one experimenter has claimed to have achieved partial success.

* By the side of his lifeless corpse a letter was found directing that "a few particles of my '*creative all-changeful essence*' be scattered over my remains, when the elements will resolve themselves into a new combination, and I will reappear a living evidence of the truth of this new discovery." If these are the words of a madman, they are those of one whose brain was turned by the study of alchemy. I have only to add that a large bottle containing the elixir was found standing by the letter (*Scientific American*, March 31, 1877). If this poor fellow was the last to offer himself as a sacrifice to the Moloch of alchemy, the last alchemist who succeeded in victimizing the public was the notorious Count Cagliostro, who, after vending his "elixir of immortal youth" in most of the courts of Europe, closed his career in a papal prison in 1795.

patience of his generous victims finally gave out; or, what is more probable, they learned from the missionaries that they had no such secret to communicate. To escape their vengeance, the crafty rogue was compelled to fly to a neighboring city, where he ended his days in a prison.

If the Chinese are the last to surrender this pleasing delusion, *there is good reason to believe that they deserve the more honorable distinction of being the first to originate the idea.*

The origin of an idea so fruitful in results is a question of great interest; and many writers have expended on it the resources of their learning. Some find it in the mythology of the Greeks, maintaining (an interpretation older than the Christian era) that the golden fleece sought for by the Argonauts was merely a sheepskin on which was inscribed the secret of making gold;* and this fancy derives, it must be confessed, a little support from the circumstance that Medea is represented as possessed of the corresponding secret of perpetuating or restoring youth, having cut to pieces and reconstructed her aged father-in-law.

Some, again, discover the origin of the idea in Egypt, the land of Thoth (Hermes Trismegistus), and allege, in corroboration of their view, that the ancient Egyptians possessed considerable skill in practical chemistry. But the advocates of its Egyptian origin are not able to trace it back further than the time of the Ptolemies, and students of Hindoo literature maintain that the Indians possessed a knowledge of it long before that date, though it must not be forgotten that there is nothing more uncertain than the chronology of ancient India.†

---

* This construction of the legend comes from Dionysius of Mitylene, who lived circa B.C. 50.

† Some instructive disclosures on this subject may be found in a lecture of the late Cardinal Wiseman entitled "Early History." It has been asserted by those who claim to be well versed in the history of India that in that country the earliest date that can be considered historical is April, B.C. 327, the date of its invasion by Alexander the Great.

Others adduce conclusive proof to show that modern Europe received it from the Arabs. They have not, however, shown that the Arabs were its authors; and seem scarcely to have entertained a suspicion that those wandering sons of the desert, like birds and bees, were nothing more than agents through whom a prolific germ was conveyed from some portion of the remoter East. What that portion is, the name of Avicenna, one of the most eminent of the Arabian scholars, might have served to suggest, if they had followed the leading of words as carefully as a certain erudite Orientalist* who not only finds in India the origin of the doctrines of Pythagoras, but recognizes his name under the disguise of Buddhaguru! For what is Avicenna but Ebn-Cinna? And what is Ebn-Cinna or Ibn Sina, as it is sometimes written, but a "Son of China?"—a designation possibly assumed by the learned physician because he was born at Bokhara, on the confines of the Chinese Empire!

If we were as ready to rest in etymologies as the above-cited Orientalist, who triumphantly concludes a chapter with that curious derivation of the name of Pythagoras, we might consider our point as carried. Our etymology is, to say the least, as good as his; but we let it go for what it is worth, and rest our argument on better evidence.†

---

* Pococke, Greece in India.

† Nothing is more fallacious than the attempt to identify words in different languages by means of a mere superficial resemblance. Some years ago, in reading the *Amour Médecin* of Molière, I fancied I had detected a translation in a combined form of the most familiar names for the Chinese elixir of life. The word *orviétan*, which is made so conspicuous in one of the scenes, describes a mysterious panacea, whose virtues the vender vaunts in strains as pompous as those of the Chinese alchemist. It struck me at once that, setting aside the accent, which goes for nothing in etymology, it might be taken as expressing 金丹 and 長生丹, golden elixir, and elixir of long life. Littré and the *Dictionnaire de l'Académie* decided against me, referring the word to the old city of Orvieto (*urbs vetus*). But, whatever the source of the name, the thing itself answers so exactly to the

It is not improbable, as we shall attempt to show, that the true cradle of alchemy was China—a country in which one of the oldest branches of the human family began their career of experience; a country in which we discover so many of the seeds of our modern arts; germs which, dwarfed and stunted in their native climate, have only been made to flourish by a change of soil. To establish this would be an interesting contribution to the history of science; and it might perhaps lead us to take an optimistic view even of the sins and follies of mankind, to discover that our modern chemistry, which is now dropping its mature fruits into the hands of Western enterprise, had its root in the religion of Tao, the most extravagant of the superstitions of the East.

We shall briefly sketch the rise and development of alchemy in China, and then conclude by comparing it with the leading phases of the same pursuit as exhibited in Western countries.

Originating at the least six hundred years before the Christian era,* the religion of Tao still exerts a powerful influence over

---

Chinese *tan*, or elixir, that I cannot forbear quoting a few lines descriptive of its qualities.

"*Sganarelle.* Monsieur, je vous prie de me donner une boite de votre orviétan, que je m'en vais vous payer.

"*L'Opérateur* (chantant).

L'or de tous les climats qu'entoure l'Océan,
Peut-il jamais payer ce secret d'importance?
Mon remède guérit, par sa rare excellence,
Plus de maux qu'on n'en peut nombrer dans tout un an:
La gale, La rogne, La teigne, La fièvre, La peste, La goutte,
Vérole, Descente, Rougeole.
O grande puissance
De l'orviétan!"

The reader may compare this with passages quoted in the sequel from Taoist books.

N.B.—*Or*, in the first line of the description, is an evident allusion to the first syllable of the name, which the vender takes to mean "golden."

* It is indigenous to China; and though we are unable to trace it to an

the mind of the Chinese. This is not the place to discuss either its sober tenets or its wild fantasies, but there is one of its doctrines that connects it closely with our present subject. It looks on the soul as only a more refined form of matter; regards the soul and body as identical in substance, and maintains the possibility of preventing their dissolution by a course of physical discipline. This is the seed-thought of Chinese alchemy; for this materialistic notion it was that first led the disciples of Lao-tsze to investigate the properties of matter.

Its development is easy to trace. Man's first desire is long life—his second is to be rich. The Taoist commenced with the former, but was not long in finding his way to the latter. As it was possible by physical discipline to lengthen the period of life, he conceived that the process might be carried on without limit, and result in corporeal immortality. Its success, in his view, depended mainly on diet and medicine; and in quest of these he ransacked the forest, penetrated the earth, and explored distant seas. The natural longing for immortality was thus made, under the guidance of Taoism, to impart a powerful impulse to the progress of discovery in three departments of science—botany, mineralogy, and geography. Nor did the other great object of pursuit remain far in the rear. A few simple experiments, such as the precipitation of copper from the oil of vitriol by the application of iron, and the blanching of metals by the fumes of mercury, suggested the possibility of transforming the baser metals into gold.* This brought on the stage an-

---

earlier date, there is good reason to believe that it is as old as the Chinese race. The connection of alchemy with Taoism did not escape the notice of the earlier Jesuit missionaries; but the Rev. Dr. Edkins, in a paper on Taoism published about twenty years ago, was the first, I believe, to suggest a Chinese origin for the alchemy of Europe.

* Science is not opposed to the abstract theory of transmutation. Indeed, the modern chemist has been led by the phenomena of allotropy and isomerism, not to speak of other considerations, almost to accept as a principle

other, and, if possible, a more energetic, motive for investigation. The bare idea of acquiring untold riches by such easy means inspired with a kind of frenzy minds that were hardly capable of the loftier conception of immortality. It had, moreover, the effect of directing attention particularly to the study of minerals, the most prolific field for chemical discovery.

Whether in the vegetable or the mineral kingdom, the researches of the Chinese alchemists were guided by one simple principle—the analogy of man to material nature. As in their view the soul was only a more refined species of matter, and was endowed with such wondrous powers, so every object in nature, they argued, must be possessed of a soul, an essence or spirit, which controls its growth and development—a something not unlike the *essentia quinta* of Western alchemy. This they believed to be the case, not only with animals, which display some of the attributes of mind, but with plants, which extract their appropriate nourishment from the earth, and transform it into fruits; and the same with minerals, which they regarded as generated in the womb of the earth. It was to this half-spiritual, half-

---

what he lately denounced as a groundless assumption of his ancient forerunner—viz., that a fundamental unity underlies many, if not all of, the forms of matter. On this subject see two interesting papers in the volume of *Nature* for 1879 (pp. 593, 625) on the question "Are the Elements Elementary?" The writer speaks approvingly of the hypothesis of *original* matter having a molecular or atomic structure; all the molecules being uniform in size and in shape, but not all possessed of the same amount of motion—the difference of their motions giving rise to all the properties of the various elements. The speculation which resolves matter into force tends in the same direction. "I must confess," says Professor Cook, "that I am rather drawn to that view of nature which has favor with many of the most eminent physicists of the present time, and which sees in the Cosmos, besides mind, only two essentially distinct beings—namely, matter and energy; which regards *all matter as one*, and all energy as one; and which refers the qualities of substances to the affections of the *one substratum modified by the varying play of forces*" (Lectures on the New Chemistry, lecture iv., International Series).

material theory that they had recourse to account for the transformations that are perpetually going on in every department of nature. As the active principle in each object was so potent in effecting the changes which we constantly observe, they imagined that it might attain to a condition of higher development and greater efficiency. Such an upward tendency was, in fact, perpetually at work; and all things were striving to "purge off their baser fires" and enter on a higher and purer state. Nor were they merely striving to clothe themselves with material forms of a higher order. Matter itself was constantly passing the limits of sense and putting on the character of conscious spirit. This idea threw over the face of nature a glow of poetry. It awakened the torpid imagination and created an epoch in literature. It kindled the fancy of Chwang-tsze, inspired the eloquence of Lü-tsu, and it figures in a thousand shapes among the graceful tales of the *Liau-chai.* It filled the earth with fairies and genii. An easy step connected them with those mysterious points of light which in all ages have excited so powerfully the hopes and fears of the human race. Astrology became wedded to alchemy, and the five principal planets bear in the current language of the present day the names of the elements over which they are regarded as presiding.

In China, as elsewhere, alchemy has always been an occult science. Its students have been pledged to secrecy, and their knowledge transmitted mainly by means of oral tradition, each adept tracing his lineage back to Hwang-te (B.C. 2700) or Kwang-ch'eng-tsze, as the Freemason deduces his pedigree from Solomon or Hiram of Tyre.*

Their doctrines, like the delicate beauties of some Eastern climes, were never allowed to go abroad without being covered with a veil. They were wrapped in folds of impenetrable mys-

* Hwang-te is at least semi-mythical. The earliest historical sovereign who became a votary of alchemy was Ts'in-she-hwang, the builder of the Great Wall, B. C. 220.

tery, and expressed, for the most part, in the measured lines and metaphorical language of poetry. Still, in spite of every precaution that pride or jealousy was able to suggest, some of their secrets would gradually ooze out, and many of the rules for working metals now in common use bear in their very terms the stamp of an alchemic parentage.

After this cursory survey, it may not be amiss to introduce a few extracts from native authors, professors of the mysterious lore, in order to ascertain how far they corroborate the foregoing views, but especially to aid us in deciding whether any real connection is to be traced between the Chinese and European schools of alchemy.

I. FROM KAO SHANG-TSZE.

*The Secret of Immortality.**

"The body is the dwelling-place of life; the spirits are the essence of life; and the soul is the master of life. When the spirits are exhausted, the body becomes sick; when the soul is in repose, the spirits keep their place; and when the spirits are concentrated, the soul becomes indestructible. Those who seek the elixir must imitate the *Yin* and *Yang* [the active and passive principles in nature] and learn the harmony of numbers. They must govern the soul and unite their spirit. If the soul is a chariot, the spirits are its horses. When the soul and spirits are properly yoked together, you are immortal."

---

* These extracts are not arranged in the order of time. The antiquity of the system will be considered in another place; and I begin with two from writers whose age I am not able to fix with precision. For the citations from both I am indebted to a compilation, in twelve volumes, entitled 百子金丹. The name, literally taken, would suggest a work specifically on the subject of alchemy; but it is figurative, and means the elixir or quintessence of the philosophers. Among the philosophers cited, those who favored alchemy are in a very small minority.

II. FROM TAN-TSZE.

The Power of Miracles.

"The clouds are a dragon, the wind a tiger. Mind is the mother, and matter the child. When the mother summons the child, will it dare to disobey? Those who would expel the spirits of evil must (by the force of their mind) summon the spirits of the five elements. Those who would conquer serpents must obtain the influences of the five planets. By this means the *Yin* and *Yang*, the dual forces of nature, may be controlled; winds and clouds collected; mountains and hills torn up by the roots; and rivers and seas made to spring out of the ground. Still the external manifestation of this power is not so good as the consciousness of its possession within."

III. FROM THE SAME.

The Adept Superior to Hunger, Cold, and Sickness.

"He inhales the fine essence of matter, how can he be hungry? He is warmed by the fire of his own soul, how can he be cold? His five vitals are fed on the essence of the five elements, how can he be sick?"

IV. FROM LÜ-TSU, OF THE TANG DYNASTY.*

Patience Essential to Success.

"Would you seek the golden *tan* [the elixir], it is not easy to obtain. The three powers [sun, moon, and stars] must seven times repeat their footsteps; and the four seasons nine times complete their circuit.

* Lü-tsu (or Lü-yien) flourished in the latter half of the eighth century. In early life respected as a scholar and a magistrate, and in later years famed for the eloquence of his style and the elevation of his character, he did much to revive the decaying credit of the "school of the genii." His works are voluminous and well known, but, like most of those ascribed to the great masters of Taoism, probably comprehend much that is not genuine.

"You must wash it white and burn it red; when one draught will give you ten thousand ages, and you will be wafted beyond the sphere of sublunary things."

V. FROM THE SAME.

The Necessity of a Living Teacher.

"Every one seeks long life, but the secret is not easy to find. If you covet the precious things of heaven, you must reject the treasures of earth. You must kindle the fire that springs from water,* and evolve the *Yin* contained within the *Yang*. One word from a sapient master, and you possess a draught of the golden water."

VI. FROM THE SAME.

The Chief Elements in Alchemy.

"All things originate from earth. If you can get at the radical principle, the spirit of the green dragon is mercury, and the water of the white tiger † is lead. The knowing ones will bring

---

* This phrase reminds us of a quaint piece of doggerel from the pen of George Ripley, a noted alchemist of England, who died in 1490, notwithstanding the medicines recommended in his two books on Alchymie and Aurum Potabile. The following are a few of his incomprehensible verses:

"The well must brenne in water clear,
Take good heed, for this they fere,
The fire with water brent shall be,
The earth on fire shall be set
And water with fire shall be knit.

. . . . .

Of the white stone and the red
Lo, here is the true deed!"

† *Yin* and *Yang* are the dual forces which control the elements of nature. Though generally referred to the sexual system, their chief symbols are the sun and moon, and the original signification of the terms is light and darkness. The "tiger" and "dragon" are synonyms for the oft-repeated *Yin* and *Yang*. Their use in this sense is comparatively ancient, as

mother and child together, when earth will become heaven, and you will be extricated from the power of matter."

VII. FROM THE SAME.

Description of the Philosopher's Stone: Self-culture Necessary to Obtain it.

"I must diligently plant my own field. There is within it a spiritual germ that may live a thousand years. Its flower is like yellow gold. Its bud is not large, but the seeds are round [globules of mercury?] and like to a spotless gem. Its growth depends on the soil of the central palace [the heart], but its irrigation must proceed from a higher fountain [the reason]. After nine years of cultivation, root and branch may be transplanted to the heaven of the greater genii."

VIII. FROM A BIOGRAPHER OF LÜ-TSU.

Speaking of the labors of his great master, he says, "Among the eight stones, he made most use of cinnabar, because from that he extracted mercury; and among the five metals, he made most use of lead, because from that he obtained silver. The fire of the heart [blood] is red as cinnabar; and the water of the kidneys [urine] is dark as lead. To these must be added sulphur, that the compound may be efficacious. Lead is the mother of silver, mercury the child of cinnabar. Lead represents the influence of the kidneys, mercury that of the heart."

But "*jam claudite rivos,*" some reader is, no doubt, ready to exclaim—"enough of this jargon, or rather gibberish." For is it not truly *gibberish*, if Dr. Johnson was correct in deriving that word from the name of Geber, the great alchemist? We must, however, plead for the privilege of introducing a few extracts

---

we may gather from the title of a book still extant called 白虎通, by the historian Panku, in the first century of our era.

from the *Wu-chen-pien*,* a work which still holds the place of a text-book among the followers of Lao-tsze. They will serve to indicate the spirit and aim of these operations, though the processes are still carefully concealed. In fact, all that is given to the public seems merely designed to inflame the imagination, and to induce readers to place themselves under the instruction of a Tauist master.

1. *The Great Motive.*—"However long this mortal life, its events are all uncertain. He who yesterday bestrode his horse so grandly at the head of the street, to-day is a corpse in the coffin. His wife and his wealth are his no longer. His sins must take their course, and self-deception will do no good. If you do not seek the great remedy, how will you find it? If you find out the method and do not prepare it, how unwise are you!"

2. *A Vindication.*—"If the virtuous follow a false doctrine, they reclaim it; but if the vicious profess a true doctrine, they pervert it. So it is with the golden elixir: a deviation of an inch leads to the error of a mile. If I succeed, then my fate is in my own hands, and my body may last as long as the heavens. But the vulgar pervert this doctrine to the gratification of low desires [such as those for wealth and pleasure]."

3. *Outline of Process.*—"In the gold-furnace you must separate the mercury from the cinnabar, and in the gemmy bath you must precipitate the silver from the water. To wield the fires of this divine work is not the task of a day. But out of the midst of the pool suddenly the sun rises." †

---

* This collection bears the name of the principal tract, 悟真篇, which dates from the beginning of the sixteenth century. It is usually bound up with the 參同契, a more weighty production which comes down from the second century. The phrase for the precipitation of silver is 下水中銀.

† A few years ago I made the acquaintance of a Kiangsi man by the name of Hiung, who had published a book of some literary merit, and was

No one at all acquainted with the operations of chemistry can fail to remark how much is implied in this reference to the precipitation of silver. Nor can any one familiar with the language of Western alchemists avoid being struck by the similarity of the terms here employed. As he reads of "separating mercury from cinnabar," "precipitating silver," "wielding the fires of the divine work," the "gemmy bath," and the "sun rising out of the pool," does he not fancy himself perusing a fragment from Lully or Albertus describing the *balneum mariæ* and the production of gold?

We add three more to our series of illustrative extracts:

1. *The Reason for Obscure and Figurative Phraseology.*—"The holy sage was afraid of betraying the secrets of heaven. He accordingly sets forth the true *Yin* and *Yang* under the images of the white tiger and the green dragon. And the harmony of the two chords he represents under the symbols of the true lead and the true mercury." *

2. *Nature of the Inward Harmony.*—"The two things to be united are *wuh* and *wo*, 物 and 我, the *me* and the *not me.* When these combine, the passions are in harmony with nature, and the elements are complete."

---

withal an ardent student of the occult science. A manuscript volume of his own compilation, which he permitted me to examine, contained, among other diagrams, one which represented the sun rising out of a smoking furnace—showing that the hermetic symbol for gold is the same in China as in Europe.

* It is curious to see how Western alchemists exhibit the same phase of feeling. Howes, an old writer, quoted in Mr. Lowell's New England of Two Centuries Ago, expresses himself thus in a familiar epistle: "Dear friend, I desire with all my heart that I might write plainer to you; but in discovering the mystery, I may diminish its majesty, and give occasion to the profane to abuse it, if it should fall into unworthy hands." The mystery was the *unity of matter.* He adds, "As there is all good to be found in unity, and all evil in duality and multiplicity, *phœnix illa admiranda sola semper existit.*"

In other passages we have noticed the outcropping of a moral idea. In this we find a materialistic doctrine suddenly metamorphosed into the most subtle form of pantheistic idealism.

3. *Self-discipline the Best Elixir* (from Tan-tsze, not in *Wu-chen-pien*).—"Among the arts of the alchemist is that of preparing an elixir which may be used as a substitute for food. This is certainly true; yet the ability to enjoy abundance or endure hunger comes not from the elixir, but from the fixed purpose of him who uses it. When a man has arrived at such a stage of progress that to have and not to have are the same; when life and death are one; when feeling is in harmony with nature, and the inner and the outer worlds united—then he can escape the thraldom of matter, and leave sun, moon, and stars behind his back. To him it will then be of no consequence whether he eat a hundred times in a day, or only once in a hundred days." We might fill volumes with similar extracts without, we fear, adding much to the information of our readers.

The composition of the elixir was a secret which the alchemist did not care to divulge. If, therefore, we seek for precise directions for its preparation in the writings of a professed adept, we seek in vain.

There is, indeed, one oft-repeated formula, which appears to be absurdly simple. It is this: "*Pb.* 8 *oz.*, *Hg.* ½ *lb.*; mix thoroughly, and the combination will result in a mass of the golden elixir." But it ceases to be simple when we learn that both metals and proportions are to be taken in a mystical sense; that, in fact, instead of indicating the materials of the elixir, they only point to the precise moment when the final touch is to be given to a complicated process—viz., one minute after the full of the moon. If this resolves itself into "moonshine," another, which has the air of being more in detail, is still less luminous. "Plant the *Yang* and grow the *Yin*; cultivate and cherish the precious seed. When it springs up, it shows a yellow bud; the bud produces mercury, and the mercury crystallizes into granules like grains of golden millet. One grain is to be taken at a dose, and the doses repeated for a hundred days, when the body will be transformed and the bones converted into gold. Body and spirit will both be endowed with miraculous properties, and their duration will have no end." These recipes are both from standard text-books of the Taoist school.*

---

* The former is from the 悟眞篇; the latter from 道法統宗. Kohhung (or Pao-pú-tsze—Simplicius), of the fourth century, is one of the most voluminous writers on the subject. He gives nine varieties of the *tan*, but no clear account of the preparation of any of them. The following extract from his work may serve to show the kind of reasoning by which he and his fellows suffered themselves to be deluded:

陳思王著釋疑論云初謂道術直呼愚民詐僞空言定矣及見武皇帝試左慈等令斷穀近一月而顏色不減氣力自若常云可五十年不食正爾復可疑哉又令甘始以藥含生魚而煮之於沸脂中其無藥者熟而可食其銜藥者遊戲終日如在水中也又以藥粉桑飼蠶蠶乃到十月不老又以住年藥食鷄雛及新生犬子皆止不復長又以還白藥食白犬百日毛盡黑乃知天下之事不可盡知而以臆斷之可任也但恨不能絕聲色專心以學長生之道耳

"I formerly thought the Taoist mystery was intended to delude simple folk, and that there was nothing in it but empty words; but when I saw the Emperor Wu subject Tso-tse and others to a fast of nearly a month—their complexion continuing fresh and their strength unabated—I said there was no reason why they should not extend the fast to fifty years.

"Another Taoist, Kan-shi, placed a number of fish in boiling oil; some of them having first swallowed a few drops of an elixir, swam about as if they were in the water, the others were boiled so that they could be eaten.

"Silk-worms taking the same medicine lived for ten months; chickens and young dogs taking it ceased to grow; and a white dog on taking it turned black; all of which shows that there are things in heaven and earth

We find a more explicit account of the composition of the elixir in the *Ko-chi king-yuen*, 格致鏡原, or Mirror of Scientific Discovery; but here again we are not favored with anything beyond a barren inventory of ingredients, without any statement of proportion or manipulation.

"The elixir of the eight precious things," says this author, "is so called because it contains cinnabar, orpiment, realgar, sulphur, saltpetre, ammonia, empty green [an ore of cobalt], and mother-of-clouds [a kind of mica]."

This and the other passages above cited throw, we confess, very little light on any question of practical science; but they are not unimportant in relation to the history of science, indicating as they do the spirit and aims of the Chinese alchemists—the most enthusiastic, and, as we think, the earliest, explorers in a region which has proved to be one of inexhaustible fertility.

The results of their labors in the way of chemical discovery it may not be easy to determine; though it is safe to affirm that, for what they knew on that subject prior to their recent intercourse with the West, the Chinese are mainly indebted to those early devotees of the experimental philosophy who passed their lives among the fumes of the alembic. The skill which the Chinese exhibit in metallurgy, their brilliant dye-stuffs and numerous pigments; their early knowledge of gunpowder,* alcohol,

---

surpassing our comprehension. Would that I could break the fetters of sense and give my whole heart to the pursuit of the elixir of life!"

* An able paper, by the late W. F. Mayers, on the origin of gunpowder, may be considered as decisive against the claims of the Chinese, unless fresh evidence be adduced in their favor. That the Chinese are not indifferent to the discussion, and that the admissions of one are not accepted by all, are sufficiently shown by the following extract from an examination-paper placed before the candidates for the doctorate in Peking, about twelve years ago: "Fire-arms began with the use of rockets in the Chau dynasty. In what book do we first meet with the word *p'ao*, 砲, for cannon? What is the difference in the two classes of engines to which it is applied? (Ap-

arsenic, Glauber's salt, calomel, and corrosive sublimate; their pyrotechny; their asphyxiating and anæsthetic compounds—all give evidence of no contemptible proficiency in practical chemistry.*

In their books of curious receipts, we find instructions for the manufacture of sympathetic inks, for removing stains, compounding and alloying metals, counterfeiting gold, whitening copper, overlaying the baser with the precious metals, etc. In some of these recipes a caution is added that neither "women, cats, nor chickens" be allowed to approach during the process, obviously a relic of alchemistic superstition.

The Hermes of China has no female disciples, though Europe can boast the names of not a few. The alchemist of China has generally been a celibate, and very frequently a religious ascetic, to whom the life-giving elixir, rather than the aurific stone, was the chief object of pursuit.

Lü-tsu, one of the most eminent, is said to have earned immortality by rejecting the art of making gold.†

---

plied also to catapults.) Is the defence of K'ai-feng-fu its first recorded use?" etc. Leaving these questions to the native scholars to whom they were addressed, I only add that gunpowder, like many other useful discoveries, probably had more than one independent origin. Its ingredients are articles of daily use, and their mode of combination is not limited to any definite proportion, so that the failure of the Chinese to hit upon it, after ages of chemical research, would be more surprising than their success.

* See Davis's Chinese, ch. xviii., for a very interesting account of the preparation of calomel (chloride of mercury) by a Chinese chemist, and by a truly China process. In the same chapter the author sketches the fantastic physical theories of the Chinese, and adds, "All this looks very much as if the philosophy of our forefathers was derived intermediately from China."

† As the legend goes, shortly after commencing the study of the art, he was met by one of the old genii, who offered to impart to him the great secret of transmutation. "But," asked the young man, "will not the artificial gold relapse to its original elements in the course of time?" "Yes," replied the genius, "but that need not concern you, as it will not happen un-

In the Chinese system there are two processes—the one inward and spiritual, the other outward and material. To obtain the greater elixir, involving the attainment of immortality, both must be combined; but the lesser elixir, which answers to the philosopher's stone, or a magical control over the powers of nature, might be procured with less pains. Both processes were pursued in seclusion, commonly in the recesses of the mountains, the term for adepts signifying "mountain men." *

In a discourse on metals in one of the works above cited, we are told that the seminal principle of gold first assumes the form of quicksilver. Exposed to the influence of the moon, it is liquid; but when subjected to the action of the pure *Yang*, the sun or the male essence, it solidifies and becomes yellow gold. Those who desire to convert quicksilver into gold should carry on their operations among the mountains, that the effluences from the stones may assist the process.

Nothing seems to be required in addition to the incidental proofs already adduced to establish the existence of a *connection* between the alchemy of Europe and that of China; still, a few considerations in the way of comparison may serve to make the nature and extent of that connection somewhat more apparent.

1. The study of alchemy did not make its appearance in Europe until it had been in full vigor in China for at least six centuries. Nor did it appear there, according to the best authorities, until the fourth century, when intercourse with the Far East had become somewhat frequent. It entered Europe, more-

---

til after ten thousand ages." "I decline it then," said Lü-tsu. "I would rather live in poverty than bring a loss on my fellow-men, though after ten thousand ages." The noble sense of right was more meritorious than any number of sham charities; and the youth who had conscience enough to spurn the gilded bait was at once admitted to the heaven of the genii.

* Probably the older form of the character is 僊, but no one can doubt that the motive which led to the substitntion of 山 for the original phonetic was not merely its simplicity, but its signification as well.

over, by way of Byzantium and Alexandria, the places in which that intercourse was chiefly centred. At a later day it was revived in the West by the irruption of the Saracens, who may be supposed to have had better opportunities for becoming acquainted with it in consequence of being nearer to its original source. One of the most renowned seats of alchemic industry was Bagdad while it was the seat of the caliphate. An extensive commerce was at that period carried on between Arabia and China. In the eighth century embassies were interchanged between the caliphs and the emperors. Colonies of Arabs were established in the seaports of the Empire; and the grave of a cousin of Mahomet remains at Canton as a monument of that early intercourse.

2. The objects of pursuit were in both schools identical, and in either case twofold—immortality and gold.

In Europe the former was the less prominent because the people, being in possession of Christianity, had a sufficiently vivid faith in a future life to satisfy their instinctive longings without having recourse to questionable arts.

3. In either school there were two elixirs, the greater and the less, and the properties ascribed to them corresponded very closely.

4. The principles underlying both systems are identical in the composite nature of the metals, and their vegetation from a seminal germ. Indeed, the characters *tsing*, 精, for the germ, and *tai*, 胎, for the matrix, which constantly occur in the writings of Chinese alchemists, might be taken for the translation of terms in the vocabulary of the Western school, did not their higher antiquity forbid the hypothesis.

5. The ends in view being the same, the means by which they were pursued were nearly identical; mercury and lead (to which sulphur was tertiary) being as conspicuous in the laboratories of the East as mercury and sulphur were in those of the West. It is of less significance to add that many other sub-

stances were common to both schools than it is to note the remarkable coincidence that in Chinese as in European alchemy the names of the principal reagents are employed in a mystical sense.*

6. Both schools, or at least individuals in both, held the strange doctrine of a cycle of changes, in the course of which the precious metals revert to their original elements.

7. Both systems were closely interwoven with astrology.

8. Both led to the practice of magical arts and unbounded charlatanism.

9. Both dealt in language of equal extravagance; and the style of European alchemists, so unlike the sobriety of thought characteristic of the Western mind, would, if considered alone, furnish ground for a probable conjecture that their science must have had its origin in the fervid fancy of an Oriental people.†

In conclusion, granting that the leading objects of alchemical pursuit are such as might have suggested themselves to the human mind in any country, as it felt its way towards an acquaintance with the forces of nature, yet the similarity of the circumstances with which they are found associated in the West and the East forbids the supposition of an independent origin. Setting aside as untenable the claims of Europe and of Western Asia, we regard alchemy as unquestionably a product of the re-

---

* Robert Boyle (quoted in *Nature*, January, 1877) is unsparing in his denunciation of "those sooty empirics, who have their eyes darkened and their brains troubled with the smoke of their furnaces; and who are wont to evince their salt, sulphur, and mercury (to which they give the canting title of hypostatical principles) to be the true principle of things."

† The whimsical idea of the homunculus, which was so prominent in the works of the later alchemists of the West, and which plays such a conspicuous rôle in the second part of Goethe's Faust, is one of which I can find no vestige in the records of Eastern alchemy. In the writings of the latter school, however, the power of synthetic creation is asserted boldly enough, and the idea of producing the homunculus, i. e. of creating a human being by an artificial process, is, in fact, only a particular application of the principle.

moter East. To the honor of being its birthplace, India and China are rival claimants. The pretensions of the former* we are not in a position to estimate by direct investigation; but they appear to us to be excluded by the proposition, of which there is abundant proof, that *the alchemy of China is not an exotic, but a genuine product of the soil of that country.*

As before remarked, it springs from Taoism, an indigenous religion; and shows itself in clearly defined outlines, if not in full maturity, at a time when there was little or no intercourse with India. Had it appeared some centuries later simultaneously with the introduction of Buddhism, there might have been more reason to look on it as a foreign importation. In polar antagonism with the idealistic philosophy of Buddha, its fundamental tenets are not only found in the ancient manual of Lao-tsze,†

* That much-lamented sinologue, the late Mr. Mayers, favors the claim of India, though, alas! it is no longer possible to question him as to the grounds of his opinion. In his essay on the origin of gunpowder, he says, "It is at least allowable to surmise that those Brahmin chemists who, it is *almost proved, inaugurated the search after the philosopher's stone and the elixir vitæ* may have been the first to discover what secret forces are developed in the fiery union between sulphur and saltpetre."

† The famous poet 白居易, Pailotien, in a well-known stanza, asserts that the extravagances of alchemy are not to be found there:

元元道德
五千言
不言藥
不言仙
不言白日
昇青天

Yet the thoughtful reader cannot fail to discover its latent principles, especially the effect of discipline in securing an ascendency over matter, and the protean power of transmutation hidden in the forces of nature. The alchemists all claim Lao-tsze as a lineal ancestor, though they derive their origin from a remoter source. Those who desire to study the relations of Chinese alchemy to primitive Taoism may, however familiar with the original, consult with advantage an excellent translation of the *Tao-teh-king*, 道德經, by Dr. John Chalmers, of Canton.

they are distinctly traceable in the oldest of the Confucian classics.

In the *Yihking*, the diagrams of which are referred to Fuhi, B.C. 2800, while the text dates from Wenwang, B.C. 1150, and the commentary from Confucius, B.C. 500, we discover at length what appears to us the true source of those prolific ideas which prepared the way for our modern chemistry. Its name, The Book of Changes, is suggestive; and we find throughout its contents the vague idea of change replaced by the more definite one of "transformation," the key-word of alchemy.

In the very first section, Wenwang descants on the "changes and transmutations of the creative principle;" and Confucius, in several chapters of his commentary, grows eloquent over the same theme. "How great," he exclaims, "is change! How wonderful is change! When heaven and earth were formed, change was throned in their midst; and should change cease to take place, heaven and earth would soon cease to exist." "The diagrams," he says again, "comprehend the profoundest secrets of the universe; and the power of exciting the various motions of the universe depends on their explanation: the power to effect *transmutation* depends on the understanding of the diagrams of changes." Here, in a word, is the leading idea of the *Yihking;* and, at the same time, the general object of Chinese students of alchemy. Indeed, so thoroughly are their works pervaded by the spirit of that venerable epitome of primitive science that it is impossible to mistake the source from which they derive their inspiration. The Taoists, without a dissenting voice, recognize it as the first book in the canon of their sect; and the Tyrant of Ts'in, a zealous votary of alchemy, spared the *Yihking* from the flames to which he consigned all the other writings of Confucius and his disciples.*

---

* The language of the above citations from the Book of Changes is taken, with some alterations, from the version of Canon McClatchie, to which the

We have therefore no hesitation in affirming that ALCHEMY IS INDIGENOUS TO CHINA AND COEVAL WITH THE DAWN OF LETTERS.

---

uninitiated reader is here referred. Those who feel inclined to go deeper into the question of the influence of that cabalistic work on the development of Taoism, and especially on alchemy, cannot do better than to read the 參同契, *Tsan-tung-chi*, a work of the second century, for an account of which see Wylie's Notes on Chinese Literature, p. 172.

REMARKS ON THE STYLE OF CHINESE PROSE.*

A PROFESSOR of Chinese in America is reported to have said that "in the Chinese language there is no such thing as a florid style or a beautiful style. Style is not taken into consideration. It is in writing the language that skill is displayed; and the man that executes the characters with dexterity and ingenuity is the one that understands the language."

Though somewhat unexpected as coming from the chair of a professor, this opinion is not novel. It expresses but too truly the estimate in which the literature of China has been generally held by the learned world.

The value of Chinese records is fully conceded. The great antiquity of the people; their accurate system of chronology; their habit of appealing to history as the only tribunal before which they can arraign their sovereigns; and especially their practice of noting as a prodigy every strange phenomenon that occurs in any department of nature—all conspire to render their annals an inexhaustible mine of curious and useful information. Add that these annals are not restricted to what is known as the history of the Empire, but that one or more such works may be found recording in minute detail whatever has been thought interesting or instructive in the history of every department and district, and we have a mass of historical literature that stands without a parallel among the nations of the earth.

It is in these that our savans may find, extending back in unbroken series for thousands of years, notices of eclipses, comets,

---

* From the *New-Englander*, April, 1872.

star-showers, aerolites, droughts, floods, earthquakes, etc., as well as a comparatively faithful account of the rise and fortunes of the most numerous branch of the human family.

But, while admitting that it is worth while to encounter all the toil of a difficult language in order to gain access to such a field of research, who ever dreams that the Chinese language contains anything else to repay the labor of acquisition? Who ever imagines that in pursuing his favorite game, instead of traversing deserts and jungles, he will find himself walking among forests filled with the songs of strange birds and perfumed with the fragrance of unknown flowers, while ever and anon he is ravished by the view of some landscape of surpassing beauty? As soon would the student of literary art expect to find the graces of diction among the hieratic inscriptions of Egypt, or the arrow-headed records of Assyria, as to meet them on pages that bristle with the ideographic symbols of China. It is with a view to correcting such prevalent impressions that this paper is written. In attempting this, however, I do not propose a disquisition on the value of Chinese literature in general, nor commit myself to the task of elucidating the principles of its rhetoric and grammar; but limit myself rather to the single topic of style, and more particularly the style of its prose composition.

This is a subject which, I am aware, it will not be easy to discuss in such a manner as to render it intelligible or interesting to those who are unacquainted with the Chinese language. Style is a volatile quality, which escapes in the process of transfusion; and illustrations of style, however carefully rendered, are at best but as dried plants and stuffed animals compared with living nature. Chinese, moreover, being from our idiom the most remote of all languages, suffers most in the process of rendering. I fear, therefore, that the best versions I may be able to offer will only have the effect of confirming the impressions which it is my object to combat. That such impressions are erroneous ought to be apparent from the mere consideration of the antiquity and extent of the Chinese literature. For, to suppose that a great people have been engaged from a time anterior to the rise of any other living language in building up a literature, unequalled in amount, which contains nothing to gratify the taste or feed the imagination, is it not to suppose its authors destitute of the attributes of our common humanity? Are we to believe that the bees of China are so different from those of other countries that they construct their curious cells from a mere love of labor, without ever depositing there the sweets on which they are wont to feed?

It is not always true that external decoration implies internal finish or furniture; still, we may assert that it would be impossible that the taste which the Chinese display in the embellishment of their handwriting and letter-press should not find its counterpart in the refinements of style.

They literally worship their letters. When letters were invented, they say, heaven rejoiced and hell trembled. Not for any consideration will they tread on a piece of lettered paper; and to foster this reverence, literary associations employ agents to go about the streets, collect waste paper, and burn it on a kind of altar with the solemnity of a sacrifice. They execute their characters with the painter's brush, and rank writing as the very highest of the fine arts. They decorate their dwellings and the temples of their gods with ornamental inscriptions; and exercise their ingenuity in varying both chirography and orthography in a hundred fantastic ways. We may well excuse them for this almost idolàtrous admiration for the greatest gift of their ancestors, for there is no other language on earth whose written characters approach the Chinese in their adaptation to pictorial effect.

Yet all this exaggerated attention to the mechanical art of writing is but an index of the ardor with which Chinese scholars devote themselves to the graces of composition.

Their style is as varied as their chirography, and as much

more elaborate than that of other nations. If they spend years in learning to write, where others give a few weeks or months to the acquisition of that accomplishment, it is equally true that, while in other countries the student acquires a style of composition almost by accident, those of China make it the earnest study of half a lifetime.

While, in the lower examinations, elegance of mechanical execution, joined to a fair proportion of other merits, is sure to achieve success, in competition for the higher degrees the essays are copied by official clerks before they meet the eye of the examiner; style is everything, and handwriting nothing. Even the matter of the essay is of little consequence in comparison with the form in which it is presented. This is perceived and lamented by the more intelligent among the Chinese themselves. They often contrast the hollow glitter of the style of the present day with the solid simplicity of the ancients; and denounce the art of producing the standard *wen-chang*, or polished essay, as no less mechanical than that of ornamental penmanship. The writer has heard Ch'ung-hau, who himself wields an elegant pen, speak of the stress which the literary tribunals lay on the superficial amenities of style as a "clever contrivance adopted by a former dynasty to prevent the literati from *thinking too much*." *

Still, however sensible to its defects, Chinese scholars, without exception, glory in the extent and high refinement of their national literature. "We yield to you the palm of science," one of them once said to me, after a discussion on their notions of nature and its forces; but he added, "You, of course, will not deny to us the meed of letters."

The Chinese language is not so ill adapted to purposes of rhetorical embellishment as might be inferred from its primitive structure. Totally destitute of inflection—its substantives with-

* The use of *wen-chang* as an official test is ascribed to Wang-an-shih, of the Sung dynasty, about 1050.

out declension, its adjectives without comparison, and its verbs without conjugation—it seems at first view "sans everything" that ought to belong to a cultivated tongue. Bound, moreover, to a strict order of collocation, which its other deficiencies make a necessity, it would seem to be a clumsy instrument for thought and expression. Nor do I deny that it is so in comparison with the leading languages of the West; but it is a marvel how fine a polish Chinese scholars have made it receive, and what dexterity they acquire in the use of it. It possesses, too, some compensating qualities. Its monosyllabic form gives it the advantage of concentrated energy; and if the value of its words must be fixed by their position, like numerals in a column of figures, or mandarins on an occasion of state ceremony, it makes amends for this inconvenience by admitting each character to do duty in all the principal parts of speech. In English, we find it to be an element of strength to be able to convert many of our nouns into verbs. In Chinese, the interchange is all but universal; and it is easy to perceive how much this circumstance must contribute to variety and vigor of expression, as well as to economy of resources.

The advice which Han-yu gives as to the treatment of the Buddhist priesthood is *jin ch'i jin lu ch'ị chü, hwo ch'i shu;* literally, *man their men, house their temples, fire their books*—an expression of which all but the last clause is as unintelligible as the original Chinese. To the Chinese reader it means "burn their books, make laity of their priests, and dwelling-houses of their sacred places;" and in its native form it is as elegant as it is terse and forcible.

Before all things, a Chinese loves conciseness. This taste he has inherited from his forefathers of forty centuries ago, who, having but a scanty stock of rude emblems, were compelled to practise economy. The complexity of the characters and the labor of writing confirmed the taste; so that though the pressure of poverty is now removed, the scholar of the present day, in regard to the expenditure of ink, continues to be as parsimonious as his ancestors. While we construct our sentences so as to guard against the possibility of mistake, he is satisfied with giving the reader a hint of his meaning. Our style is a ferry-boat that carries the reader over without danger or effort on his part; his is only a succession of stepping-stones which test the agility of the passenger in leaping from one to another.

The Chinese writer is not ignorant of the Horatian canon, that in "striving after brevity he becomes obscure;" but with him obscurity is a less fault than redundancy. Accordingly, in Chinese, those latent ideas to which a French writer has lately drawn attention play an important part.* In return for a few hints, the reader himself supplies all the links that are necessary for the continuity of thought. This intense brevity is better adapted to a language which is addressed to the eye than it would be to one which is expected to be equally intelligible to the ear. Light is quicker than sound. *Segnius irritant animos demissa per aurem.*

Next to conciseness, or perhaps in preference to it, the Chinese writer is bound to keep in view the law of symmetry. He loves a kind of parallelism; but it is not that of the Hebrew poets, whose tautology he abhors. It may consist of a simile; but more frequently it merely amounts to the expression of correlated ideas in nicely corresponding phrases. Every sentence is balanced with the utmost precision; every word having its proper counterpoise, and the whole composition moving on with the measured tread of a troop of soldiers.

---

* To say that latent ideas form an essential, often a principal, part of human speech is as much a paradox, and yet as true, as to affirm that in reading we depend on the absence of light, and that the letters are precisely what we do not see. In case of an inscription lit up by an electric current, the metallic letters, though necessary to convey the fluid, remain invisible, and we see only the illuminated intervals. The greater the interstices consistent with the passage of the spark, the more brilliant the effects.

Dr. Johnson's famous parallel between Pope and Dryden, and the studied antitheses of Lord Macaulay, are quite in accordance with the taste of the Chinese. When they meet with such a passage in a foreign book, they usually exclaim, "This writer knows something of the art of composition." And where, in addition to a superfluity of words, they find, as they often do, a neglect of their cardinal principle, they do not fail to express their disgust.

A difficulty in rendering the Christian Scriptures is that the translator is not at liberty to measure off his periods according to the canons of Chinese taste; and he not unfrequently gives unnecessary offence by retaining all the circumstances of gender, number, and tense where the sense does not require them, and where the genius of the Chinese language and the rules of Chinese rhetoric alike reject them. In this respect, the earlier translations were particularly faulty; and of the more recent versions, one at least (that of the Delegates) is distinguished for classical taste.

In such a task, the distinction between the *Dolmetscher* and the *Uebersetzer* which Schleiermacher has so clearly drawn should always be kept in view. For, difficult as is the task of translating out of a foreign language, that of translation into it is still more so; and still more essential is it that the translator be thoroughly imbued with its spirit. He must himself be in a manner naturalized, in order that his literary offspring may enjoy the privileges of citizenship.

The bane of Chinese style is a servile imitation of antiquity. This not only confines the writer within a narrow circle of threadbare thoughts; it has the effect of disfiguring modern literature by spurious ornaments borrowed from the ancients. The authors of the Thirteen Classics are canonized. Infallible in letters as in doctrine, every expression which they have employed becomes a model, or rather, I should say, a portion of the current vocabulary. But, like the waters of the *King* and *Wei*, the diverse elements refuse to mingle, giving to the most admired composition a heterogeneous aspect which mars its beauty in our eyes as much as it enhances it in those of the Chinese. A premium is thus placed on pedantry, and fetters are imposed on the feet of genius. The peculiar dialect which we sometimes hear from the pulpit, made up of fragments of the sacred text skilfully incorporated with the language of every-day life, may serve as an illustration of this singular compound.

In spite of this imitation of antiquity, they are, age after age, insensibly drifting away from their standard. A law of movement seems to be impressed on all things, which even the Chinese are unable to resist. By consequence, each century in their long history, or, more properly, each dynasty, has formed a style of its own. The authors of the Chau, Han, Tang, and Sung periods are broadly discriminated.

China abounds in literary adventurers of the stamp of Constantine Simonides, and the prevalent antiquity-worship affords them encouragement; but happily she has her critics too, as acute as Aristarchus of old.

The great schools of religious philosophy are also strongly differentiated in their style of expression. The Confucian, dealing with the things of common life, aims at perspicuity. The Tauist, occupied with magic and mystery, veils his thoughts in symbols and far-fetched metaphors. The Buddhist, to the obscurity inseparable from the imported metaphysics of India, adds an opaque medium by the constant use of Sanscrit phrases which are ill understood. Subdivisions of these great schools have likewise their peculiarities of style. Of these, however, I shall not speak, but hasten to indicate certain species of composition, each of which is characterized by a style of its own.

In no country are private correspondence, official despatches, and didactic and narrative writings distinguished by more marked peculiarities.

In China, the style of epistolary intercourse, instead of approaching, as with us, to that of familiar conversation, is singularly stiff and affected. Whatever the subject, it is ushered in by a formal parade of set phrases, and finished off by a conclusion equally stereotyped and unmeaning. Form dominates everything in China. It is seldom that a letter flows freely from the heart and pen even of an able writer; and as for the less educated, though quite capable of expressing their own thoughts in their own way, they never think of such a thing as throwing off the constraint of prescribed forms. It is amusing to see how carefully one who hears of the death of a relative culls from the letter-book a form exactly suited to the degree of his affliction. If the Chinese wrote love-letters (which they never do), they would all employ the same honeyed phrases; or, like Falstaff in the Merry Wives, address the same epistle to all the different objects of their admiration.

By way of sample, here is a "note of congratulation on the birthday of a friend:"

"The Book of History lauds the five kinds of happiness, and the Book of Odes makes use of the nine similes. Both extol the honors of old age. Rejoicing at the anniversary of your advent, I utter the prayer of Hwa-fung; and, by way of recording my tally in the seaside cottage, I lay my tribute at your feet, by retaining the whole of which you will shed lustre on him who offers it."

In this short note we have five classic allusions, two of which require a word of explanation. The prayer of Hwa-fung was for the Emperor Yau, that he might be blessed with a happy old age and numerous posterity. The "tally in the seaside cottage" refers to a legend in which one of the genii, when asked his age, replied that he "could not reckon it by years; but as often as the azure sea became a field for the planting of mulberry groves he was accustomed to note the event by depositing a tally. Those tallies now filled ten chambers of his dwelling."

The reply to the foregoing ran as follows:

"My trifling life has passed away in vanity, unmarked by a single trait of excellence. On my birthday especially this fills me with shame. How dare I, then, accept your congratulatory gifts? I beg to decline them, and, prostrate, pray for indulgence."

The official correspondence and state-papers of the Chinese are, for the most part, dignified, clear, and free from those pedantic allusions with which they love to adorn their other writings. Whoever has read, even in the form of a translation, the memorials on the opium trade laid before the Emperor Tau-kwang, or the papers of Commissioner Lin on the same subject, cannot have failed to be struck with their manifest ability. Some of them are eloquent in style and masterly in argument. Imperial edicts are generally well written; but those of the Emperor Yung-ching are of such conspicuous merit that they are collected in a series of volumes and studied as models of composition.

The didactic style, whether that of commentaries on the classic texts or of treatises on science, morals, and practical arts, is always formed in accordance with the maxim of Confucius, *Tsze tah erh ye*, "Enough if you are clear." Such writings are as lucid as the nature of the subject, the genius of the language, and the brain of the author will admit. The commentaries on the classics are admirable specimens of textual exposition.

The narrative style ranges from the gravity of history to the description of scenery and humorous anecdote. Its ideal is the combination of the graphic with simplicity. Of the historical writings of the Chinese, so far as their style is concerned, nothing more can be said than that they are simple and perspicuous. Interesting they are not; for their bondage to the annal and journal form has prevented their giving us comprehensive *tableaux;* while the idea of a philosophy of history has never dawned on their minds. In descriptions of scenery the Chinese excel. They have an eye for the picturesque in nature; and nature throws her varied charms over the pages of their literature with a profusion unknown among the pagan nations of the West. Chinese writers are particularly fond of relating incidents that are susceptible of a practical application. Of this allow me to furnish one or two illustrations:

"Confucius was passing the foot of the Tai-shan when he heard a woman weeping beside a new-made grave. There was something so sad in the tones of her voice that the sage leaned his head on his hand and listened. Then sending Tsz'-lu (one of his disciples), he said to her, 'Madam, you weep as though you were loaded with many sorrows.' She replied, 'What you say is true. First, my husband's brother was devoured by a tiger, then my husband was killed, and now my son has been eaten.' 'But why do you not leave this fatal spot?' 'Because,' said the woman, 'here among the mountains there are no oppressive magistrates.' 'Mark that, my children,' said the sage, addressing his disciples; 'oppressive magistrates are dreaded more than tigers.'"

This is from Tan-kung, of the Chau dynasty. Liu-tsung-yuen, of the Tang period, has a similar narrative in which a poisonous reptile takes the place of the tiger. A poor man was employed to capture the spotted snake for medicinal purposes, and had his taxes remitted on condition of supplying the Imperial college of physicians with two every year. The author expressing his sympathy for his perilous occupation, the man replied, "'My grandfather died in this way, my father also, and I, during the twelve years in which I have been so engaged, have more than once been near dying by the bite of serpents.' As he uttered this with a very sorrowful expression of countenance, 'Do you wish,' said I, 'that I should speak to the magistrates and have you released from this hard service?' His look became more sorrowful, and, bursting into tears, he exclaimed, 'If you pity me, allow me, I pray you, to pursue my present occupation; for be assured that my lot, hard as it is, is by no means so pitiable as that of those who suffer the exactions of tax-gatherers.'"

I add a specimen, in the same vein, from Liu-ki, a writer of the Ming period, who flourished no more than five hundred years ago. "I saw," he says, "oranges exposed on a fruit-stand in midsummer, and sold at a fabulous price. They looked fresh and tempting, and I bought one. On breaking it open, a puff of something like smoke filled my mouth and nose. Turning to the seller, I demanded, 'Why do you sell such fruit? It is fit for nothing but to offer to the gods or to set before strangers. What a shame! What a disgraceful cheat!' 'Well were it,' replied the fruit-seller, 'if my oranges were the only shams.' And he went on to show how we have sham soldiers in the field, sham statesmen in the cabinet, and shams everywhere. I went away silently, musing whether this fruit-seller might not be, after all, a philosopher who had taken to selling rotten oranges in order to have a text from which to preach on the subject of shams."

The last two pieces, though separated from it by a space of from twelve to sixteen hundred years, are evidently modelled after the first. I have quoted them to show that Chinese writers are not always servile in their imitation, or timid in denouncing the corruptions of their government.

Another kind of style is that of the *wen-chang*, or polished essay—a brief treatise on any subject, constructed according to fixed rules, and limited to six or eight hundred words. In our own literature it answers to the short papers such as those of the *Spectator* and *Rambler*, which were so much in vogue in the last century—invariably ushered in by a classic motto, and expected to be a model of fine writing.

The production of these is the leading test of literary ability. The schoolboy writes *wen-chang* as soon as he is able to construe the native classics; and the gray-haired competitor for the doctorate in the examinations at the capital is still found writing *wen-chang*. In all the world there is no kind of literature produced in equal quantity—excepting, perhaps, sermons. Nor is their prodigious quantity their only point of resemblance to the productions of the Western pulpit. They always have a text from the sacred books, which they analyze in a most artificial manner, and uniformly reduce to eight heads. They aim at nothing beyond exposition, on the principle that the moderns can do nothing more than unfold the germs of ancient wisdom; originality is renounced, and, as already intimated, their chief adornment consists in the artful interweaving of sacred and modern phraseology. Like the inlaid wares of the Japanese or the mosaic pictures of the West, the more numerous and minute their component parts, the more are these compositions admired. Of no practical utility except as a mental gymnastic, the style of these essays exerts an influence through the whole range of literature. Indeed, the term which is commonly employed to cover the whole field of *belles-lettres* is no other than *wen-chang.*

Here is an opening paragraph of an essay which took the first honor in a recent examination for the doctorate:

Subject—Good-faith and Dignity. "When we begin, we should look to the end. Good-faith and dignity of carriage should therefore be objects of our care. By faith we mean that our acts should respond to our promise; and by dignity that our bearing should be such as to repel any approach towards insolent familiarity. This is only obtained by cherishing a sense of right, cultivating a regard for propriety, and at the same time maintaining a sympathy for our fellow-men. In this earthly pilgrimage, what we most desire is to escape the blame of being untrue. We choose our words with care, for fear we should be untrue to our fellows. We choose our actions with care, for fear we should be untrue to ourselves. And we choose our companions with care, lest we should prove unfaithful to our friends or they should prove unfaithful to us. By so doing we can fulfil our obligations, maintain our dignity of character, and yet preserve inviolate our social attachments. Within we shall have a heart that feels its self-imposed engagements as much as if it were bound by the stipulations of a solemn covenant; while without we shall wear an aspect that will command the respect of those who approach us."

"Enough," you will say; "those thoughts are all very commonplace. It is of no use to translate any further." And truly; for a translation can never do justice to the subtle qualities which caused this performance to be crowned among seven thousand competitors. The delicate sutures which blend its various elements into an harmonious whole must, of course, like the wavy lines of a Damascus blade, disappear when cast into the crucible of the translator.

From what has been said of the style of schools, periods, and different provinces in the empire of letters, it follows that, notwithstanding their propensity for imitation, Chinese writers must be as strongly individualized as those of other countries. If gifted with original genius, they form a style of their own; if not, they produce in new and undesigned combinations the traits of earlier authors by whom they have been most deeply impressed. Confucius professed to be an imitator, but he was eminently original. Direct, practical, and comprehensive, his thoughts are expressed in language at once concise and rhythmical—resembling as much as anything else those choice lines of Shakespeare which by their combined felicity of idea and expression have become transformed into popular proverbs. Whether, like the Hindoo *guru*, he threw them into this form as the text for his daily discourse, or whether they were reduced by his disciples, it is not in all cases easy to determine. But certain it is that, stripped of their attractive dress, whatever their intrinsic merit, they never could have attained such universal currency. The teachings of Confucius owe as much to style as those of Mahomet. The extent to which style was studied in his time we may infer from the account he gives us of the manner in which the elegant state-papers of the principality of Cheng were produced. They were the work of four men with long, strange names. One "drew out a rough draft," a second "sifted the arguments," another "added rhetorical embellishments," and the fourth finished them by "polishing off the periods."

Lau-tse, the contemporary of Confucius, though somewhat his senior, left his instructions to posterity in "five thousand words," cast in a semi-poetical mould. Obscure and paradoxical like Heraclitus of Ephesus, surnamed the Dark (a writer with whom it would not be difficult to trace other points of analogy besides their common partiality for enigma), his dark pages are illumined by many a flash of far-reaching light. Each of these great masters impressed his style on the school which he founded.

Mencius is Confucius with less dogmatism and more vehemence; while the wild fancy of Chwang-tse reproduces the characteristics of Lau-tse in exaggerated proportions.

With both, the current of their diction flows like a river, but in each case it wears the complexion of its distant source.

As another example of a contrast in manner, I may adduce two historians of the Chau period. Kung-yang-kau and Tso-chew-ming both confine themselves to the rôle of expositors, taking the Confucian annals as their text; but the first often commences with a minute analysis of the text, while the other proceeds at once to a narrative of facts. The former, for instance, thus expounds the heading of a chapter:

Text—"*First year, spring, royal first moon.*" "Why the first year? Because it was the commencement of a new reign. Why does he mention spring? Because the year began at that season. Why, in speaking of the month, does he prefix the word royal? To indicate that it was fixed by the Imperial calendar. Why refer to the Imperial calendar? To show that all the states are united under one sovereign," etc.

From Tso-chew-ming I cite a passage which, whether it do or do not exhibit any other peculiarity, will at least show the absence of interrogation-marks.

Text—"*The Prince of Cheng conquers Toan at Yien.*" Premising that the belligerents were brothers; that their mother had abetted the rebellion of Toan the younger; and that the Prince, pronouncing against her a sentence of banishment, had taken a solemn oath never to see her again until they should both be under the ground, the historian continues, "The Prince soon repented of his hasty oath. The Governor of Ying-ku heard it, and came with a present. The Prince detained him to dine. Ying-ku put aside a portion of the meats. The Prince inquired the reason. Said Ying-ku, 'They are for my mother, who has never tasted such royal dainties.' 'You have a mother, then,' said the Prince; 'alas! I have none.' He then told him of his oath, at the same time informing him of his repentance.

"'Why need your Majesty be troubled on that account?" exclaimed Ying-ku. 'If you will only make a subterranean chamber with two doors, and meet there, who will say that you have not kept your oath?'

"The Prince took the counsel, and, meeting his mother beneath the ground, they became mother and son as before. How perfect the piety of Ying-ku, who devised the plan!"

The great masters of style are a thousand years later than these last; and then we find philosophers, poets, and historians in such constellations as to make the dynasties of Tang and Sung a Golden Age for Chinese letters. Then flourished such writers as Han-yu, surnamed the Prince of Literature; Li-po, in whom the planet Venus was believed to be incarnate; the three Su, father and sons; and a host of others whose light has not yet reached the Western shores, and whose names it would be tedious to recount. Their names, musical enough in the tones of their native land, are harsh to Occidental ears. What a pity they have not all been clothed in graceful Latin, like those of Confucius and Mencius! These sages, if they owe to their style in a great degree their popularity at home, are almost equally indebted for their fame abroad to the classical terminations of their names. Name is fame in more than one sense, and more than one language—in Chinese as in Hebrew; and it is obvious that in the Western world no amount of merit would be sufficient to confer celebrity on a man bearing the name of *K'oong-foo-tsze!*

I refrain from further extracts. For reasons already given, no translation can do justice to the style of a Chinese writer; and a volume, instead of a brief essay, would be required to give an approximate idea of the other qualities of what the Chinese describe as their *elegant literature.*

To their poets we have made no reference, as that would open up a distinct field of inquiry. It is on their poetry that they especially pique themselves; but, as I think, with mistaken judgment. For while their prose-writers, like those of France, are unsurpassed in felicity of style, their poetry, like that of France, is stiff and constrained. Like their own women, their poetical muses have cramped feet and no wings.

For variety in prose composition, the nature of the language affords a boundless scope. For, not to speak of local dialects, the language of scholars, or the written language, ranges in its choice of expressions from the familiar *patois* up to the most archaic forms. In China nothing becomes obsolete; and a writer is thus enabled to pitch his composition, at option, on a high or low key, and to carry it through consistently. There are, for example, three sets of personal pronouns that correspond to as many grades of style; while there are other styles in which the personal pronoun is dispensed with, and substantives employed instead.

Founded on pictorial representation, the language is, in many of its features, highly poetical, the strange beauties with which it charms the fancy at every step suggesting a ramble among the gardens of the sea-nymphs. Nor is it a dead language, though in its written form no longer generally spoken. It contains "thoughts that breathe, and words that burn"—writers whom the student will gladly acknowledge as worthy compeers of the most admired authors of the ancient West. I say "ancient," for China is essentially ancient. She is not yet modernized, and finds fitter parallels in pagan antiquity than in modern Christendom.

The time, I trust, is not far distant when her language will find a place in all our principal seats of learning, and when her classic writers will be known and appreciated.

ON THE STYLE OF CHINESE EPISTOLARY COMPOSITION.*

In no other language is the style of private correspondence so widely separated from that of official or public documents as in the Chinese. The latter, simple and direct in expression, eschews ornament, and aims chiefly at clearness and force; the former, artificial to the last degree, bristles with trite allusions which are rather pedantic than elegant.

With us, in this as in so many other things, the reverse is not far from the truth. It is the official despatch that is cast in iron moulds; and the familiar letter is left free to take any shape the easy play of thought and feeling may impress upon it. Authors accordingly sometimes choose to throw their compositions into the convenient form of epistles when they wish to invest them with the double charm of clearness and vivacity. By employing the form of letters, Pascal imparted to polemic discussion the grace and humor of the comic drama; while Swift and Junius availed themselves of the same weapon in their terrible attacks on the government.

Not so the Chinese: while necessity leads to the discussion of grave topics in the form of letters, and the teachings of some of their ancient philosophers were communicated in the way of correspondence, among them no modern author ever thinks of throwing his ideas into such a shape. Neither does any author treat a grave subject under the form of the modern prize essay;

---

* Read before the North China Branch of the Royal Asiatic Society on the 8th December, 1876.

and thoughtful men denounce the regulation essay as utterly useless; but they never denounce the conventional style of letter-writing, though both have a family likeness. The reason is that the letter of friendship or business is a social necessity, and the literary ornament with which it is tricked out is deemed essential to save it from vulgarity.

In friendly correspondence the opening paragraphs are always consecrated to the expression of high-flown sentiments, real or assumed, and not unfrequently the falsetto pitch of the exordium is painfully sustained to the very close. Nothing is more offensive to our taste, or less calculated to encourage the labor of acquisition. If a letter contains any serious business, the foreign reader, if he does not, as in most cases, rely on a native teacher for explanation, finds that he can arrive at it by a process of elimination, i. e. by leaving out of account all the unintelligible rhetoric. But this is not merely unscholarly; it limits the use of correspondence, and shuts out the student (he does not deserve the name of student if willing to be shut out) from a department of literature which more than any other presents us with pictures of individual character and social life.

The student who desires to enter this field will find numerous private collections of more or less celebrity soliciting his attention. If any of them were from the pens of gifted women; and if the canons of Chinese taste (for the fault is not in the language) permitted them, like their sisters of the West, to write as they talk, he might, even in this department, verify the quaint old maxim, "The sweetness of the lips increaseth knowledge." But, alas! there is no Sévigné who, by her brilliant gossip, can shed the dews of immortal youth over the ephemeral intrigues of a court, and by her wit give a value to things that are worthless, as amber does to the insects which it embalms; there is no Wortley who chats with equal charm of literature and love; no Lady Duff Gordon, who, by her genius and enterprise, puts us in love with boat-life and Bedouins.

The paths of epistolary literature, where the choicest flowers are dropped from female hands, are in China all untrodden by female feet; and a reason gravely given for withholding from women the key of knowledge is that men are *afraid they will learn to write letters.* It is not nature, but man, that is ungenerous to the daughters of the East.

> "Knowledge to their eyes her ample page,
> Rich with the spoils of time, did ne'er unroll;
> Chill *jealousy* repressed their noble rage,
> And froze the genial current of the soul."

Nor, it must be confessed, is there any such indemnity in store for our student as the epistles of a moralizing Seneca; or the correspondence of a malignant and intriguing Walpole, which lifts the veil from the mysteries of contemporary politics, and from the writer's own bosom, so that Macaulay ingeniously compares the flavor of the letters of the great minister to that of *patés de foie gras*, because derived from a disease of the liver in the animal that produced them. But as some of our most eminent poets, such as Dryden, Gray, and Cowper, have left behind them letters that are preserved as models of elegance in which fancy and feeling are no less happily blended than in their poetical works, so we find that in China the list of distinguished letter-writers is headed by the names of poets, showing that they enjoyed the favor of the *musa pedestris* as well as of her winged sisters.

The earliest collection of letters, or at least the most famous of those that are accepted as models of epistolary style, came from the pens of two celebrated poets of the Sung dynasty, Su-tung-p'o, 蘇東坡, and Hwang-t'ing-kien, 黃庭堅. Under the joint name of Su-Hwang-ch'i-tuh, 蘇黃尺牘, though not properly a *Briefwechsel*, or correspondence between the two authors, it has ever since the battle of Hastings given law to this species of composition.

The stream of time, like that which floated the borrowed axe of the prophet, usually carries down the weightier matters, and deposits the less important as sediment; yet in this instance we have reason to regret that, like natural rivers, it has only brought down to us the lighter material on its surface. Both writers held high offices, and one of them was especially honored at the Imperial Court; but their letters have little to do with State policy; and the selection has obviously been made on the principle that if one of their merits is in the elegance of their form, another ought to be in the absence of facts. Still, even these shining husks, if carefully sifted, will be found to yield some grains of valuable information.

A book of letters of more modern date, and scarcely inferior in reputation, is the *Ch'i-tuh* of Siao-ts'ang, 小倉山房尺牘, or of Sui-yuen, 隨園尺牘, as it is variously styled. The author, Yuen-mei, 袁枚, a native of Che-kiang, won a seat in the Imperial Academy in the reign of Kien-lung; and declining office, passed his life at Nanking, chiefly engaged in scholastic pursuits, boasting that for thirty years he never appeared at court.

Known mainly as a professor of *belles-lettres*, with pupils dispersed over several provinces, instead of collected into one lecture-room, and communicating by post instead of *viva voce*, this worthy man has not merely left models of composition, but set an example, both as scholar and instructor, which is much admired though little followed.

A poet of refined taste, and not without talent, it is interesting to know that he gave instruction in the art of poetry to numerous ladies of high family and culture, making, from time to time, the circuit of the cities where they resided—a fact the rarity of which rather supports than invalidates the view above given of the deficiencies of female education.

There are numerous works passing under the general name of *Ch'i-tuh*, which were prepared expressly for form-books, and will repay perusal for that purpose. Of these I may mention the *Yen-chi-mutan*, 胭脂牡丹, *Hai-shang-hung-ni*, 海上鴻泥,

and *Liu-ts'ing-tsi*, 留青集; but they have not the merit of a history.

It is, however, with a view to drawing attention to a more recent collection that this article is written.

The *Tsze-yuen Ch'i-tuh*, 雜園尺牘, published at Peking a few years ago in four thin volumes, consists of a selection from the letters of Liu-kia-chu, 劉家柱.

This is a name which, being unknown, carries no weight; and our author, like Hawthorne in one of his earlier works, might speak of himself as enjoying the distinction of being one of the obscurest men of letters in all China. A native of Hunan, he passed many years in the Yamen of the Governor of Canton; a representative of that nameless but influential class who transact the business while their superiors enjoy the honors of official station.

During this period he wrote, he tells us, heaps of papers higher than his head, among which one might play hide-and-seek in more senses than one. Most of them were, of course, sent forth in the name of others, and the writer facetiously compares himself to a milliner who prepares the clothing for a bride, or a go-between who arranges for her nuptials. Of these he gives us none, unless, indeed, by surreptitiously changing their address and adapting them to his own use.

The most of his papers bear unmistakable marks of having been culled from his private portfolio; affording such incidental glimpses of life and manners that one is compelled to accept them as a genuine record—a portion of the writer's autobiography. This gives the work an element of interest of no mean order, and a value of its own, as a mirror held up to the face of Chinese life by the hand of a native. So frank, indeed, are its disclosures, so little care is taken to draw a veil over things that are deemed discreditable, that one might almost regard the work as belonging to the category of "confessions"—originated by St. Augustine, and rendered popular by Rousseau.

As to the literary merits of the performance, it is sufficient to cite the names of the two sponsors under whose patronage the author comes before the public—Kwo Sung-tao, Minister to England, and Wang K'ai-tai, the late enlightened governor of the Province of Fohkien—each of them having filled the post of Governor of Canton, and employed Liu-kia-chu as a confidential secretary.

Other great names are invoked in a long list of laudatory notices; and some that we meet with incidentally in the course of the correspondence, such as Tseng Kwo-fan, Tsiang Ih-li, Li Hung-chang, and Liu Ch'ang-yiu, the present viceroy of Yunnan and Kweichau, impart to it an air of historical truth that is much in its favor.

Without pausing longer to discourse about the book, let us open its pages and see what we shall find there.

To begin, we shall find a meteoric shower of allusions. This is the most prominent characteristic of this species of writing; and its primary object is to hide the nakedness of commonplace. Employed in excess or handled clumsily, it aggravates the evil by exposing the poverty of the writer, or substitutes the graver faults of pedantry and cant; used with skill and taste, it throws over the page a glitter of iridescent hues, or, it may be, contributes largely to the significance and force of language.

These allusions are of various kinds. Some suggest whole chapters of history; others bring up the words or actions of real or mythical personages; while others still, by a single word or phrase, cast a beam of light on some poetical tableau, which brings its entire effect to bear on the subject in hand. For instance, when Dryden says of Thais that,

> "Like another Helen, she fired another Troy,"

what a crowd of teeming associations he condenses into the space of a single line! How much is expressed by such brief phrases as "a Barmecide feast," "a Bellerophon letter," "a Judas kiss!"

The Chinese language—I do not say literature—abounds in such; and no one can be said to understand the language who is not in some degree familiar with them. Then there are curt allusions of a purely literary kind—catch-words which suggest any one of the three hundred classic odes, or refer to thousands of well-known passages in later literature. To these we may add a vocabulary of metaphorical words and phrases, the use of which is *de rigeur* in a certain style which makes it a point of taste not to call things by their right names. Thus the poet or the elegant letter-writer never speaks of copper cash, but calls them "green beetles;" a sheet of paper he calls "a flowery scroll;" an epistle is "a wild-goose." Husband and wife are *Ch'ang-sue*, bass and treble; *K'ang-li*, strength and beauty; *Yuen-yang*, duck and drake; and a hundred other pretty things, at the poet's option. A man is a prince and his wife a princess; his house a palace and his children a phœnix brood. To repay the kindness of parents is to emulate the stork; to return a borrowed article is to restore the gem; and a man of genius employed in a work of drudgery—as Charles Lamb in the India Office—is a race-horse in a salt-wagon.

These are but a few specimens of a sort of dialect that has its own dictionaries without number or limit; and of which every reader of Chinese is under the necessity of knowing something, if he does not master it. Perhaps the best key to it for any student, native or foreign, is a collection of *wen-chang*, or of well-written letters, such as those of our obscure friend Liu-kia-chu.

In dictionaries and cyclopædias, or in such a useful hand-book as Mr. Mayer's Chinese Reader's Manual, he will find gems arranged as in a mineralogical cabinet; but in these compositions he meets them in their proper setting. The object of such works is to aid, not to supersede, the reading of difficult authors—as a certain learned Dutchman proposed to supersede Homer by presenting the Homeric archæology in a tabulated form.

We now proceed to the substratum of facts underlying the gold and tinsel of which we have been speaking. Of little importance in themselves, and not by any means thick-sown through these pages, they are still not devoid of interest as illustrations of character, personal and national.

It was from the letters of Cicero that Mr. Middleton drew the principal materials for his admirable life of the great Roman statesman. But even the letters of Chu-fu-tsze or Su-tung-p'o would furnish scanty materials for a history of their lives; and meagre, indeed, are the outlines of biography which we are able to extract from the sentimental effusions of Liu-kia-chu.

Our author first drew his breath, and with it what poetic inspiration he possessed, amidst the mountain scenery of Southern Hunan, about the middle of the reign of Kia-king (circa 1810). Born in a rustic village not far from the city of Sin-hwa, 新化, he came of a family distinguished for scholarship—a fact of which he never ceases to remind the reader; and there can be no doubt that he inherited talent, though his patrimony included little else.

Boasting somewhat of his early precocity, he hints at youthful dissipations as having proved fatal to his career as a scholar, and planted the seeds of unending regrets. He failed—probably from a defective chirography, as many a worthier man has done—to win the first or lowest degree in the civil-service examinations; and about the age of thirty he removed with his family to Canton, forgetting, it seems, to liquidate certain debts of honor.

Concerned in the conduct of a charity-school, Liu, thinking that charity ought to begin at home, "borrowed" a portion of the funds to meet his own necessities. Arrived at Canton, he learned with much regret that the slight liberty he had taken with its capital was likely to occasion the dissolution of the school. Against this he protests with much eloquence; but has nothing more substantial to encourage the good work than "promises to pay." In this connection his reference to himself as a good example of the benefits of education is, to say the least, a little naïve.

After this, we are not surprised to find many epistles filled with complaints of poverty. He has work enough, but scant remuneration. Great men admire his genius, and load him with compliments; but, like virtue, which he does not much resemble in any other respect, *laudatur et alget.*

From one friend he begs the loan of a "few hundred pieces of gold," and from another he borrows a suit of decent apparel. Good models these letters for one who has much to do in the line of begging or borrowing!

All this time Liu's family is increasing at a rather alarming rate; not that he has any children born, but from time to time he takes a new beauty into his harem in the hope that children will follow. One is presented to him by a friend; another, not unnaturally, runs away, or, as he euphemistically terms it, "carries her guitar to another door."

A correspondent of comparatively severe morals expostulates with Liu on this seeming abandonment to a life of sensuality; and the latter replies by drawing an affecting picture of an aged father who cannot die in peace without the joy of embracing a grandson!

At length his hopes are awakened only to meet with disappointment—one of his wives presenting him with a daughter. The little creature appears not to be altogether unwelcome, and, in fact, makes for herself a warm place in her father's heart; though he frequently alludes to her in terms borrowed from one of the odes of which the following couplet gives the leading idea:

"A girl is born; in coarse cloth wound,
With a tile for a toy, let her lie on the ground," etc.

The spell broken, another of his ladies crowns his desires by giving him a son, whose advent is duly hailed by a flourish of trumpets, and further quotations from the Book of Odes:

"A son is born; on an ivory bed,
Wrap him in raiment of purple and red;
Gold and jewels for playthings bring
To the noble boy who shall serve the king."

In a few months this child of many hopes sickens and dies. The disconsolate father mourns deeply, and fills many sheets with melodious *tristia.*

About this time the doors of official preferment, before which he had been so long waiting (having failed to find the key in his earlier youth), began slowly to open before him. Appointed magistrate of a sub-district in the country, called *Loh-kang*, he contrived to send some one to act in his stead (perhaps sub-letting the profits of the position), while he remained at the capital in the midst of the literary society which he loved so much.

Another time, appointed to Kowloon on the main opposite to Hongkong, Liu finds excuses for not repairing to his post; and the governor, offended by his tardiness, cancels the appointment. After due penance, he is restored to favor and offered another post, such as Cæsar himself would have preferred to being the second man at Rome. Taught by experience, he lost no time in installing himself in his new yamen. Its roof leaks, its walls are crumbling, and all its apartments filled with rubbish; but, to compensate for all this, it contains a *throne*, which, if he had read Milton, he might have compared to that of the "anarch old" who ruled the realms of chaos.

Here he finds a new order of talents called into requisition: he has to deal with facts instead of words, and is evidently proud of the success with which he performs the functions of a judge—favoring us with one of his judgments as a model of its kind. It betrays, however, the fact that his right hand has not forgotten its cunning; that he continues to be a rhetorician in spite of himself, and is more at home in reading a lecture than in pronouncing a sentence.

Unique among the rose-water productions of his epistolary pen, his report of this lawsuit reminds us that Liu has also given us a few specimens of another species of composition.

In the course of his career he is sometimes assistant examiner, and sometimes appears in the character of a competitor; not, indeed, in the ordinary examinations, but in those special trials which expectant officers are required to pass at the provincial capital. On one of these occasions Liu's essays were endorsed by the high authorities in terms which placed them on a level with the best productions of the classic ages.

These eulogies he not only repeats in many of his letters, but favors his friends with copies of the fortunate papers, that they may judge for themselves whether the praise is merited; pleasing himself with the reflection that but for the injustice of the lower courts he might long since have worn the highest honors of the literary arena.

Liu's literary ability is also duly recognized by a host of junior aspirants, who solicit copies of his MSS., send presents on his fête-days, and institute theatricals in his honor.

His moral character is more doubtful. A polygamist on principle, he disclaims the virtues of an ascetic philosopher in order to emulate the libertinism of certain dissolute poets. Had he, indeed, done nothing worse than fill his own cage with bright-winged songsters, he would have been walking too closely in the footsteps of saints and sages to attract attention. To vindicate for himself the reputation of being a free spirit—one that spurns what he denominates the "minor morals"—he mingles occasionally with the "soiled doves."

For this, his best apology is found in the fact that the silly occupants of his own dove-cot are incapable of appreciating his genius; while some of these unappropriated, like the hetæræ of Greece, had their charms enhanced by the advantages of education. He gives us a letter which he wrote to one of this class, with hypocritical morality recommending her to take refuge in a house of religion.

In an epistle to another friend, he gives us reason to suspect that even the vestals of Buddha were not sacred in his eyes; and that with him sacrilege was necessary to give the highest flavor to license. Freely unfolding his inner life, and trenching often on forbidden ground, it is something in his favor that he is always elegant and never indecent.

After this account of his morals, it would be useless to inquire for his religion. He says, indeed, very little on the subject. He alludes to a "Creator" more than once, but in language of studied levity, showing that to him the author of nature is not a "living God."

As to outward observances, he conforms to popular usage; he believes in fate, and, impatient to know its decrees, applies to a professional fortune-teller; in all these points only too true a type of the average literati of his country.

Our hasty sketch may serve to indicate the range and variety of his correspondence, which, with all its finish, resembles a Chinese garden, where *artis est* NATURAM *celare* by twisting flower and plant into the grotesque shape of bird and beast.

The boundary-line between friendly and official correspondence is not easy to trace. It is to the former that we confine ourselves in the present communication; but it will not be amiss to remark that much of the best writing in the Chinese language may be found on intermediate ground between formal business documents and friendly letters.

In this class of compositions vaguely described as official letters, the grace of the polished epistle is often added to the directness and force of the despatch style—a happy combination, of which some of the best specimens may be seen in the published correspondence of Hu-lin-yeh, canonized under the title of Hu-wen-cheng-kung; and in that of Ch'en Wen Chung-kung, who, having won three times in succession the first literary honor of his province and of the Empire, received from that circumstance the sobriquet of Ch'en San Yuen, 陳三元.

CHINESE FABLES.*

The student of Chinese inquires in vain for any collection of native fables; and he feels their absence as a personal inconvenience when he recalls his obligations to Æsop and Phædrus, Lessing and La Fontaine, for alleviating the toil of his earlier studies in the classic languages of ancient and modern Europe. This deficiency is the more disappointing, as the constant occurrence of the word *pifang* in our colloquial exercises leads us to expect to find the fields of literature thick-sown with every variety of similitude. Parables and allegories are, indeed, not wanting, but their congener, the fable, seems never to have existed, or in some mysterious way to have become well-nigh extinct.

Nor is this last supposition a mere idle fancy. We turn up from time to time what seem to be fossil fragments enough to give it, to say the least, as good a foundation as some scientific theories have to rest on. For what are those numerous proverbial expressions drawn from the habits of animals but the ghosts, or rather the skeletons, of vanished fables. But whether such originals ever existed, certain it is that nothing is more easy or natural than to expand these phrases into the full dimensions of the proper apologue.

Take, for instance, "the sheep in a tiger's skin," "when the hare dies the fox weeps," "he who nurses a tiger's cub will rue his kindness," etc. Do not these seem to point back to ancient fables as their source; just as we know "the fox and the grapes,"

---

* Written for the *Celestial Empire* in 1871.

"the ass in a lion's skin," and other proverbial expressions current among us were derived from fables?

But how did such originals, supposing them to have existed, come to be lost? We reply, they were either never reduced to writing, or not written in a style adapted to the taste of the country. For ages past the Chinese have affected an extreme sententiousness in the style of their literary composition. This would naturally lead them to extract the living spirit and to reject the cumbrous form of such fables as might spring up in the humbler walks of their folk-lore. Thus they may have had their unknown Pilpays and their mute, inglorious Æsops.

At all events, the defect of which we are speaking was not occasioned, as some would have us infer, by a want of imagination. For Chinese literature, while it contains nothing that rises to the dignity of the epic muse, yet teems with the productions of a fertile fancy—metamorphoses as numerous (if not as elegant) as those of Ovid; fairy tales more monstrous than Grimm's; and narratives of adventure (generally accepted as sober history) as strange as those of Sindbad or Gulliver. It is, we repeat, a question of taste rather than talent; and this, we think, is borne out by the reception which the Chinese gave to Mr. Thom's excellent translation of Æsop, a work which, instead of finding its way into every household, is rarely to be met with even in the stalls of a bookseller. The mandarins suspected that wolves and bears were masks for dangerous doctrines and biting satire; while neither prince nor peasant has cared enough about the production to keep it alive.

As to talent, while we will not assert that the Chinese could have excelled in this department of literature, there is proof, we think, that they are not wholly destitute of a capacity for it. This will be found in the following fables, derived from various sources, which we give by way of specimen, hoping that our readers will add to the number any that happen to come under their notice:

1. The King of Ch'oo inquiring with some surprise why the people of the North were so frightened at the approach of Chou-si-hü, one of his ministers replied as follows: "A tiger who happened to be preceded by a fox was greatly astonished to see all the animals running away from the fox, little suspecting that their terror was inspired by himself. It is not Chou, but your Majesty, of whom the people of the North are in dread."

2. "I may go out and play without any danger now," said a little mouse to its mother. "The old cat has become religious; I see her with her eyes shut, engaged in praying to Buddha."

Grimalkin's devotions, however, did not prevent her seizing the silly little creature as soon as it ventured near.

3. A tiger who had never seen an ass was terrified at the sound of his voice, and was about to run away, when the latter turned his heels and prepared to kick.

"If that is your mode of attack," said the tiger, "I know how to deal with you."

4. A tiger having clapped his paw on an unlucky monkey, the latter begged to be released on the score of his insignificance, and promised to show the tiger where he might find a more valuable prey. The tiger complied, and the monkey conducted him to a hill-side where an ass was feeding—an animal which the tiger, till then, had never seen.

"My good brother," said the ass to the monkey, "hitherto you have always brought me two tigers, how is it that you have only brought me one to-day?"

Hearing these words, the tiger fled for his life. Thus a ready wit may often ward off great dangers.

5. A tiger, finding a cat very prolific in devices for catching game, placed himself under her instruction. At length he was told there was nothing more to be learned. "Have you, then, taught me all your tricks?" he inquired. "Yes," replied the cat. "Then," said the tiger, "you are of no further use, and so I shall eat you." The cat, however, sprang lightly into the

branches of a tree, and smiled at his disappointment. She had not taught him *all* her tricks.

The Chinese apply this to their foreign instructors in the art of war, and evidently suspect that some master secret is always held in reserve.

THE RENAISSANCE IN CHINA.*

As link after link is added to that chain of communication which brings China nearer to us than Europe was before the rise of steam navigation, it is interesting to know that a mental awakening is taking place among the people of China by which the Chinese mind will be brought proportionally nearer to our own.

The announcement of this fact will be received with distrust by some who are sceptical as to the doctrine of human progress. It will be questioned by others who deride as visionary the efforts of Christian enterprise. Nor will it be readily admitted by that large class who are wont to regard the Chinese mind as hopelessly incrusted with the prejudices of antiquity.

Never have a great people been more misunderstood. They are denounced as stolid, because we are not in possession of a medium sufficiently transparent to convey our ideas to them or transmit theirs to us; and stigmatized as barbarians, because we want the breadth to comprehend a civilization different from our own. They are represented as servile imitators, though they have borrowed less than any other people; as destitute of the inventive faculty, though the world is indebted to them for a long catalogue of the most useful discoveries; and as clinging

* This paper was originally delivered as an address before the American Oriental Society, October, 1868; and subsequently published in the *New-Englander* quarterly magazine, January, 1869. It is reproduced without alteration, because, in the writer's opinion, the history of the past twelve years serves to confirm and verify the views here given.

with unquestioning tenacity to a heritage of traditions, though they have passed through many and profound changes in the course of their history.

They have not been stationary, as generally supposed, through the long past of their national life. The national mind has advanced from age to age with a stately march; not, indeed, always in a direct course, but at each of its great epochs recording, as we think, a decided gain; like the dawn of an arctic morning, in which the first blush of the eastern sky disappears for many hours, only to be succeeded by a brighter glow, growing brighter yet after each interval of darkness as the time of sunrise approaches.

The existence in such a country of such a thing as a national mind is itself an evidence of a susceptibility to change, and at the same time a guarantee for the comparative stability of its institutions. It proves that China is not an immense congeries of polyps, each encased in his narrow cell, a workshop and a tomb, and all toiling on without the stimulus of common sympathy or mental reaction. It proves that China is not, like Africa and aboriginal America, or even like British India, an assemblage of tribes with little or no community of feeling. It is a unit, and through all its members there sweeps the mighty tide of a common life.

In the progress of its enormous growth, it has absorbed many a heterogeneous element, which has always been transformed into its own substance by an assimilative power that attests the marvellous energy of the Chinese civilization. It has, too, undergone many modifications, in consequence of influences operating *ab extra* as well as from within; and though the process of transmission has often been slow, those influences have always extended to the whole body. Within the bounds of China proper there is no such thing as the waves of Buddhism or Taoism being arrested at the confines of a particular province; nor is there any district in which the pulsations from the great heart of the empire do not, by virtue of a common language and common feeling, meet with a prompt response.

Yet the existence of this oneness and sympathy—this nationality of mind, which brings modifications on a vast scale within the range of possibility, necessarily interposes an obstacle in the way of their speedy consummation. Planted on the deep foundations of antiquity, extending over so wide an area, and proudly conscious of its own greatness, its very inertia is opposed to change. In China, accordingly, great revolutions, whether political, religious, or intellectual, have always been slow of accomplishment. Compared with the facility with which these are brought about in some Occidental countries, they resemble the slow revolution of those huge planets on the outskirts of the solar system, which require more than the period of a human life to make the circuit of the sun, while the little planet Mercury wheels round the centre once in a few months.

The great dynastic changes, involving as they do a period of disintegration and another of reconstruction, have usually occupied from one to three generations; while the growth of those grand revolutions which resulted in the ascendency of a religion or a philosophy must be reckoned by centuries.

A brief review of some of the more remarkable changes that have occurred in the progress of Chinese civilization will enable us better to understand the nature of the intellectual movement now going on.

To begin with the development of political ideas. Instead of being wedded to a uniform system of despotic government, the Chinese have lived under as many forms of government as ancient Rome or modern France. While the Romans passed under their kings, consuls, and emperors, the Chinese had their *tees*, their *wangs*, and their *hwangtees*. And as France has passed through the various phases of a feudal and centralized monarchy, a republic, and a military despotism, so China exhibits an equal variety in the forms of her civil government.

When the hand of history first lifts the curtain, two thousand years before the Christian era, it discloses to us an elective monarchy, in which the voice of the people was admitted to express the will of Heaven. Thus Yaou, the model monarch of antiquity, was raised to the throne by the voice of the nobles, in lieu of his elder brother, who was set aside on account of his disorderly life. Yaou in turn set aside his own son, and called on the nobles to name a successor, when Shun was chosen. Again, Shun, passing by an unworthy son, transmitted the Imperial yellow to an able minister, the great Yu.

Yu, though a good sovereign, departed from these illustrious precedents, and incurred the censure of "converting the Empire into a family estate." The hereditary principle became fixed. Branches of the Imperial family were assigned portions of the Empire, and, their descendants succeeding to their principalities, the feudal system was confirmed.

This, in China, is the classical form of government; Confucius himself compares the majesty of the sovereign to the polar star, which keeps its steadfast place while all the constellations revolve around it. It prevailed under the dynasty of Chow, when the Classics were produced; and a large part of the classic writings is occupied with questions relating to the balance of power among the feudal lords and the regulation of their relations to the Emperor. Transplanted to Japan, it exists till the present day, where a war among the nobles is now exciting the attention of the public.* But in China it was overthrown completely two thousand years ago by one of the most sweeping revolutions on the records of history.

---

* This conflict resulted in the overthrow of the usurpation of the Shogun, and the restoration of the Mikado to all his ancient rights and to more than his ancient power; the great barons by common consent surrendering their territorial sovereignty, and converting their country into a centralized empire, instead of a congeries of vassal states.

Lücheng,* an ambitious noble, sweeping all rival princes from the chess-board, dethroned the last degenerate scions of the house of Chow, and proclaimed himself under the title of the First Whangtee. Finding that the literary class were wedded to feudal institutions, he carried on a relentless persecution against the disciples of Confucius; and, fearing that the traces of them contained in the Confucian books might lead the people to restore the obliterated principalities, he proceeded to destroy, as far as possible, every vestige of classic literature. His object was to cut loose from the leading-strings of antiquity, and to inaugurate a totally new system in the politics of the Empire. He further signalized his reign by the erection of that huge barrier on the north which to this day continues to be a wonder of the world. It is only just to add that the system of centralized power which he introduced was as firmly established as the Great Wall itself. The very title of *Whangtee*, first assumed by Lücheng, continues to be that of the emperors of China at the present day.

Under the dynasty of Han, about the commencement of the Christian era, a still more important modification was introduced into the constitution of the Empire—viz., a democratic element, in virtue of which appointments to office were not left to the caprice of the sovereign and his favorites. This consisted in testing the capacity of candidates by a literary examination; and it operated so well that it was not only adopted, but greatly improved, by succeeding dynasties, and continues in force at the present day. Americans would as soon surrender their ballot-box as the Chinese that noble system of literary competition which makes public office the reward of scholarship, and gives every man an opportunity of elevating himself by his own exertions.

Nor are the Chinese less familiar with the idea of change in

* This name implies an opprobrious and, no doubt, fictitious account of the great man's parentage. I employ it notwithstanding, because it is that which is most frequently used by native historians.

the region of religious thought, three systems of religion having appeared on the arena of the Empire and struggled for ascendency since the sixth century before the Christian era. Confucianism was persecuted under the dynasty of Ts'in; and Taoism and Buddhism, alternately persecuting and persecuted, kept up the conflict for ages, each in turn seating its own disciples on the throne of the Empire. The last of these is of foreign origin; and its universal prevalence does much to reconcile the people to the introduction of religious ideas from abroad; while it stands forth as a visible proof of the possibility of converting the Chinese to a foreign creed. A leading statesman* of China has recently made use of this as an argument that the Emperor should not object to the propagation of Christianity. "From the time of Ts'in and Han," he says, "the doctrines of Confucius began to be obscured, and the religion of Buddha spread. Now Buddhism originated in India, but many of the Hindoos have renounced Buddhism and embraced Mahometanism. The Roman Catholic faith originated in the West, but some nations of the West have adopted Protestantism, and set themselves in opposition to the faith of Rome. Whence we see that other religions rise and fall from age to age, but the doctrine of Confucius survives unimpaired throughout all ages." The writer is careful to disavow any sympathy for Christianity, and he by no means recommends its adoption; but he wishes to assure his Majesty that there is no serious evil to be apprehended even if Christianity should succeed in supplanting Buddhism, as long as the people adhere to the cardinal doctrines of their ancient sage. It is a great thing for the leading minds to acknowledge the possibility of a change even in this hypothetical form.

Aside from these religious revolutions, and altogether distinct from them, are several periods of intellectual awakening that constitute marked epochs in the history of literature.

---

* Tseng Kuo-fan, Viceroy of Nanking.

The first of these was occasioned by the publication of the Confucian Classics. Another occurred in the time of Mencius, when the ethical basis of the school underwent a searching revision, the great question of the original goodness or depravity of human nature being discussed with acuteness and power. A third and more powerful awakening took place when the classic books which Lücheng had burned rose, phœnix-like, from their ashes, or, to speak more correctly, issued, Minerva-like, from the retentive brain of those venerable scholars who had committed them to memory in their early boyhood.

This was the age of criticism, the very circumstances which roused the national mind to activity directing its efforts to the settlement of the text of their ancient records. But it did not stop here. Slips of bamboo and tablets of wood, the clumsy materials of ancient books, gave place to linen, silk, and paper. The convenience and elegance of the material contributed to multiply books and stimulate literary labor.

The great work which laid the foundation of all the existing histories of the Empire was produced in this age; as also a dictionary, the pioneer of Chinese lexicography, since followed by more voluminous works, but so complete and lucid that it is still reckoned among standard authorities.

But the grandest of all the revivals of learning was, as might be expected, that which ensued on the discovery of the art of printing. In the period above referred to, about A.D. 177, the revised text of the sacred books was engraved on tablets of stone, by Imperial order, as a precaution to secure it against the danger of another conflagration. Impressions must have been taken from these, and the art of printing thus practised to a limited extent at that early date; but it was not till the eighth century that it came into general use for the manufacture of books. At that time the number of old works described in the official record of the Imperial Library was 53,915, to which were added 28,468 that were characterized as recent. But it was not so much this vastly augmented rate of production that marked the epoch as the improved character of its original literature. This was eminently the age of poetry, when Letaipe and Tufu, and a whole constellation of lesser lights, rose above the horizon. The poems of Tang are still recognized as forming the text-book of standard poetry.

This period was succeeded by another in the reign of the Sung dynasty (960–1279), when the mind of China exhibited itself in a new development. It became seized with a mania for philosophical speculation, and grappled with the deepest questions of ontology. Chowtsze, Chengtsze, and, above all, the famous Chuhe, distinguished themselves by the penetrating subtlety and the daring freedom of their inquiries. Professing to elucidate the ancient philosophy, they in reality founded a new one—a school of pantheistic idealism, which has continued dominant to the present hour.

The last two dynasties have not been unfruitful in the products of the intellect; indeed, there seems to be no end or abatement to the teeming fertility of the Chinese mind. Less daringly original than in the preceding period, it has yet, under each of these dynasties, appeared in a new style—the writers of the Ming being distinguished for masculine energy of expression, and those of the Ts'ing for graceful elegance. Each period was introduced by a gigantic work—that of the Mings by the codification of the laws of the Empire, the Pandects of Yunglo; and that of the Ts'ings by the compilation of Kanghe's Imperial Dictionary, the "Webster unabridged" of the Chinese language. The writers of the Ts'ing (the present) dynasty are displaying a little independence, if not originality, in revolting against the authority of Chuhe as an expositor of their canonical Scriptures—a reaction against the pantheism, or rather atheism, of the Sung philosophers. Whether this tendency is due in any degree to the influence of Mahometans and Christians, it is certain that from both sources, especially the latter, the Chinese have received powerful impulses in the way of mathematics and astronomy.

Enough has been said to show that the Chinese have not maintained through all the ages that character of cast-iron uniformity so generally ascribed to them. Worshippers of antiquity they certainly are, and strongly conservative in their mental tendencies; but they have not been content, as is too commonly supposed, to hand down from the earliest times a small stock of crystallized ideas without increase or modification. The germs of their civilization, like those of any civilization worth preserving, are not precious stones to be kept in a casket, but seeds to be cultivated and improved. In fact, modifications have taken place on an extensive scale, foreign elements have from time to time been engrafted on the native root, and the native scholar, as he follows back the pathway of history, fails to discover anything like uniformity or constancy, except in a few of the most fundamental principles. The doctrine of filial piety, carried to the point of religious devotion, extends like a golden thread through all the ages, as the foundation of family ties and social order; while the principle of the divine origin of government, administered by one man as the representative of Heaven, and modified by the corresponding doctrine that the will of Heaven is expressed in the will of the people, is found alike in every period as the basis of their civil institutions.

Though not so much given to change as their more mercurial antipodes, it is still true that the constant factors of their civilization have been few, and the variable ones many. Bold innovations and radical revolutions rise to view all along in the retrospect of their far-reaching past, and prepare them to anticipate the same for the future. With such antecedents, and such a character for intellectual activity, it would be next to impossible that they should not be profoundly affected by their contacts and collisions with the civilization of Christendom.

In point of fact, the impression is profound, though it was

not immediately apparent. For more than thirty years the West has been acting on China by the combined influence of its arms, its commerce, its religion, and its science. Some of these influences commenced to operate at a much earlier date, and their effects were by no means insignificant; but of late years all of them have been combined with an oxyhydrogen-blow-pipe intensity that one would think sufficient to melt a mountain of adamant. They could not, in the nature of things, have been brought to bear on China so effectively at any earlier period, on account of her geographical isolation.

In some respects a great advantage, this was, in others, a serious drawback. Almost separated from the whole world, as the Romans said of Britain, she had a magnificent arena in which to grow undisturbed and develop her peculiar culture. The mountains of Thibet rose like a giant breakwater between her and that tide-wave of Western conquest which swept away the coeval empires of Babylon and Persia; while an ocean not yet ploughed by the keels of civilized commerce washed her eastern shore, and a vast expanse of inhospitable plains stretched away to the north. She grew up, of consequence, without a rival—a giant surrounded by pygmies, a pyramid in the midst of molehills. The weak nationalities and wandering tribes by whom she was surrounded rendered her a willing homage, more impressed by the spectacle of her greatness than affected by dread of her military power; and China, on her part, was accustomed to treat them with condescending patronage or disdainful contempt. Thus, when she first became aware of the existence of the great nations of the West, she judged of them by the tribes on her own frontiers; and when they approached her by embassies, she employed towards them the forms and language she had been accustomed to use in dealing with her semi-barbarous neighbors. She assumed a tone of superiority, pronounced them barbarians, and demanded tribute.

For a long time they were too remote to cause her great uneasiness, or to do anything that could materially alter this state of feeling. She saw, it is true, the Russians extending their frontiers from the Ural to Kamtschatka, and England pushing her conquests to the banks of the Irrawaddy. But the fate of scattered nomads and decayed nationalities was no warning to her. Even when those great powers approached her in hostile array, she was still confident of her ability to resist them. Hence the arrogant tone which she assumed in intercourse with them, and, until very recently, continued to maintain.

It was this arrogance that precipitated the Opium war of 1839; and the result did so little to overcome it that in 1856 a display of equal or greater arrogance brought on another collision. For more than three years the Chinese government persisted in applying their old policy to the Anglo-French invaders, still hoping to terminate the conflict by their expulsion rather than by conceding the points in dispute. When, however, their last army had been beaten, their Emperor had fled, and his palace lay in ruins, the Chinese awoke to the reality of their situation. They opened the gates of their capital, and from that day to this no serious thought of trying the issue of another such conflict has crossed the mind of any of their statesmen.

This lesson was decisive—an experience of inestimable value, without which all the attempts of Western nations to benefit the Chinese must have proved like attempting to irrigate the side of a mountain by projecting water from its base.

The effect was immediate. The Chinese were, for the first time, convinced that they had something to learn; and within less than a year from the close of hostilities, large bodies of Chinese troops might have been seen learning foreign tactics under foreign drill-masters, on the very battle-grounds where they had been defeated. Arsenals, well supplied with machinery from foreign countries, were put in operation at four important points, one of them employing as many as nine hundred workmen; and navy-yards were established at two of the principal seaports, where the construction of steam gunboats, entirely by native mechanics, is now going forward.*

But does not all this wear rather an aspect of hostility? Does it not indicate that the Chinese, worsted in the late contest, are preparing for another?

The necessity, we answer, of providing themselves with more efficient means for suppressing their own rebellions is sufficient to account for it. But, after all, the motive is of little consequence—the important fact is that the Chinese are learning. With them the day of bows and arrows, bamboo spears, and lumbering war-junks has passed away, and they intend henceforth to make war like other nations, in a Christian style. They mean to be able to keep the peace within their own borders, and to maintain their self-respect in the face of the world.

But they do not stop here; if they did, there might be ground for suspicion. But they are a pacific people, both from disposition and tradition, using war neither as a pastime nor a business, but resorting to it solely as a matter of necessity. As such they are now learning it, and applying themselves at the same time to the cultivation of the arts of peace.

At three of the open ports they have established schools for the study of the languages and sciences of the West; and, in connection with the arsenal at Shanghai, the mandarins have employed three gentlemen, skilled in the Chinese language, to translate works on science and the useful arts.

These institutions, it might be said, are established at important outposts, under the auspices of provincial viceroys; but they are hardly sufficient to justify the conclusion that the central

* Two other arsenals have since been opened at provincial capitals in the interior—one of them, however, being speedily suppressed by orders from the throne; the other, at Tsinanfu, in Shantung, is described by an English engineer as in successful operation—a fact worth noting, as no foreign hand had any share in its construction. No better proof could be given of the capacity of the Chinese to acquire the arts of the West.

government is adopting an enlightened and liberal policy. But has not the Imperial government at length afforded this evidence by the college which it has established in the capital for the introduction of Western science, and the embassy it has sent forth to cultivate friendly relations with the nations of the West?

The embassy,* and especially the treaties it is now negotiating, are sufficient evidence of liberality in the policy of the government; but the college in which graduates in the schools of Confucius are invited to become pupils is the most undeniable proof of a great intellectual movement.† It was established at the instance of Prince Kung, uncle to the Emperor, and the most influential man in the Empire.

Two memorials of the Prince, one containing the proposal and the other explaining and vindicating it, were laid before his Majesty and published in the official gazette, after receiving the Imperial sanction, constituting them a charter for the new institution. The second of these papers we translate from the pages of the gazette, and here insert, as affording a photograph of the attitude of the Chinese mind in relation to these subjects. Four of the ministers who joined the Prince in presenting it are heads of departments in the government.

"*Memorial of Prince Kung on the Establishment of a College for the Cultivation of Western Science.*

"Your Majesty's servant, and other ministers of the Council

---

* Instead of that "Ecumenical Embassy" with its special objects, we now see permanent Chinese legations established in the principal capitals of the West, and diplomatic intercourse conducted on a basis of reciprocity. In addition, a consular system has been inaugurated, the future extent and influence of which it would be difficult to foretell.

† Since the date of the above this tendency has shown itself in a new direction in the sending of large numbers of youth for education to the United States and other countries, Mr. Yung-wing, himself a graduate of an American college, being a principal leader of the movement.

for Foreign Affairs, on their knees present this memorial in regard to regulations for teaching astronomy and mathematics, and the selection of students.

"These sciences being indispensable to the understanding of machinery and the manufacture of fire-arms, we have resolved on erecting for this purpose a special department in the Tung-wen College, to which scholars of a high grade may be admitted, and in which men from the West shall be invited to give instruction.

"The scheme having met with your Majesty's approval, we beg to state that it did not originate in a fondness for novelties or in admiration for the abstract subtleties of Western science; but solely from the consideration that the mechanical arts of the West all have their source in the science of mathematics. Now, if the Chinese government desires to introduce the building of steamers and construction of machinery, and yet declines to borrow instruction from the men of the West, there is danger lest, following our own ideas, we should squander funds to no purpose.

"We have weighed the matter maturely before laying it before the throne. But among persons who are unacquainted with the subject, there are some who will regard this matter as unimportant; some who will censure us as wrong in abandoning the methods of China for those of the West; and some who will even denounce the proposal that Chinese should submit to be instructed by the people of the West as shameful in the extreme. Those who urge such objections are ignorant of the demands of the times.

"In the first place, it is high time that some plan should be devised for infusing new elements of strength into the government of China. Those who understand the times are of opinion that the only way for effecting this is to introduce the learning and mechanical arts of Western nations. Provincial governors, such as Tsotsungtang and Lehungchang, are firm in this conviction, and constantly presenting it in their addresses to the throne.

The last-mentioned officer last year opened an arsenal for the manufacture of arms, and invited men and officers from the metropolitan garrison to go there for instruction; while the other established in Fuchau a school for the study of foreign languages and arts, with a view to the instruction of young men in ship-building and the manufacture of engines. The urgency of such studies is therefore an opinion which is not confined to us your servants.

"Should it be said that the purchase of fire-arms and steamers has been tried, and found to be both cheap and convenient, so that we may spare ourselves the trouble and expense of home production, we reply that it is not merely the manufacture of arms and the construction of ships that China needs to learn. But in respect to these two objects, which is the wiser course, in view of the future—to content ourselves with purchase, and leave the source of supply in the hands of others, or to render ourselves independent by making ourselves masters of their arts—it is hardly necessary to inquire.

"As to the imputation of abandoning the methods of China, is it not altogether a fictitious charge? For, on inquiry, it will be found that Western science had its root in the astronomy of China, which Western scholars confess themselves to have derived from Eastern lands. They have minds adapted to reasoning and abstruse study, so that they were able to deduce from it new arts which shed a lustre on those nations; but, in reality, the original belonged to China, and Europeans learned them from us. If, therefore, we apply ourselves to those studies, our future progress will be built on our own foundation. Having the root in our possession, we shall not need to look to others for assistance—an advantage which it is impossible to overestimate.

"As to the value to be set on the science of the West, your illustrious ancestor Kanghe gave it his hearty approbation, promoting its teachers to offices of conspicuous dignity, and employing them to prepare the Imperial calendar; thus setting an example of liberality equalled only by the vastness of his all-comprehending wisdom. Our dynasty ought not to forget its own precedents, especially in relation to a matter which occupied the first place among the studies of the ancients.

"In olden times yeomen and common soldiers were all acquainted with astronomy; but in later ages an interdict was put upon it, and those who cultivated this branch of science became few. In the reign of Kanghe, the prohibition was removed and astronomical science once more began to flourish. Mathematics were studied together with the classics, the evidence of which we find in the published works of several schools. A proverb says, 'A thing unknown is a scholar's shame.' Now, when a man of letters, on stepping from his door, raises his eyes to the stars and is unable to tell what they are, is not this enough to make him blush? Even if no schools were established, the educated ought to apply themselves to such studies; how much more so when a goal is proposed for them to aim at?

"As to the allegation that it is a shame to learn from the people of the West, this is the absurdest charge of all. For, under the whole heaven, the deepest disgrace is that of being content to lag in the rear of others. For some tens of years the nations of the West have applied themselves to the study of steam navigation, each imitating the others and daily producing some new improvement. Recently, too, the government of Japan has sent men to England for the purpose of acquiring the language and science of Great Britain. This was with a view to the building of steamers, and it will not be many years before they succeed.

"Of the jealous rivalry among the nations of the Western Ocean it is unnecessary to speak; but when so small a country as Japan is putting forth all its energies, if China alone continues to tread indolently in the beaten track, without a single effort in the way of improvement, what can be more disgraceful than this? Now, not to be ashamed of our inferiority, but, when a measure is proposed by which we may equal or even surpass our neighbors, to object the shame of learning from them, and, forever refusing to learn, to be content with our inferiority—is not such meanness of spirit itself an indelible reproach?

"If it be said that machinery belongs to artisans, and that scholars should not condescend to such employments, in answer to this, we have a word to say. Why is it that the book in the Chowle on the structure of chariots has for some thousands of years been a recognized text-book in all the schools? Is it not because, while mechanics do the work, scholars ought to understand the principles? When principles are understood, their application will be extended. The object which we propose for study to-day is the principles of things. To invite educated men to enlarge the sphere of their knowledge by investigating the laws of nature is a very different thing from compelling them to take hold of the tools of the workingman. What other point of doubt is left for us to clear up?

"In conclusion, we would say that the object of study is utility, and its value must be judged by its adaptation to the wants of the times. Outsiders may vent their doubts and criticisms, but the measure is one that calls for decisive action. Your servants have considered it maturely. As the enterprise is a new one, its principles ought to be carefully examined. To stimulate candidates to enter in earnest on the proposed curriculum, they ought to have a liberal allowance from the public treasury to defray their current expenses, and have the door of promotion set wide open before them. We have accordingly agreed on six regulations, which we herewith submit to the eye of your Majesty, and wait reverently for the Imperial sanction.

"We are of opinion that the junior members of the Hanlin Institute, being men of superior attainments, while their duties are not onerous, if they were appointed to study astronomy and mathematics, would find those sciences an easy acquisition. With regard to scholars of the second and third grades, as also mandarins of the lower ranks, we request your Majesty to open the portals and admit them to be examined as candidates, that we may have a larger number from whom to select men of ability for the public service.

"Laying this memorial before the throne, we beseech the Empresses regent and the Emperor to cast on it their sacred glance, and to give us their instructions."

The Imperial placet is added with the "vermilion pencil." It says, "Let the measures proposed in the memorial be adopted."

This remarkable document shows us the humiliation felt by the Chinese mind to find itself, on awakening, in the rear of the age; and exhibits in an amusing light the sophistical artifices resorted to by the friends of progress to avert the odium which their proposed movement was certain to excite. It shows us the two parties in conflict, and acquaints us with the position occupied by each. The conservatives take their stand within the old intrenchments of pride and prejudice, while their assailants are attempting to dislodge them by the force of arguments drawn from necessity.

The latter are the party in power; and this paper, designed at once to vindicate the action of the government and to refute the narrow views of those who would adhere to the policy of its predecessors, goes forth to the people of the Empire under the seal of their sovereign, and endorsed by governors and viceroys.

The minds that are thus enlightened are few, but they are the most eminent in the State; and when we see the rays of morning glancing on the highest peaks of a mountain-range, we may be sure that it will not be long before the light reaches those of lesser elevation, or penetrates to the valleys that lie between them. Under a government constituted like that of China, an immense advantage lies on the side of those in power. Whatever cause they advocate is sure to be respected by the people; and in this case, convinced that ignorance is the bane of their people, they are in earnest in endeavoring to apply the remedy.

Nor are these enlightened views confined to the heads of the government. An increasing avidity for books of science is perceptible among the literary classes; some of whom contribute liberally for the publication of scientific works, and feel repaid by the honor of having their names associated with the advancement of learning.

To meet this growing taste for real knowledge, the Viceroy of Kiangnan is now bringing out a series of works on scientific subjects, mostly by European authors, employing at a high salary, in the capacity of editor, a learned native who was instructed by English missionaries. One of the works last published is Ricci's translation of Euclid, enlarged by A. Wylie, Esq., late of the London mission. It contains a preface by the last-named gentleman, in which he replies to the common charge that missionaries take advantage of mathematics to propagate Christianity by admitting the fact and setting forth the transcendent value of religious truth. This preface is reprinted entire without the alteration of a word; nor does the viceroy, in the introduction from his own pen, bring forward anything to counteract its influence.

The views of the more advanced members of this scholarly class are well set forth in an essay lately published in a Chinese newspaper by Chang-lu-seng,* a gentleman of wealth and titular rank, who has lately published two small volumes, one on engineering and the other on chemistry.

As a testimony to the scientific labors of missionaries as well as an index of intellectual progress, it is of sufficient value to justify us in translating a few paragraphs. He is discussing a question much mooted among the Chinese, that of the advantages and disadvantages of foreign intercourse.

"Commencing," he says, "with the last years of the Ming dynasty, we opened the seaports of Kwangtung to foreign trade,

* Now 副使, or Vice-minister to Japan.

doing a profitable business in tea and silks, receiving in return fabrics of woollen and cotton suited to our wants; as well as clocks, matches, mirrors, and other articles of luxury. But opium came in at the same time, and its poisonous streams have penetrated to the core of the Flowery Land. The blame of this partly rests on us; but when we go to the root of the evil, it is impossible to exculpate the English from the guilt of originating the traffic."

"Foreigners, with their ships and steamers, have, moreover, monopolized the carrying trade of the sea-coast and the great rivers; throwing thousands of seafaring natives out of employ, and causing great distress."

To the advantage derived from the purchase of foreign arms, from the assistance of foreigners in suppressing the late rebellion, and, above all, from the protection which they extended over the open ports, he does ample justice. Yet in striking a balance-sheet, he still concludes that the "advantages derived from foreign commerce are not sufficient to make amends for the evils to which it has given rise. But the benefits which we derive from the teachings of missionaries are more than we can enumerate."

He then recapitulates the publications of missionaries on scientific subjects, commencing with those of the Jesuit fathers of two centuries ago, and coming down to those of the Protestants of the present day; and closes the catalogue with the remark, "All these are the works of missionaries: they are well adapted to augment the knowledge and quicken the intellect of China. Their influence on our future will be unbounded."

He does not stop with the scientific teachings of missionaries. "China," he says, "is much given to idolatry, which is to us a source of wasteful and foolish practices. Now Christianity teaches men to renounce the worship of idols, in conformity with the maxim of Confucius, 'that he who sins against Heaven will pray in vain to any other.' Should we attend to these instructions, our women would cease to frequent the temples, and we should waste no more money on idolatrous processions. Monasteries would be converted into private residences, and their yellow-capped occupants would not be seen fleecing the people by their deceptions. Their sorceries and charms would be laughed at, and this would indeed be a great gain."

The author of these paragraphs has very little sympathy with the spiritual elements of our holy faith, but, like many of his countrymen, he views it with favor, as a powerful agency, co-operating with the diffusion of science, to emancipate his country from the bondage of superstition.

Such views as these, it is hardly necessary to say, have not yet become the staple of public opinion. The opposition outnumbers the administration, and pamphlets against Christianity and science are more numerous than those in their favor. Still, enough, we think, has been said to show that the tide is turning. Chinese statesmen of both schools recognize the incipient change. Some exert all their influence to check its progress; while others, who describe their illiberal opponents as *tso tsing kwan tien,* "looking at the sky from the bottom of a well," are doing all in their power to help it forward.

There is a word of frequent occurrence in the state-papers of the day which must prove a talisman of might to the progressive party. This is *chunghing,* a term allied in signification to that which we have placed at the head of this article. It relates specifically to dynastic renovations, such as that which occurred in the dynasty of Han, when that illustrious house, reviving after a period of decay, entered afresh on a career of glory. In the present case the Manchu family, which has given to the Empire some of its most distinguished sovereigns, was reduced to the verge of extinction by the combined influence of foreign wars and domestic rebellion. The late Emperor, Hienfung, having fled to Tartary, and died of chagrin and despair, the victorious allies strove with laudable moderation to heal the wounds, so nearly fatal, which they had themselves inflicted; and when his infant son, Tungche, succeeded to the throne, they afforded him both moral support and military aid.

With peace abroad, and no longer any powerful enemy at home, the statesmen of China believe (and they have good grounds for the opinion) that their young Emperor comes to power at a most auspicious epoch. Favored with the friendship of powerful nations, and with sources of power unknown to antiquity placed within his reach, it is possible, as they think, and even probable, that his reign, by the splendor of its intellectual progress, may eclipse the military glory of his most illustrious ancestors. They desire to make the present reign the commencement of a new career, and are constantly exhorting one another to co-operate in the work of renovation. This is what they mean by *chunghing;* and when they seek to effect it by the intellectual regeneration of their people, it acquires the full dignity of a national renaissance.

But is it within the bounds of possibility that such a renaissance should be achieved without the whole empire first passing through a period of disintegration? Is it possible that this ancient people, hoary with years, and bowed beneath a load of traditions, should descend into the fountain of youth and emerge with all the freshness of manhood's prime, without undergoing the painful process of dismemberment and reconstruction? Or must they be cut piecemeal, like Æson of old, and thrown into the seething caldron before they can come forth a renovated people?

This is the great problem of the day, the question of "to be or not to be" in the politics of China. But, however it may be solved, as it relates to the government, the Chinese people must, and will, be renovated. Foreign diplomatists and statesmen feel that a mighty change must pass over the people, sweeping away their old superstitions, unchaining them from the oars of custom, and setting their minds free to labor in productive fields, before they can be qualified to develop the resources of their magnificent patrimony. The most intelligent of them believe that such a change, though gradual in its approach, is certain to take place. Such men as H. B. M. Minister in Peking, whose experience in China dates back a quarter of a century; such men as the chief of the Chinese Embassy, whose experience extends over seven years; and such men as the Inspector-general of Imperial Customs, who has resided in China twice that length of time—all have faith in the future of China, and favor well-devised schemes for the improvement of the Chinese people.*

We have adverted to the encouragement which the advocates of progress among the Chinese derive from a prevailing impression that the present is a time favorable for *chunghing*, or renovation. In addition to this, they have a powerful support in a saying of their Sage, expressed in the first sentence of the *Tahio*, or Great Study, that "it is the prime duty of the sovereign to seek the renovation of his people."

To the renovation of the Chinese people, the most formidable obstacle is the use of opium, a vice of recent growth, for the prevalence of which they have to thank the unscrupulous cupidity of Christian nations. It undermines the physical system, impairs the mental faculties, and smites the moral nature with a kind of paralysis. It impoverishes the individual and the public, and hangs as a dead weight on the prosperity of the State. A little cloud at the commencement of the present century, it has expanded with alarming rapidity, until it casts heavy shadows over the prospect of the future and on the hearts of the well-wishers of China. It threatens to sap the vigor of the Chinese race—a race that has seen the Egyptians and Assyrians laid in their graves, and continued till our own day with unimpaired vitality, sending forth fresh swarms from the old hive to

* The gentlemen referred to are Sir R. Alcock, the Hon. Anson Burlingame, and Robert Hart, Esq. The last named still remains at his important post.

colonize the steppes of Tartary and the islands of the sea, and to compete with European immigration on our own Pacific coast.

But happily an antidote is in the field. The Chinese have not attempted, like the Japanese, to weave their code of international intercourse into a network which shall admit civilization and exclude Christianity.* On the contrary, the government has pledged itself in all its recent treaties to protect the propagators and professors of the Christian religion. Already is Christianity in some localities getting a hold on the popular mind; and though it encounters violent opposition, culminating now and then in a furious outbreak, the Imperial power may at any time be invoked for its defence by the representative of a "Treaty" nation. It is working its way up through the lower strata of society, preparing its triumph from afar, proving itself a moral antiseptic to counteract the growth of corruption; or rather a new principle of life, which will not merely conserve, but renovate, the Chinese race. To this grand result the intellectual movement which it is the special object of this article to indicate will prove itself a powerful auxiliary, like the revival of letters in modern Europe, preparing the way for a work of spiritual reform.

Can this renovation, we again ask, be effected under the sceptre of the reigning house? Without venturing a categorical answer, we only say that many propitious circumstances appear to concur in a remarkable manner.

The present is a minority reign; and the influential men who surround the throne are leaders in a movement to "infuse new elements of strength into the government of China." The Emperor, a lad of thirteen years, may imbibe their spirit and

* How great a change has taken place in the attitude of Japan towards Christianity is apparent from the fact that a large body of missionaries are now engaged in openly and successfully carrying on their work in that country.

shape his policy on theirs; and in a few years, when he takes the reins of power into his own hands, he will receive in person, as by treaty bound, the ambassadors of foreign powers. He will thus have an opportunity of acquiring new ideas, such as his fathers never enjoyed.

The government, though rudely shaken and much exhausted, gives unmistakable signs of convalescence. With its growing superiority in discipline and arms, it can smile at the menaces of border tribes, and hold in check the seeds of domestic revolution. China's greatest danger is from the great powers of the West.

Russia covets her sunny plains and fine harbors, and France would not be averse to accepting China as an offset to British India. But England is too jealous of her great rivals to consent to any encroachment of this nature by either of them. The doctrine of the balance of power, formerly limited in its application to the map of Europe, is now transferred to Eastern Asia; and it is under the shield of this principle alone that either China or Japan can hope to maintain her independence, or to go forward in that career of progress on which both have so auspiciously entered.

NOTE.

Let the reader who may feel inclined to censure as over-sanguine the statements and anticipations of eleven years ago compare them with the following paragraphs, which I copy from an editorial article in the *Shanghai Courier* of January 7, 1880:

"China is moving. She is moving in the path of progress, knowledge, and civilization. The rate of movement may be slow, much slower than her truest friends desire; but the fact is beyond dispute.

"A single illustration will show this. For the first time in the world's history the Chinese flag has lately been seen in the middle of the Pacific. That one fact, viewed in the light of the past, is in some respects more pregnant and suggestive than any which has occurred in connection with this Empire. That the nation which but the other day was content to conduct its commerce by means of the old-fashioned junk, which rarely ventured very far from the shore, should send a steamer across the Pacific, and thus enter into competition with foreigners on what might almost be called their own element, is really an important historical fact.

"But a few years ago China prohibited emigration, while other lands were seeking the services of the industrious Chinamen, and in a way maintaining their right to leave their native land. To-day those same countries are exerting themselves to repel the influx of the yellow race, while China is defending their right to foreign residence and good treatment.

"In nearly all the courts of the civilized world there are representatives of China. Instead of being a feeble power tottering to ruin, and likely to fall a prey to any adventurer, she has shown her ability to crush out the most serious rebellions; and when a Western empire, taking advantage of a temporary weakness, annexed one of her distant provinces, her diplomacy—which, indeed, has rarely failed her—enabled her to obtain its restoration. Instead of being looked upon with contempt as a military power, as a country which a single regiment of skilled soldiers might overrun and hold in subjection, she has come to be considered as a factor not only in Asiatic, but in European, politics; and it would seem that more than one of the most powerful nations of Europe were now courting her as a possible ally in some future momentous struggle. Her long sea-coasts and rivers are buoyed and lighted; some of her coal-mines are being worked under the superintendence of foreign engineers; a short telegraph-line is in successful operation;

a company of native merchants own one of the largest fleets of steamers in the world; and many millions of the natives are clothed with the produce of foreign manufactures.

"We need not pursue the comparison further; for we have, we think, mentioned sufficient to show that China is progressing, that she occupies a very different position to-day to what she did only a few years ago, and that there are indications of still greater changes in the not distant future. That foreign improvements and inventions should not be adopted more readily is to many a matter of disappointment and vexation; but it should not be forgotten that national evolution is a slow process. China has been for some years, and is now, serving a kind of apprenticeship to true civilization; and the knowledge which she is acquiring in various ways she will one day apply to her advantage. The young Chinese who are being trained in foreign systems, whether at home or abroad, and who in time will fill official positions; the thousands who emigrate to foreign countries and return to live in their fatherland; the increasing number of Chinese who are becoming familiar in China with Western modes of life and government; in fact, all ways by which East and West are virtually brought into closer contact, must cause the general, if gradual, adoption of Western ideas; and the adoption of Western ideas means individual liberty, national safety, and increased comfort and prosperity."

APPENDIX

THE WORSHIP OF ANCESTORS IN CHINA.*

RITUAL TENDENCIES OF THE CHINESE.

As the Chinese language has preserved for the student of philology one of the simplest forms of human speech, so in China the investigator of what has been called the science of religion may find certain phases of primitive religion conserved to the present day in a state of arrested development.

This has been effected by the agency of a settled government ruling over the same people for thousands of years, with only occasional interruptions, and these at long intervals; a government which early conceived the idea of ruling by inspiring its subjects with a respect for traditional forms as a substitute for military force. It has been said that the bamboo rules China, but it would be nearer the truth to assert that the Chinese are governed by custom. Among them more than anywhere else, custom has the force of law; and they more than any other people have moulded all the relations of social life into conformity with a complicated code of ritual observances. Etiquette with them becomes a kind of religion, and instead of being restricted to the narrow circle over which, in other countries, fashion reigns supreme, it is made a serious study in all the schools of the land. Sages have not disdained to teach it; and a high court exists, and has existed from the earliest ages, which takes cognizance of all questions relating to official manners, State ceremony, and religious ritual.

* Read before the American Oriental Society in New York, Oct. 28, 1880.

This court is called the Board of Rites, and has nothing answering to it in the political constitutions of the West.

We find it in full operation at the beginning of the third dynasty, B.C. 1150; and the idea of what has been denominated ceremonial government meets us a thousand years earlier in the opening pages of the *Shuking*, a book which presents us with the prologue to the long drama of Chinese history.

The Emperor Shun, after an unsuccessful campaign against a rebellious district, is represented as bringing his refractory subjects to submission by the celebration of a religious pageant in the temple of his ancestors. Later writers say that the monarchs of that halcyon period knew how to employ moral forces in place of physical; or, as they express it, they secured the peace of the Empire by merely displaying their embroidered robes; which means that they maintained in their palaces an imposing ceremonial, and caused their example to be followed as far as possible by officers and people.

A government so wide-awake to the efficacy of the sentiment of reverence as a means for controlling the multitude could not fail to assign a large place to the regulation of religious rites. We are accordingly told in distinct terms that the dynasty of Shang, the second of the great houses which swayed the sceptre over the whole Empire, "employed the worship of the gods as an instrument of government."

What gods were worshipped, and with what rites, in those early days when Moses was going to school to the priests of Memphis, and when Cecrops had not yet landed on the shores of Attica, we are not minutely informed; but in the next era, that of the long dynasty of Chau, B.C. 1150–300, under which the civilization of China was crystallized into its permanent and distinctive shape, we find the national religion consisting of three elements: 1. The worship of Shangti, the Supreme Ruler; 2. The worship of powers supposed to preside over the principal departments of material nature; and 3. The worship of deceased ancestors.

RISE AND PROGRESS OF THE SYSTEM.

The first two of these divisions I shall pass by as not belonging to our present subject, merely observing that they both meet us at the dawn of Chinese history in a much more distinct form than that which is assumed by the worship of ancestors. This is what we should expect from the order of mental development. Man opens his eyes on the external world before he learns to reflect on the phenomena of his own mind. He personifies the forces of nature, and marshals them into a hierarchy under the hegemony of some supreme divinity—"Jehovah, Jove, or Lord"—before he arrives at a conception of his own personal immortality. This done, the idea of a renewed or continued existence in some unseen world in the company of the gods is one which is not slow to rise; suggested, as it is, by a thousand analogies, and gratifying, as it does, our instinctive love of life, and aspirations after progress.

Few tribes have been found so rude as not to have formed some notion of a heaven or hell. The Zulus, prior to their contact with the white settlers of the Cape, were accustomed to account for disturbing dreams and bodily disease by saying that they were troubled by the spirits of their ancestors. The North American Indian expects to rejoin his forefathers in the "happy hunting-ground;" and the rude progenitors of our own race in the wilds of Northern Europe had their courage fired by the promise of a place in Walhalla by the side of Odin. At the dawn of history we find the same belief already rooted in the Chinese mind.

Thus, in the first chapter of the *Shuking*, their earliest historical record, we read the simple statement, "The Emperor died;" but the ideograph by which the notion of death is here expressed, besides being different from the common character, is composed of two parts which convey the idea of being "gathered to one's fathers." The authorized commentary, without referring to etymology, explains it as signifying the return of the physical elements to earth, and the ascent of the spiritual part to heaven. But, not to cite other passages, the traditional view of the ancient Chinese is more clearly indicated by a poet who flourished about the epoch of the Trojan war, who sees in vision Wen-wang, the founder of the house of Chau, promoted to be a ministering spirit in the palace of the Supreme Ruler. Nor is this merely a poetical apotheosis which springs from flattery of the great. Not long after that date, we find it a common belief that children meet their parents in a state of conscious existence in some subterranean Elysium. Thus Chuang-kung, the Duke of Cheng, enraged at the conduct of his mother, who had abetted a conspiracy of his younger brother (another Parysatis favoring another Cyrus), makes a hasty vow that he will never see her face until he meets her under the earth. Repenting his rashness, and longing for reconciliation, he eagerly embraces an expedient for evading the fulfilment of his vow by meeting his mother in a subterranean grotto. Shallow and almost comical as is the artifice by which he imposes on conscience in favor of affection, it points to a national belief as distinctly as does Homer's narrative of Ulysses seeking his father among the Cimmerian shades, or Virgil's story of Æneas's descent into Avernus.

From faith in a future state, the practice of presenting offerings to the dead came into use as a matter of course; nor among the ancient Chinese were the offerings confined to fruits and flowers. At the time when Polyxena was immolated on the tomb of Achilles, it was the custom to despatch a retinue of slaves and favorite concubines to follow the spirit of a prince or noble into the world of shades. This was abolished, we are told, about B.C. 700; and the occasion is thus related:

A prince of one of the feudal states having deceased, his principal wife proposed to give him a magnificent funeral, and to offer an unusual number of men and maidens to accompany his manes. The Prince's brother replied, "If any one is to be sacrificed, your Ladyship shall be the first, for his Highness loved no one better than you." The Princess declined the honor, and the spell of custom was broken forever.

A reminiscence of the cruel rite was, however, long retained in the substitution of effigies made of straw which were buried with the corpse; a trace of it may even be discovered in the present day in the burning of paper images, and perhaps also in the suicide of widows. Against the interment of effigies, Confucius raised an energetic protest, because they bore the semblance of human victims; and now and then a *censor morum* lifts his voice against the self-immolation of Chinese widows; but such acts of conjugal devotion are always rewarded by popular applause, and not unfrequently signalized by marks of Imperial favor.

Considerable amounts of jewelry and treasure are sometimes enclosed in the coffins of the rich; and a premium is thus offered to the commission of what in Chinese law is treated as a capital crime. But in general the Chinese, in making offerings to the dead, have an eye to the wants of the living; of the fruits and meats, enough remains, after their spiritual essence has been enjoyed by the soul of the departed, to provide a feast for the family; and instead of silver and gold, masses of gilt paper are made to do duty; and on passing through the flames they are supposed to be transmuted into the metals which they simulate.

The offerings at the tombs are renewed every spring and autumn; and on fine days the population of a city may be seen pouring forth in all directions, seeking out the sepulchres of their ancestors, and combining religious duty with much-needed recreation. But there is another place where the offerings are more frequent. This is the ancestral temple. Here the deceased are represented, not by images or pictures, but by slips of wood inscribed with their names. Tablets representing near relatives are preserved in a shrine in the family residence. Those common to a clan or tribe are honored with a temple of more or less extent, according to the wealth of the community.

Before these memorial tablets every member of the household prostrates himself at least twice a month—viz., at the new and full moon. Every important event affecting the family is solemnly announced to the ancestors; marriages are solemnized in their presence; and a new bride presents offerings to her husband's ancestors in token of adoption into their family.

RELATION TO THE SAN KIAO, OR THREE RELIGIONS.

Such, in outline, is the system of ancestral worship, which constitutes the central division, and, as it were, the very heart, of the religion of China. The Supreme Ruler is too august to be approached by ordinary mortals. As to other divinities, their worship is incumbent only on priests or magistrates; but the worship of ancestors is obligatory upon all. They are the penates of every household. To honor them is religion; to neglect them the highest impiety.

We have seen how usages of this kind spring as naturally as the grass from the graves of the deceased; and that in ancient times the funeral rites of the Chinese differed little from those of other nations. That by which they are justly distinguished is that, instead of suffering them to be overshadowed by polytheism, they alone have shaped their offices for the dead into an all-pervading and potent cult which moulds the social and spiritual life of every individual in the Empire.

Spontaneous in its origin, in its progressive development it is the slow growth of thirty centuries. It is probable that it was practised in the Golden Age of Chinese history, two thousand years before the Christian era; and in the rites of Chow, a thousand years later, we find it reduced to a precise and complicated code; but it was not so stereotyped as to be incapable of further alteration. It was then disfigured by grotesque ceremonies, the reproduction of which at the present day would be regarded as hardly less shocking than the restoration of human sacrifices—I allude particularly to that curious arrangement by which a solemn act of religion was converted into a ridiculous masquerade—young children being made to personate their ancestors, and, habited in ghostly costume, receiving the homage of their own parents. Nor was it then clothed with the imperious authority which it now exercises. In the life of Confucius we find recorded the remarkable fact that when arrived at manhood he was ignorant of the burial-place of his father, who had died when he was an infant, and it was not until the death of his mother that he took pains to ascertain it. This indicates a degree of laxity which would not be possible at the present day, when semi-annual offerings are required to be made at the tombs of ancestors.

Yet it is to Confucius more than to any other man that China is indebted for the strictness with which the rites of this worship are now universally observed. Making filial piety the corner-stone of his ethical system, and only vaguely recognizing the personality of the supreme power, whom he styles *Tien*, or Heaven, he was led to seek in the worship of ancestors for the religious sanctions required to confirm it. "If," said he, "funeral rites are performed with scrupulous care, and remote ancestors duly recognized, the virtues of the people will be strengthened." This is a maxim which lies at the foundation of the religious polity of the Chinese Empire.

The more objectionable features in ancestral worship are not due to Confucius, and derive no sanction from his authority; I mean the belief in an active interest taken by the deceased in the fortunes of their posterity, which leads to their virtual deification, and the absurd doctrine that the destinies of the family are determined by the location of the family tombs.

The first of these springs so readily from the human heart that it is unnecessary to look for its origin in the teachings of any particular school. It is touching to read on a tombstone that a mourning family, having laid an aged parent in his last resting-place, beseech his spirit to hover over them as a protecting power. But the Chinese are not so taught by Confucius, who, when interrogated as to the survival of the soul, refused to admit that it possesses any conscious existence after the death of the body; and who, while exhorting to sincerity in sacrifices, went no further than to say, "Sacrifice to the spirits *as if* they were present."

The other tenet is derived from *fung-shui*, or geomancy, the debasing offshoot of a degenerate Taoism. This false science, which bears to geology a relation similar to that which astrology bears to astronomy, assumes the existence of certain influences connected with the configuration of the surface which affect the destinies of the inhabitants of any given locality. These must be taken account of in selecting the site of a dwelling-house, a school, a shop, or even a stable, and especially a burial-place. So strong is the conviction on this last point that families who are overtaken by a series of misfortunes are often persuaded to exhume the bones of their forefathers, and shift them, perhaps more than once, to a new location, in hopes of hitting on the focus of auspicious influences. This superstition is even carried into the domain of politics; so that the government, on suppressing a rebellious *emeute*, has been known to order the destruction of the family tombs of the rebel chief, in order to strike at what is supposed to be the fountain-head of the disturbing influence.

Buddhism has also exerted a profound influence on the worship of ancestors, strengthening, as it has done, the instinctive faith in a future state, and introducing an elaborate liturgy for the repose of the departed.

RELATION TO SOCIAL ORDER.

After the rapid sketch which we have now given of the rise of ancestral worship, and its relation to the Three Religions, it may be worth while to inquire what influence it has exerted on the civilization of China. If we were to attempt an answer in a single sentence, we should say, it has been deeper than that of all other religions combined. It forms the essence of the State religion; and while other religious systems are simply tolerated, this alone is inculcated by Imperial authority.

The Imperial house sets the example in what it regards as the highest form of filial piety. Not only are separate shrines erected for the ancestors of the reigning family; the Emperor, according to immemorial usage, even associates them with Shangti, the Supreme Ruler, in the sacrifices which, as high-priest of the Empire, he makes at the Temple of Heaven.

The visitor who is fortunate enough to gain access to an azure-colored pagoda on the north of the principal altar may see there a tablet inscribed with the name of Shangti occupying the central place of honor, while the tablets of ten generations of the reigning family are ranged on the right and left. Three of these never set foot in China, nor in any proper sense can they be said to have occupied the Imperial throne.

Two of them reigned in Liaotung, over a single province, and one was the chief of a roving tribe in the wilds of Manchuria; yet on the occupation of China by their descendants, they were all canonized or raised by Imperial decree to the dignity of Emperor.

This tendency of the stream of honor to flow upwards is peculiar to China. There alone is it possible for a distinguished son to lift his deceased parents out of obscurity, and to confer on their names the reflected lustre of his own rank.

It is not easy for us to understand the force of the motive which is thus brought to bear on a generous mind nurtured under the influence of such traditions. *Kwang-tsung-yau-tsu*, "Be careful to reflect glory on your forefathers," is a hortatory formula, addressed alike to the soldier on the battle-field and the student in the halls of learning.

If, as President Hayes asserted in a recent speech at San Francisco, "those who show the greatest respect for their ancestors are most likely to be distinguished by their regard for posterity," the Chinese ought to excel all men in that sentiment, so essential to the well-being of a State; certain it is that their worship of ancestors fosters the sentiment in a most effectual manner.

The man who worships his forefathers, and believes in their conscious existence, naturally desires to leave offspring who shall keep the fires burning on the family altar, and regale his own spirit with periodical oblations. Mencius accordingly lays it down as a maxim that "of the three offences against filial piety, the greatest is to be childless"—a dictum which has contributed not a little to promote the practice of early marriage, and the consequent enormous expansion of the population of China. Viewed in this latter aspect, the reflex influence of ancestral worship may be considered as a doubtful boon; but as to the underlying sentiment, were it wisely directed to providing for the welfare of coming generations as well as to bringing them into existence, its beneficial effects would be of inestimable value.

The worship of ancestors strengthens the ties of kinship, and binds together those family and tribal groups on which the government so much relies for the control of its individual subjects. The family temple serves for a church, theatre, school-house, council-room, and indeed for all the varied objects required by the exigencies of a village community. Domains attached to it for the maintenance of the sacrifices are held as common property; and glebe-lands are often appended which are devoted to the support of needy members of the widely extended connection. I have seen a town of twenty-five thousand people, all belonging to the same clan, and bearing the same family name. A conspicuous edifice near the centre bore the name of *She-tsu-miao*, i. e. temple of our first ancestor. Here the divergent branches of the family tree met in a common root; and all the citizens, under the cloud of incense arising from a common sacrifice, were led to feel the oneness of their origin; though separated, it might be, by half a millennium. Such a village resembles the growth of a banyan-tree—the most distant column in the living arcade, though resting on a root of its own, still maintaining a vital connection with the parent stock.

Aside from its social and economic relations, this form of worship exerts a religious and moral influence beyond any other system of doctrines hitherto known to the Chinese Empire. In a sceptical world, and through ages not favored with that revelation which has "brought life and immortality to light," it has kept alive the faith in a future life. The orthodox son of Han regards himself as living and acting in the sight of his ancestors. He refers his conduct to their supposed judgment, and the comfort of his dying hour is largely determined by the view he takes of the kind of welcome he is likely to receive when he meets the shades of his forefathers.

"How could I look my ancestors in the face if I should consent to such a proposition?" is a reply which many an officer has given to a temptation to betray his trust. A motive which has such power to deter from baseness may also be potent as a stimulus to good; indeed, in respect to moral efficacy it would appear to be only second to that of faith in the presence of an all-seeing Deity. How effective it must be may be inferred from the fact that a Chinaman bent on wounding his adversary in the keenest point curses, not the obnoxious individual, but his ancestors; because respect for them is the deepest of all his religious sentiments.

RELATION TO CHRISTIANITY.

In conclusion, the spectacle of a great nation with its whole population gathered round the altars of their ancestors, tracing their lineage up to the hundredth generation, and recognizing the ties of kindred to the hundredth degree, is one that partakes of the sublime. It suggests, moreover, two questions of no little interest: 1. May there not be some feature in the Chinese system which we might with advantage engraft on our Western civilization? 2. In propagating Christianity in China, what attitude ought missionaries to assume towards that venerable institution?

If it be objected that a sufficient answer to both is found in the tendency of ancestral worship to fetter progress by pledging men to the imitation of the past, we reply that such an effect is by no means necessary; that Chinese conservatism is due to other causes, and that men of the present generation may gratefully acknowledge their obligations to the past, while conscious that they themselves constitute the highest stage in the skyward column of our growing humanity. The Vrilya, we are told in the instructive romance of Lord Lytton, with all their advanced ideas, still preserved with reverence the portraits of their early ancestors who had not yet attained the human shape.

But the question of adopting such an institution is quite distinct from that of uprooting it from a soil in which it has been prolific of blessings. Is it merely one of the many phases of pagan religion, which, however they may have subserved the cause of morality in a twilight age, must be regarded as purely obstructive in the light of Christian day, or may we not recognize in it some element of permanent good worthy to survive all changes in the national faith? As a matter of fact, all missionary bodies, the Jesuits excepted, have taken the former view. Perceiving unmistakable evidence that filial-reverence had grown into idolatrous devotion, and memorial tablets become converted into objects of idolatrous homage, they have declared war against the entire system.

It is, I confess, a suspicious circumstance to find the Jesuits tolerating the traditional rites, while Dominican and Franciscan, Greek and Protestant, all concur in rejecting them. Yet I cannot bring myself to feel that the latter have been wholly right, or the former altogether wrong. Had the policy of the Jesuits been followed, the adherents of the Church of Rome might have been spared a century of persecution, and it is probable that the religion of India might have been supplanted by that of Europe; for nothing has ever aroused such active opposition to Christianity as the discovery that it stands in irreconcilable antagonism to the worship of ancestors. The decision of the Sovereign Pontiff committing his Church to this position reminds us of the unfortunate reply of a Saxon missionary to Radbod, the King of Friesland. The King, with one foot in the baptismal font, as a last question, asked the missionary whether he must think of his ancestors as in heaven or in hell. "In hell," was the reply. "Then I shall go with my fathers," exclaimed the King, as he drew back and refused the Christian rite. Millions of Chinese on the brink of a Christian profession have been held back by a similar motive.

The question, I admit, is one of duty, not of expediency. Yet, in view of all our obligations to truth and righteousness, there appears to me to be no necessity for placing them in this cruel dilemma. The idolatrous elements involved in ancestral worship are, as we have seen, excrescences, and not of the essence of the system. Why not prune them off and retain all that is good and beautiful in the institution? A tablet inscribed with a name and a date is in itself a simple memorial not more dangerous than the urns of ashes which cremationists are supposed to preserve in their dwellings, and not half so much so as pictures and statues: why should the native convert be required to surrender or destroy it? The semi-annual visit to the family cemetery is a becoming act of respect to the dead: why should that be forbidden? As to offerings of meats and drinks, why should they not be replaced by bouquets of flowers, or the periodical planting of flower-seeds and flowering shrubs? Even the act of prostration before the tomb or tablet can hardly be regarded as objectionable in a country where children are required to kneel before their living parents.

That which is really objectionable is geomancy and the invocation of departed spirits. The simplest ideas of science are sufficient to dispel the one form of superstition, and a very small amount of religious knowledge supplies an effectual antidote to the other. The worship of ancestors would thus be restored to the state in which Confucius left it, or rather to that in which he himself practised it—as merely a system of commemorative rites.

Whatever party takes this position will have an immense advantage in the competition for proselytes. Missionaries may never accept it. They may even, in combating ancestral worship, believe themselves to be like St. Boniface, felling the trees that shelter the spirit of idolatry, instead of, as we think, clearing away those forests that are necessary to the fertility and beauty of the land. But the native Church cannot be expected to follow servilely in the footsteps of its foreign leaders. When the higher classes come to embrace Christianity in great numbers, they will readily leave behind them their Buddhism and their Taoism; but the worship of ancestors they will never consent to abandon, though they may submit to some such modifications as those which I have endeavored to indicate.

SECULAR LITERATURE.*

(Viewed as a Missionary Agency.)

In those good old days when ready wit and prompt expression were more prized in the pulpit than they are in this age of written sermons, it was the custom in the Kirk of Scotland to serve a candidate with a text just as he rose to deliver his trial discourse. On one such occasion, the youthful preacher received instead of a text only a slip of blank paper. Holding it up before his audience, and turning it slowly round, he exclaimed, "On this side there is nothing, and on that side there is nothing, and *out of nothing God made the world.*"

In undertaking to discuss the subject of "secular literature"† assigned me by the committee, I find myself in a similar predicament. While there is no room to complain that there is nothing on this side and nothing on that, the subject is so polyhedral that the writer is altogether in doubt as to the aspects under which he is expected to treat it.

Is it native literature or foreign literature? Is it extant, or only existing in the possibilities of the future? These and many more such questions are suggested by the studied ambiguity of the proposed theme—a theme which involves no proposition; a subject without a predicate! I run no risk, however, in con-

* This paper was written, by request, for the General Conference of Missionaries which met in Shanghai, May, 1877. It is reproduced here, not to show the present state of the Chinese, but to indicate what remains to be done to impart a new stimulus to their intellectual life.

† The subject as given was expressed in the two words that stand at the head of this page.

cluding that the subject was intended to be of a practical character, and to have a bearing on the great question of missionary duty.

This, then, is the sense in which I shall understand it—viz., as affording a basis for the inquiry, To what extent is it desirable that missionaries should endeavor to contribute to the creation of a new secular literature for China?

The literature in question is, I would premise, understood to be a Christian literature, notwithstanding the descriptive prefix "Secular." Not professedly religious, it is, or ought to be, leavened with religion, as the atmosphere is impregnated with ozone; not as an extraneous element, but as something evolved from itself, endowed with a higher energy, and enhancing its salutary influence.

So far, however, is the secular literature of the most favored nations of Christendom from realizing our ideal in point of purity and spiritual elevation that we sometimes doubt the propriety of calling it Christian. But bring it into comparison with the literature of a heathen people, and mark how it glows with the warm light of a higher world.

Whence, for example, come those noble sentiments which pervade every branch of our literature—law, philosophy, poetry, fiction, and history? The sentiment of the brotherhood of mankind, so effective in checking oppression and promoting international justice—whence comes it, but from that Gospel which teaches us that "God made of one blood all nations for to dwell on all the face of the earth?" That sense of responsibility which extends to the minutest affairs of daily life, and inspires the sublimest achievements of heroism—making "duty" a watchword in the day of battle—whence comes it but from those lessons of responsibility to a higher power which constitute the Alpha and the Omega of the Christian system?

Again, the idea of rights as correlative to obligations, if not peculiar to Christianity, belongs at present exclusively to the moral and political systems of Christendom. In China the conception is wanting, and the language contains no word for its expression.

Finally, while self-sacrifice for the good of others is not only taught, but beautifully illustrated, in some of the religions of the pagan world, it was reserved for Christianity to give it a place in the hearts and homes of mankind—teaching the humblest of them to cherish the spirit and imitate the example of its Divine Founder. Such are some of the golden threads which the fingers of religion have wrought into the tissue of our Western thought, and they sparkle on every page of our standard literature.

M. Troplong,* a learned jurist of France, has shown how Christianity infused itself into the body of Roman law, and thence passed into the jurisprudence of Europe. Chateaubriand,† in his eloquent pages, points out how it inspires modern art, and fills the domain of taste and imagination with new elements of spiritual beauty.

Christianity has made epic poetry almost exclusively her own, inspiring her Dantes, her Miltons, and her Klopstocks to sing of spiritual conflicts in loftier strains than those which describe the barbarous wars of ancient Greece. Cowper, Wordsworth, and Coleridge breathe the very essence of Christianity, and even Shakespeare is full of it. No one can fail to perceive that though he had "little Latin and less Greek," he was a diligent student of the English Bible. What a precious little Gospel he compresses into three lines when he speaks of

> "Those holy fields,
> Over whose acres walked those blessed feet
> Which fourteen hundred years ago were nailed,
> For our advantage, on the bitter cross!"

Goethe's Faust deals with the great problem of human probation; and though he drew his subject from mediæval legends, those legends were founded on the allegory of the Book of Job.

* *L'Influence du Christianisme sur le Droit Civil des Romains.*

† *Génie du Christianisme.*

The latest poem but one from the pen of England's laureate is religious, or, more properly, theological; and one of the latest compositions of the laureate of the other hemisphere, the Divine Tragedy, is merely a versification of the Gospel history.

Of the poet it may be said that, laboring under the influence of a kind of inspiration, "Himself from God he cannot free"* —he must be religious or irreligious; and, according to the circumstances of his age, pagan or Christian. But there is no such necessity laid on the historian, who may, if he choose, marshal his facts in the spirit of the positive philosophy, and leave the nations to work out their own destiny, independent of what is called providential control. Yet, in general, writers of this class have not failed to recognize the hand of God in the rise and fall of empires; Cicero makes his doubting Academic admit its presence in great affairs of national moment, though he denies its extension to the interests of the individual man. Let two of the most eminent speak for their order.

Says M. Guizot,† "In the very nature of human reason, and of the relations of the human race to it, lies the idea of the destination of the race for a supermundane and eternal sphere. . . . It is equally clear that humanity can realize the idea of social perfection only as a rational society by the union and brotherhood of the human family. How far it may be the intention of Divine Providence that the human race shall realize this perfection, it may be impossible to determine. Certain it is that it can never be brought about by any mere political institutions: only Christianity can effect this universal brotherhood of nations, and bind the human family together in a rational, i.e. a free, moral society."

Says Mr. Bancroft,‡ "That God rules in the affairs of men is as certain as any truth of physical science. . . .

---

* Emerson. † History of Civilization.

‡ Discourse on the Character of President Lincoln.

"Eternal wisdom marshals the great procession of the nations, working in patient continuity through the ages; never halting and never abrupt; encompassing all events in its oversight; and even effecting its will, though mortals may slumber in apathy or oppose with madness."

So much for history. Time would fail me to indicate how completely the entire body of our higher philosophy is pervaded with a spirit of religion, which in general, if not always, is distinctively Christian.

Waiving, then, further illustrations, such is the religious character even of the secular literature of Christendom—a literature which, with all its imperfections, is the fitting expression of the intellectual life of a Christian people; and such is my idea of the new secular literature which we desire to see springing up on the soil of China.

If the missionary can do aught to bring about this result, who will dare to assert that his efforts are misdirected? The missionary, it will be said, is already laboring to bring about this result, and that in the most effective way.

This I admit in a general sense. I would not have him, like one of the early fathers, expend his energies in the vain attempt to produce Christian plays which shall supersede the profane productions of the pagan stage. Nor would I have him, under the impulse of religious zeal, intrude into certain other departments to which the taste of a native and native genius are the only passports. Works of that kind—*nascuntur, non fiunt*—will spring up spontaneously when the soil is once prepared. Columba and Augustine were predecessors of Shakespeare and Milton; and in this country, whatever works most efficiently for the implanting of Christian thought in the heart of the nation will also lead most speedily to the growth of a secular literature which shall be Christian in its essential characteristics.

But are there not other departments of literary effort within the general field described as *secular* from which the missionary is not debarred by any such irreversible decree of nature, and which he is impelled to enter in order to insure the success of his leading enterprise?

That there are such will, no doubt, be conceded by the great majority of the members of this Conference; and what they are I shall endeavor to indicate in the sequel of this paper. In the meantime, permit me to dispose of a familiar objection, which grows out of a narrow interpretation of the great commission, and fortifies itself by the citation of honored but inappropriate examples. The missionary, it is said, is sent forth to *preach*, and, like St. Paul, he should know nothing beyond the special subject of his mission.

Those who urge this objection appear to forget that, in the lapse of ages, the relations of the Church to the heathen world have undergone a complete revolution. In the days of St. Paul, the followers of Christ were few and despised; now they are numerous and powerful, and hold in their hands the destinies of the nations of the earth. Then they were less cultivated than those to whom they were sent, and had but one book to give to mankind. Now it is they who stand upon the higher plane and have possession of the keys of knowledge. They are no longer armed with the power of miracles; but are they not clothed with other powers which may be made to serve as an ample substitute in the way of attesting and enforcing their principal message?

When they go to the savage tribes of Africa, or to the still ruder savages of the southern seas, their superiority is at once recognized.

The unlettered native worships as a fetich the chips of wood which the missionary has taught to talk by means of mysterious marks which he has traced on their surface. They are welcomed as the apostles of civilization, and no narrow prejudice has ever been permitted to deter them from instructing the natives in the arts of civilized life.

In this country we meet with a very different reception; we come to a people who were highly civilized before our forefathers had emerged from barbarism—a people who still assume, tacitly or openly, that they occupy a position of unquestionable superiority. Here, therefore, more than anywhere in the world, do we need to avail ourselves of every circumstance that may help to turn the scale. We are required to prove our commission to teach men spiritual things by showing our ability to instruct them in worldly matters.

It was observed by one of the Jesuit fathers, a long time ago, that the Chinese were so advanced in culture that there was nothing in which Europeans could claim pre-eminence save the knowledge of mathematical science and the verities of the Christian faith.

The advantages derived from these two sources have been rendered all the more conspicuous by the marvellous progress of the last three centuries; and where, I ask, is the necessity of renouncing those of the one class in order to communicate the other? Who can doubt that the melancholy fact that the Nestorian missions appear to have sunk like a stone in the mighty waters, without leaving so much as a ripple on the surface, was mainly owing to the circumstance that their civilization was of a lower type than that of China? On the other hand, is it not equally evident that it is to the learned labors of her early missionaries, more than to anything else, that the Catholic Church owes her strong foothold in this Empire? The lesson is obvious. In the work of converting the nations, religion and science are, or ought to be, a wedded pair, each lending its aid to the other; and what God hath joined together, let man not put asunder.

This brings me to point out those departments in which it is not only possible, but almost imperative, for the missionary to make contributions to the secular literature of the land we live in. They may be considered under three general heads:

1. History and geography.

2. The mathematical and physical sciences.

3. The mental and social sciences.

Books of the first class, however secular in character, may fairly be regarded as an indispensable preparation for the propagation of the Gospel. For every fact, to borrow the language of geometrical analysis, requires the aid of two co-ordinates to determine its position. These are time and place, history and geography; and without these, the statements of the Gospel narrative would be as vague as objects floating in space, which the eye is unable to refer to any definite distance, or compare with any certain standard of magnitude.

So generally is this recognized that missionaries have, in fact, made sundry efforts to supply the desiderata in both divisions. A sketch of general or universal history was prepared by the late Dr. Gutzlaff; but it was left in such a meagre, imperfect state that I am glad to be able to announce that two distinct enterprises in the same direction are now in progress—one based on the work of the German professor Weber, the other on that of the English historian Tytler.

Of particular histories, I may mention that of the United States, by Dr. Bridgman; and a history of England, by a living missionary.* Both, if I mistake not, have enjoyed the honorable distinction of being reprinted in Japan. But what are these among so many? There are at least a score of other nations, ancient and modern, who have acted, or are now acting, conspicuous parts in the great march of humanity; and all these are waiting for the muse of history to inspire some competent pen to make them known to the Chinese, and to emphasize the providential lesson of their national life.

In geography, the first place is due to the excellent work of the late Seu Keyu, a former governor of Fuhkien. Combining

* The Rev. W. Muirhead, London Miss. Soc.

historical notices with topographical description, and full of valuable information expressed in the choicest style (though equally replete with minor blemishes), it produced a marked sensation on its first appearance, nearly thirty years ago; and its influence has gone on extending to the present hour. Its liberal and appreciative views of foreign countries are reputed to have occasioned the dismissal of the author from the public service; and the same qualities caused him to be recalled after a retirement of eighteen years, and made a member of the Board of Foreign Affairs, by whose authority an edition of his book was published in Peking.

My apology for mentioning this work, if it required any, would be found in the fact that in his introduction the author refers in terms of high commendation to the Rev. Dr. Abeel, as the chief source of his information. Does any one imagine that, fervent and devoted as he was, the direct evangelistic labors of the lamented missionary were ever half as effective as those spare half-hours which he placed at the service of the inquisitive mandarin?

Three smaller works on this subject have been prepared and published by missionaries, not to mention several in provincial dialects. Of these, two* are composed in such a style as to commend themselves to general readers; and they have both enjoyed a wide popularity.

But no one has thus far so hit the mark as to matter and manner as to supersede the necessity of further efforts in the same line. The sketching of physical characteristics is comparatively easy; but the delineation of the varying phases of civilization is a task of great delicacy, and one which, if well performed, cannot fail to exert a profound influence.

In astronomy and mathematics, all honor is due to the labors of the Catholic missionaries. But how much remains to be

---

* By the Rev. W. Muirhead and the Rev. R. Q. Way.

done may be inferred from the fact, for which those pioneers of Western science are partly answerable, that in the official text-books the earth still occupies the centre of the universe; and that other fact, for which they are not responsible, that the Imperial calendar continues to be encumbered by the rubbish of mediæval astrology.

For the only considerable work on what we may call modern astronomy, the Chinese are indebted to a Protestant missionary,* who has also given them a pretty full course of modern mathematics, including the higher branches of analytical geometry and the infinitesimal calculus.

The worthy author of these excellent translations would be the last to claim a monopoly of the field; and to me it appears that there is still room for a double series of works on the same subjects—one of them simple and popular, the other more complete and extensive.

When the literary corporation becomes inoculated with a love of exact science, the most salutary reforms may be anticipated in the general character of the national education; but not until the new astronomy succeeds in expelling the earth from the place which belongs to the sun can we expect their earth-born pantheon to yield the throne to the rightful Sovereign of the Universe.

As to the other branches of physical science new to the Western world, it is but a few years since their very names were unknown to the Chinese. Yet already are there indications that China is swinging to the tide—a tide which no anchor of Oriental conservatism will ever be able to resist. On these subjects we cannot have too many books, provided they are good ones.

It is to the diffusion of just ideas as to the laws of nature by means of scientific publications that we are to look for the abolition of that degrading system of geomancy which never fails

* A. Wylie, Esq., London Miss. Soc.

to throw its shapeless form athwart the pathway of material progress.

It is from the same influence, and from that only, that we are to expect the extinction of popular panics and judicial executions connected with a superstitious belief in witchcraft.

The sad tragedy of Tientsin witnesses to the danger of the one; and at least four heads—one that of a woman—which have fallen under the axe of the executioner within the last four years testify to the disgrace of the other.

It was science, and not religion, that broke the power of such delusions among our own people; rendering impossible a repetition of the horrible scenes in which good men like Sir Matthew Hale and Dr. Cotton Mather earned an unenviable notoriety. In this connection I cannot forbear paying a passing tribute to those periodicals, monthlies and dailies, scientific and popular, which are now so actively employed in disseminating the hellebore required by the national mind.

Medical science, in particular, strikes at the roots of a host of superstitious errors; and it is not easy to overestimate the value of the books which our medical missionaries, in the midst of their philanthropic labors, have found time to prepare and publish.

As yet, however, they are only on the threshold of their work. Their mission will not be complete until the present generation of unlicensed empirics shall be superseded by a native faculty well versed in all the arts and sciences that belong to their profession.

The group of sciences which I have comprehended under the general designation of mental and social occupies a border-land so close on the confines of religion that one is surprised to find it almost as untrodden as the arctic snows. Practical ethics have, of course, not been neglected; and certain metaphysical speculations have also come forward in connection with topics of theology; but the scientific treatment of any one in the whole circle is still a desideratum.

Indeed, native scholars are apt to insinuate that the whole domain of what they call *singli* is in our Western literature a barren waste; a suspicion which, while it flatters their own pride, enables them to treat with patronizing disdain a style of learning whose highest fruit they consider to be the production of a cunning artificer.

In the face of such a charge, what is more natural than that we should feel a desire to vindicate the credit of our Christian culture—to show the sceptical followers of Chufutse that we are familiar with subtleties of thought which their language, with all its boasted refinement, is powerless to express?

But there is a higher motive for taking up the gage; I mean the influence exercised by writers in this department over the weightier interests of human society. The cloudy heights of speculation may, indeed, appear to be cold and barren; yet from them issue streams which sweep over the lower plains of human life like a desolating flood, or, like the Nile, diffuse beauty and abundance.

In the ancient world, the triumph of Epicurus was fatal to the liberties of Rome. In modern France, the guillotine reaped the harvest sown by the hands of an atheistic philosophy. After the restoration of the Stuarts, the materialism of Hobbes strengthened the tyranny and encouraged the excesses of a dissolute court; nor can it be doubted that the Scotch philosophy of common-sense contributed much to impart that intelligent sobriety which characterizes the British mind.

It will be a sad day for Germany when men of the stamp of Schopenhauer are accepted as masters in her schools of philosophy.

The Sung philosophers have made a far more complete conquest of China than the Encyclopædists did of France—the speculative atheism which, after the lapse of a thousand years, still steeps the educated mind of this country being mainly derived from that source.

Books on these subjects, if well composed, would command the attention of the leading classes in the Empire. A good treatise on the analysis of the mental powers would call them away from groping among the mists of ontology, and teach them to interrogate the facts of their own consciousness; astonishing them not less by revealing to them their hitherto unsuspected mental anatomy than works of another class do by unveiling the structure of their physical frame. The grand corollary would be the nature and destiny of the human soul. A treatise on formal logic would scarcely prove less fascinating by its novelty, or less revolutionary in its effect? On this point *fas est ab hoste*, etc. The late Mr. J. S. Mill informs us that his father warned him against making any open attack on the Christian faith, as likely to prove abortive and to recoil upon his own head; but suggested that a successful assault might be made from the masked batteries of a work on logic.

With Christianity this method has been tried, and without any serious result; but a missile which rebounds harmless from the plates of an iron-clad will crush through the timbers of a wooden junk. It is certain that the medley of incompatible opinions which make up the creed of a Confucianist, however formidable when approached from without, could not long hold out against the force of logical principles applied from within. In a word, with the learned classes, anything which tends to show them how to investigate their own mental processes, to weigh arguments and try evidence, cannot fail to contribute powerfully to their abandonment of error and adoption of truth.

In the field of political economy, soil was broken some five-and-twenty years ago by the publication of a small brochure under the auspices of the Morrison school.* Thus far this effort has not been followed up; and yet a weighty writer in the *Fortnightly Review*, referring to the late centennial of the

* By the Rev. S. R. Brown, D.D., late of Japan.

Wealth of Nations, does not hesitate to affirm that "political economy has contributed to the wealth of England a hundred-fold more than any other science."

Dr. Chalmers, though the first preacher in Europe, did not disdain to write a book on political economy; and in America, Dr. Wayland, alike eminent as a scholar and a pulpit orator, also prepared a text-book on the same subject. A science which so conspicuously improves the temporal well-being of all classes must of necessity promote their higher interests.

While on this branch of the subject, I cannot refrain from expressing the pleasure I have had in perusing two books from the pen of a German missionary—one of them a view of the educational institutions of Germany, the other a discourse on civilization. Both are calculated to make a decided impression on native scholars, though the latter may perhaps awaken a feeling of resentment by the severity of its criticism, appearing to assert superiority without proving it; while the former proves it without advancing any such irritating claim.

Not only is it desirable that the learned classes of China should be made acquainted with the educational institutions of the West, it is of equal importance that they should obtain some idea of the nature and extent of our polite literature. The only satisfactory way for them to arrive at this is by learning to read it. Yot if the missionary, in the intervals of more serious work, would now and then translate a poem like Pope's Essay on Man, or a prose composition like some of the best of Johnson or Addison, the effect could hardly be otherwise than happy—*especially on the translator.*

In conclusion, we have taken a kind of balloon voyage over a wide region, in the course of which we have seen how the land lies without pausing to map down its minute features. We have given no names of living authors, and no catalogue of books; our sole object being to ascertain in what departments of secular authorship a missionary may engage with most advantage to the great cause. Already is the triumph of that cause foreshadowed by what a secular writer describes as a "tendency towards homogeneity of civilization."*

Japan has openly adopted the Western type; and China, without committing herself, is slowly moving in the same direction. The growing demand for books on scientific subjects is but one among many signs which point to an approaching intellectual revolution.

This demand, it is true, the government is endeavoring to supply at its own expense; and many excellent works are produced by the translators whom it employs. But there is, as we have shown, still room for the missionary, and a call for his labors in this department which scarcely anything but conscious inability would justify him in declining. He can hardly stop for a night in a city of the interior without some of its best inhabitants applying to him for books of science and for instruction on scientific subjects. Is it wise to turn a deaf ear to such appeals for intellectual food? Can the missionary afford to do so without losing prestige as a representative of liberal culture? His preaching will lose nothing in its power by the consecration of a portion of his time to such scientific and literary labors as lie outside of the beaten path of pulpit duty.

In view of the intellectual movement now beginning to show itself all over this Empire, I would urge upon missionary societies

---

* The phrase in the text is due, I believe, to a writer in the *Edinburgh Review*. A similar expression occurs in the 7th article of the original draft of what is known as the Burlingame Treaty, drawn up, not as generally supposed by Mr. Burlingame, but by the late Secretary Seward—a fact which I had from Mr. Seward himself. The article was rejected by China, because she was not prepared to commit herself to a change of coinage. It commences thus: "The United States and the Emperor of China, recognizing in the present progress of nations a favorable *tendency* towards *unity of civilization*, and regarding a unit of money, etc." *Vide* Mayers' Treaties, p. 95.

to send into this field none but their best men, and upon missionaries now on the ground to endeavor to rise to the occasion; to take for their models such men as Chalmers and Wayland, and to emulate them in the breadth of their views as well as in the fervor of their devotion.

ACCOUNT OF A VISIT TO THE JEWS IN HONAN,

FEBRUARY, 1866.*

An intimate relation must always subsist between the civil capital and the commercial metropolis of a great empire. Not closer, indeed, is the connection between the throbbing heart and the scheming brain; and, however remote their geographical situation, the trade that centres in the one is sure to suggest, and in the end control, the legislation which emanates from the other; while political influences cannot fail, in their turn, to react on the interests of commerce.

The subject, therefore, on which I am called to address you is one that may justly challenge a deeper interest than that which is given to some unpractical abstraction, or even to the most entertaining narrative of scenery and manners. Not altogether devoid of matter for the studies of the antiquarian and the physical geographer, its chief interest lies in developing a new relation between Shanghai and Peking, and I shall deem my forty days of lonely travel well employed if they shall contribute in any degree to pave a pathway for the locomotive or open a channel for the steamer.

What I have to lay before you in relation to my journey may be comprised under the following topics:

---

* This paper was prepared for the North China Branch of the Royal Asiatic Society, and, after being read at a special meeting on the 29th of March, 1866, was published in the Society's *Journal*. It is reproduced here chiefly on account of the information it contains concerning the Jews in China—a subject not out of keeping with the foregoing notices of various systems of religion and philosophy.

1st. The Imperial road leading south from Peking.

2d. The present condition of the Jews in Honan.

3d. The navigation of the Yellow River.

4th. The central section of the Grand Canal.

I. As to the importance of the road referred to, the idea the Chinese entertain of it is expressed by an inscription at the head of a superb bridge near the city of Choh-chau—萬國梯航, "A Thoroughfare for a Myriad Nations." It is crossed by the envoys of several feudal states as they bear tribute to the Emperor; and we saw, as illustrating the inscription, shortly after it had passed the bridge, the Lewchewan embassy approaching the capital in twelve carts adorned with yellow flags, on which were inscribed the characters 貢使, "tribute-bearers." The ministers of our Western countries have never crossed that bridge, but (dare we allude to it, in their present altered position?) some of them have actually borne those yellow banners!

Not far from Pau-ting-fu, seat of the provincial government of Chihli, and about a hundred miles to the south of Peking, the road that leads to the maritime provinces branches off from that which conducts to the heart of the Empire. The former bears to the southeast until it strikes the Grand Canal in the vicinity of Tientsin in Shantung; the latter pursues its southward course for more than three hundred miles farther until it crosses the Yellow River at K'ai-fung-fu. This is the road over which I passed, as a main object of my journey was to make inquiries respecting the Jews in Honan.

The distance from Peking to K'ai-fung is 1400 *li*, or about 470 English miles, through the greater part of which the highroad, as it winds through the plain, presents to the distant view the aspect of a river with wooded banks—a row of trees, mostly willow and aspen, being planted on either side to supply shade to travellers and timber for the repair of bridges. Its course is also traced by other landmarks, which, if less graceful, are more striking to the eye of a foreign observer. I allude to the police-stations and watch-towers that line the road at intervals of from three to five *li*.

The police-stations, though presenting in conspicuous characters a list of the force, together with an official statement of their duty to "protect the traveller and arrest robbers," were nearly all deserted. The tranquillity of the country, however, is not such as to justify this official negligence; for, not to adduce other evidence, we were informed that at one point of the road several carts had, not long before, been carried away by robbers. The watch-towers, built of brick and resembling the bastions of a city wall, are intended not only for observation, but defence. In front of each are several little structures of brick, surmounted by a cone or semi-oval elevation covered with lime and resembling a huge egg. These are always five in number, for what reason I am unable to say, unless it is because the Chinese reckon five colors in the rainbow and five virtues in their moral code. They are the depositories of fuel, which is supposed to be ready for the lighting of signal-fires on the occurrence of any sudden alarm. It is not, however, the flame, but the smoke, that they use for signals; and the substance which they profess to employ for this purpose as possessing certain remarkable properties is 狼糞, "excrement of wolves." Both towers and beacons are alike falling to decay, and the impression made by their neglected ruins is that the day is not far distant when the telegraph of wolf's dung will be superseded by the electric wire.

Through this portion of my journey, the eye of the traveller rests on but one natural object that can truly be denominated picturesque—this is the long range of Si-shan hills which, meeting him outside the gates of Peking, runs parallel to his course for nearly four hundred miles. The highest peaks crowned with snow and glittering like a thousand gilded domes, and their rugged sides resembling the wave-worn shore of a long-retired ocean, they form at first a pleasing contrast to the unvarying level of the subjacent plain. But when the traveller has looked out on what seems to be the same landscape each morning for half a month, he grows weary of their uniformity, and seeks relief in speculating on the varied wealth that lies concealed beneath their monotonous surface.

Silver they certainly do contain, but the mines of Shan-si, whether from defective engineering or other causes, are no longer remunerative, and have ceased to be worked. Of gold we have no notice; but the "black diamond" is found there in rich deposits, and along with it an abundance of iron, the most precious of all metals. Iron-foundries are in operation in at least two districts—one in Peking and the other in Hoh-lu-hien, 獲鹿, about two hundred miles to the south. As we passed the latter place, we met a vast number of carts conveying its productions to all parts of the province. These ranged from kitchen utensils up to salt-boilers five or six feet in diameter. They appeared to be well executed, and the metal of good quality.

Of coal-deposits there seems to be a continuous chain, extending from the verge of the Mongolian plateau to the banks of the Yellow River. In the vicinity of Peking there are beds of both bituminous and anthracite, but at other points I met only with the latter variety. With the exception of places near the Hwang-ho, it is transported mainly by land carriage—near Peking, on the backs of camels; farther south, on mules, donkeys, and wheelbarrows. The consequence is that, while at some points it is cheap and abundant, at intermediate places it becomes so costly that the people are obliged to burn reeds and millet-stalks, or glean a scanty supply of fuel from their stubble-fields.

Here, then, on the line of this Imperial road, and along the base of this range of hills, is the track for *the first grand trunk railway in the Chinese Empire.* Not only would it find close at hand iron for its rails and coal for its motive power, but the carriage of coal and iron to all the cities on the line, including

Peking and Tientsin, would constitute one of the richest sources of its revenue. With Ta-ku for one terminus and K'ai-fung-fu for the other, it would pass through the capital of the Empire, through two provincial capitals, six *fu* cities, and an indefinite number of *chows* and *hiens.**

Between these places the amount of local travel is immense. At some points I estimated the number of vehicles passing in the course of a day at two hundred, employing from four to five hundred mules; while caravans of pilgrims mounted on camels were flocking to the shrines of Shan-si, as the Hindoos do to those of Benares. The supposed railway would soon supersede these slow and painful modes of locomotion. Troops would be despatched by rail instead of marching by easy stages; and scholars attending the metropolitan examinations, and mandarins with their large retinues, always good customers, would cease to creep through the Grand Canal, or jolt for months in lumbering carts, and learn to appreciate our locomotives as they do our steamers.

My friend, Mr. Morrison, late her Majesty's Consul at Che-foo, proposes the extension of the road to Hankow, and is perhaps at this very moment engaged in exploring the route in that direction.

But why indulge in dreams of railways into the heart of the Empire, when the Chinese government refuses to tolerate a telegraphic line to the mouth of the Shanghai River? †

They may not, I confess, be destined to a speedy realization, but to me they are worth all they cost, as a relief from thoughts of present discomfort. What better preparation for such dreaming than to arrive at a miserable inn with sore feet and aching head, after driving from five in the morning till nine at night to

* Cities of the third and fourth orders.

† A telegraph between those points is now in operation, and a railway was not long ago opened in the same place by foreign enterprise; but official jealousy soon put an end to its existence.

make out the distance of forty miles? You throw yourself down in an apartment without floor and without windows; without a fire, as I found in many places, to mitigate the rigor of the season, and without a softer spot than a pavement of brick on which to rest your weary limbs. Weird fancy waves over you her creative wand, and old memories mingle with present realities. Instead of the shout of your mule-driver and the rumbling of his cart-wheels, you hear the shriek of the steam-whistle, the rush of the train, and the click of the telegraph. The dingy hovel rises into a stately station-house—its carpeted saloons thronged by people of all the provinces, and the ticket-office besieged by an eager crowd. You press to the front, hear your money clink on the counter, and are just clutching the coupon that promises you a passage over the rails to Hankow at the rate of 1000 *li* per diem, when the crowing cock awakes you to another day of toil and pain.

II. The existence in Honan of a colony of Jews, who profess to have entered China as early as the dynasty of Han, has long been known to the Christian world. They were discovered by Father Ricci in the seventeenth century, and full inquiries concerning their usages and history subsequently made by Jesuit missionaries who resided at Kai-fung-fu.* In 1850 a deputation of native Christians was sent among them by the Bishop of Victoria and the late Dr. Medhurst. Two of the Jews were induced to come to Shanghai, and some of their Hebrew manuscripts were obtained; but up to the date of my journey, for more than a century and a half, they had not, so far as we are informed, been visited by any European. It became, therefore, a matter of interest to ascertain their present condition; and this, as I

* There is reason to believe that in earlier ages there were many other congregations of Jews located in different parts of China. A synagogue at Ningpo, now extinct, formerly contributed one or more copies of the Law to their brethren in Honan; and Chinese writers speak of a sect called 祆教, supposed to be Jews.

have remarked, was the chief consideration that induced me to make K'ai-fung-fu a point in the course of my inland travels. What others may have published I shall not repeat, but as concisely as possible lay before you a résumé of my own observations.

Arriving in their city on the 17th of February, I inquired for the Jewish synagogue, but, getting no satisfactory answer from the pagan innkeeper, I went for information to one of the Mahometan mosques, of which there are six within the walls. I was well received by the mufti, and the advent of a stranger from the West, who was reported to be a worshipper of the True Lord, drew together a large concourse of the faithful. At the request of the mufti, holding a New Testament in my hand, I addressed them in relation to the contents of the Holy Book of Jesus Christ, whose name he pronounced with reverence as that of one of the most illustrious of their prophets. The Jews he denounced as Kafirs (unbelievers), and evinced no very poignant sorrow when he informed me that their synagogue had come to desolation. It was, he assured me, utterly demolished, and the people who had worshipped there were impoverished and scattered abroad. "Then," said I, "I will go and see the spot on which it stood;" and, directing my bearers to proceed to the place indicated by the mufti, I passed through streets crowded with curious spectators to an open square, in the centre of which there stood a solitary stone.

On one side was an inscription commemorating the erection of the synagogue in the period Lung-hing, of the Sung dynasty, about A.D. 1183, and on the other a record of its rebuilding in the reign of Hung-che, of the Ming dynasty; but to my eye it uttered a sadder tale—not of building and rebuilding, but of decay and ruin. It was inscribed with *Ichabod*—"The glory is departed." Standing on the pedestal, and resting my right hand on the head of that stone, which was to be a silent witness of the truths I was about to utter, I explained to the expectant multitude my reasons for "taking pleasure in the stones of Israel and favoring the dust thereof." *

"Are there among you any of the family of Israel?" I inquired. "I am one," responded a young man, whose face corroborated his assertion; and then another and another stepped forth, until I saw before me representatives of six out of the seven families into which the colony is divided. There, on that melancholy spot where the very foundations of the synagogue had been torn from the ground, and there no longer remained one stone upon another, they confessed with shame and grief that their holy and beautiful house had been demolished by their own hands. It had, they said, for a long time been in a ruinous condition. They had no money to make repairs; they had lost all knowledge of the sacred tongue; the traditions of the fathers were no longer handed down, and their ritual worship had ceased to be observed. In this state of things, they had yielded to the

* Much interesting information touching the Jews in China may be found in the twentieth volume of the Chinese Repository, which contains also the report of the deputation above referred to. From this source I borrow an extract from the inscription on that monumental stone: "With respect to the religion of Israel, we find that our first ancestor was Adam. The founder of the religion was Abraham; then came Moses, who established the Law and handed down the sacred writings. During the dynasty of Han [B.C. 200–A.D. 226] this religion entered China. In the second year of Hiao-tseng, of the Sung dynasty [A.D. 1164], a synagogue was erected in K'ai-fung-fu. Those who attempt to represent God by images or pictures do but vainly occupy themselves with empty forms. Those who honor and obey the sacred writings know the origin of all things; and eternal reason and the sacred writings mutually sustain each other in testifying whence men derived their being. All those who profess this religion aim at the practice of goodness, and avoid the commission of vice." It is affecting to think of this solitary stone continuing to bear its silent testimony after the synagogue has fallen, and the voice of its worshippers has ceased to be heard. Like that which records the story of the Nestorian missions in China, it deserves to be regarded as one of the most precious monuments of religious history.

pressure of necessity, and disposed of the timbers and stones of that venerable edifice to obtain relief for their bodily wants.

In the evening some of them came to my lodgings, bringing for my inspection a copy of the Law inscribed on a roll of parchment, without the points, and in a style of manuscript which I was unable to make out, though I had told them rather imprudently that I was acquainted with the language of their sacred books.* The next day, the Christian Sabbath, they repeated their visit, listening respectfully to what I had to say concerning the Law and the Gospel, and answering as far as they were able my inquiries as to their past history and present state.

Two of them appeared in official costume, one wearing a gilt and the other a crystal button; but, far from sustaining the character of this people for thrift and worldly prosperity, they number among them none that are rich and but few who are honorable. Some, indeed, true to their hereditary instincts, are employed in a small way in banking establishments (the first man I met was a money-changer); others keep fruit-stores and cake-shops, drive a business in old clothes, or pursue various handicrafts, while a few find employment in military service. The prevalence of rebellion in the central provinces for the last thirteen years has told sadly on the prosperity of K'ai-fung-fu, and the Jews have, not unlikely owing to the nature of their occupations, been the greatest sufferers.

Their number they estimated, though not very exactly, at from three to four hundred. They were unable to trace their tribal pedigree, keep no register, and never on any occasion assemble together as one congregation. Until recently they had a com-

---

* I afterwards obtained from them two rolls of the Law, and after a little practice found myself able to read them with sufficient ease; the chief difficulty being the want of the vowel-points. One of these rolls I procured for my friend Dr. S. Wells Williams, who presented it to the American Bible Society.

mon centre in their synagogue, though their liturgical service had long been discontinued. But the congregation seems to be following the fate of its building. No bond of union remains, and they are in danger of being speedily absorbed by Mahometanism or heathenism. One of them has lately become a priest of Buddha, taking for his title *pen tau* (本道), which signifies "one who is rooted in the knowledge of the Truth!" The large tablet that once adorned the entrance of the synagogue, bearing in gilded characters the name Israel (一賜樂業, E-sz-lo-yeh), has been appropriated by one of the Mahometan mosques; and some efforts have been made to draw over the people, who differ from the Moslems so little that their heathen neighbors have never been able to distinguish them by any other circumstance than that of their picking the sinews out of the flesh they eat — a custom commemorative of Jacob's conflict with the angel.*

One of my visitors was a son of the last of their rabbis, who, some thirty or forty years ago, died in the province of Kan-suh. With him perished the last vestige of their acquaintance with the sacred tongue. Though they still preserve several copies of the Law and Prophets, there is not a man among them who can read a word of Hebrew; and not long ago it was seriously proposed to expose their parchments in the market-place, in hopes they might attract the attention of some wandering Jew who would be able to restore to them the language of their fathers. Since the cessation of their ritual worship, their children all

---

* These Jews, in commemoration of the principal land of their sojourn on their way to China, formerly called their religion 天竺教, the "religion of India." This name, being in sound, though not in orthography, liable to be confounded with that of the Roman Catholics, was later on abandoned through fear of being involved in the fierce persecutions which fell on the Christians of China. They then called themselves 挑筋教, *Tiao-kin-kiao*, "sinew-pickers," from a name first given them in derision by their heathen neighbors. See Gen. xxii. 32.

grow up without the seal of the covenant. The young generation are uncircumcised, and, as might be expected, they no longer take pains to keep their blood pure from intermixture with Gentiles. One of them confessed to me that his wife was a heathen. They remember the names of the Feast of Tabernacles, the Feast of Unleavened Bread, and a few other ceremonial rites that were still practised by a former generation; but all such usages are now neglected, and the next half-century is not unlikely to put a period to their existence as a distinct people.

Near the margin of the Poyang lake there stands a lofty rock, so peculiar and solitary that it is known by the name of the "little orphan." The adjacent shore is low and level, and its kindred rocks are all on the opposite side of the lake, whence it seems to have been torn away by some violent convulsion, and planted immovably in the bosom of the waters. Such to me appeared that fragment of the Israelitish nation. A rock rent from the sides of Mount Zion by some great national catastrophe and projected into the central plain of China, it has stood there, while the centuries rolled by, sublime in its antiquity and solitude. It is now on the verge of being swallowed up by the flood of paganism, and the spectacle is a mournful one. The Jews themselves are deeply conscious of their sad situation, and the shadow of an inevitable destiny seems to be resting upon them.

Poor unhappy people! as they inquired about the destruction of the holy city and the dispersion of their tribes, and referred to their own decaying condition, I endeavored to comfort them by pointing to Him who is the consolation of Israel. I told them the straw had not been trodden underfoot until the ripe grain had been gathered to disseminate in other fields. The dikes had not been broken down until the time came for pouring their fertilizing waters over the face of the earth. Christian civilization, with all its grand results, had sprung from a Jewish root, and the promise to Abraham was already fulfilled that "in his seed all the nations of the earth should be blessed." *

III. From K'ai-fung-fu I proceeded in a northeasterly direction as far as Kiuh-fu, the Mecca of the Empire, which I reached after a circuitous journey of eight days. It is here that the remains of Confucius have slept for three-and-twenty centuries, while his doctrines have swayed the mind of the nation with undiminished authority, and his memory continued as green as the cypress grove that shades his sepulchre. I yield to few in respect for the character of that illustrious sage, who in the inscriptions that surround his temple is styled 萬世師表, "the model teacher of all ages," and of whom an emperor of the Mings has said with some truth that "but for Confucius, China would have remained shrouded in the gloom of a rayless night." I shall not, however, pause to describe his mausoleum, because it is a leading topic in the paper of my friend Mr. Williamson, whose path I crossed at that point, and especially because in this part of my journey I met with a more interesting object—the Yellow River.†

* Three years after the date of this visit, I addressed a letter to the editor of the *Jewish Times* of New York, embodying the observations here given, and proposing the formation of a Jewish mission. The appeal excited some discussion among the Jews, but produced no further result, if I except sundry letters in Hebrew, which I was requested to forward to a people who had forgotten the language of their fathers. In my letter to the *Jewish Times*, I said, and now repeat, that "the rebuilding of the synagogue is indispensable to give this moribund colony a rallying-point and bond of union; and that without this nothing else can save them from extinction."

† The mausoleum of the Sage surpasses in grandeur anything I had before seen in China. Extending in a series of courts, each enclosed by buildings, along an entire side of the city, it presents the aspect of a little city in itself; though ordinarily a deserted one, for it is only on the days of the new and full moon that it is visited by worshippers; and the pilgrims are few for a place of such renown. The architecture is like that of most Confucian temples, but on a larger scale. The whole space is girdled and intersected by canals without water, which appear to have been excavated solely

The sepulchre of wisdom would detain us with the hoary past; but the fierce and turbid stream carries our thoughts irresistibly to the future. Spurning the feeble efforts of the natives, it waits to be subdued by the science of Western engineers; and, too rapid for the creeping junk, it has rushed into the sea at a more accessible point than its ancient mouth, seemingly for the very purpose of inviting our steam-navigation. I crossed it at three points—once near K'ai-fung, where it still continues in its old channel; once at Ts'ing-kiang-pu, where I walked over dry-shod at a place where the junks that carried "Lord Amherst" in 1816 offered incense to secure a favorable passage; the third point was near Tung-ping-chau, where it was hastening in its new course towards the Gulf of Pe-chi-li.

When I first saw it, I felt disappointed. The huge embankment, crenellated like the wall of a fortress, winding through the plain as the Great Wall winds over the mountains of the North, almost as huge a monument of industry, and vastly more expensive, excited my expectations. But the river itself lay hidden between its banks, waiting for the melting of the winter snows to call it forth. Equal in length to the Yang-tsze-kiang,

---

for the purpose of furnishing an occasion for the construction of a number of pretty bridges. The principal shrine is surrounded by a grove of venerable cedars, one of which is said to have been planted by the hand of Confucius himself. In another court stands a forest of marble columns all covered with inscriptions in praise of the great master. Each of these was erected by an Imperial hand; and dynasties as far back as the beginning of the Christian era are here represented; but the legends are in many cases altogether obliterated. What is stone or brass to a man who has an empire for his monument? Outside of the city, and approached by an avenue of stately cedars, is seen the spacious cemetery of the family of K'ung. Here, beneath a mound which has grown to the dimensions of a small hill, sleep the mortal remains of the Great Sage, surrounded by the graves of thousands of his posterity. The very grass on this mound is deemed holy, and stalks of it put up in small packets are carried to all parts of the country to be used in divination.

it could not at that season boast one twentieth of its volume of water. The diagonal pursued by the ferry-boat at K'ai-fung-fu, as it is swept down by the current, is estimated in the Chinese guide-book at no more than two *li;* the actual width opposite the ferry-landing is less than half that distance; and where its volume is contracted by a sudden bend, the breadth is reduced, if I may trust to ocular measurement, to less than one hundred yards. The greatest depth at the K'ai-fung crossing at the then low stage of water did not exceed six or seven feet, so that the ferrymen were able to use their poles all the way from one bank to the other. The Peiho below Tientsin makes quite as respectable a figure; and I could hardly have realized that I was viewing one of the chief rivers of the East but for the enormous embankments, which are so wide apart as to make allowance for an expansion of seven miles. At the point where I crossed it in Shantung, it had gained considerably both in breadth and depth, and thence to the sea it is, no doubt, much better adapted to navigation by large vessels.

In this part of its course the number of junks is greatly increased; but in Honan there appeared to be little communication between distant points. Numerous boats were carrying coal to Fung-hien, not far from the capital; but I was unable to discover one that was bound for a more distant port. I was resolved, if I could obtain any kind of craft, to commit myself to the current and explore the river through its new channel; but my efforts were in vain. No boat was lying at the crossing except those that belonged to the ferry; and I was informed that all the intercourse between the capitals of Honan and Shantung, distant only three hundred miles, and both situated on the bank of the river, is carried on by land. Of the truth of this statement I had ocular evidence in the large number of carts and wheelbarrows which we met on the way, a whole fleet of the latter with sails spread scudding before the wind, and reminding us of what Milton says of the—

"Barren plains
Of Sericana, where Chineses drive
With wind and sails their cany wagons light."

This deficiency of junk-navigation is to be ascribed in part to the rapidity of the current, which makes the downward trip dangerous and the return voyage next to impossible; or it may be due to obstructions in the river where it breaks away from its old channel; but the best explanation is, no doubt, to be found in the unsettled state of the country through which it flows, its banks until recently being infested by ferocious hordes of banditti. We have never heard that its upper waters are obstructed by any impassable cataract; and if civil barriers were removed, it is not impossible that steamers of light draught might make their way to Lan-chau, or even beyond the northwestern boundaries of China proper; traversing *en route* five great provinces, and communicating with three provincial capitals and with departmental and district cities without number.

In a geographical point of view, the exploration of the Yellow River is one of the most interesting problems of the age; and in its political and commercial aspects it is one of the pressing questions of the hour. Natives and foreigners would both profit by the opening of the Hwang-ho to steam-navigation. To the foreign merchant it would open a market not reached by any of the affluents of the Yang-tsze-kiang, while to the natives it would bring a termination of that terrible brigandage under which they have been suffering for so many years. Let us hope that our ministers will bear this in mind in the negotiations of 1868.*

* My anticipations in regard to the navigation of the Yellow River are, I fear, not destined to be realized. The bar at the mouth forms so rapidly and shifts so capriciously that it is doubtful if a steam-dredge would prove of any permanent utility. Possibly the species of hydraulic engineering which Captain Eads has applied with so much success to the mouth of the Mississippi might prove equally effectual in the case of the Yellow River. As to the upper course of this famous stream, we now know that it is so

Two questions require attention before we allow ourselves to dismiss the subject of the Hwang-ho—the course pursued by its new channel, and the cause of that wonderful change which has thrown five hundred miles of sea-coast between its present and its former embouchure.

According to the best information I was able to collect, the breach that opened the new channel occurred near E-fung-hien, thirty or forty miles to the east of K'ai-fung-fu. From that point, washing the city of K'au-ching, it flows north, passing under the walls of Ts'au-chou-fu, as far as Fan-hien, where it spreads into a lagoon some thirty *li*, or ten miles, in width. I passed near this place, and should have crossed the river here but for the ice that had formed on the lagoon. Turning in an easterly direction, it intersects the Grand Canal at Chang-ch'iu-chen, 張秋. It was at Li-liang-k'iau, a little beyond this place, that I crossed it—it had there diverged from the canal to the distance of fifteen *li*. A stone bridge that gave name to the locality, and which in former years sufficed to carry passengers over a small tributary of the Ta-ts'ing, was lying in ruins, the advent of the Hwang-ho having tossed it aside with little ceremony. From this point, it not only usurps the bed of the Ta-ts'ing, but obliterates its very name—the natives everywhere speaking of that startling phenomenon, the "Coming of the Yellow Waters."

As to the cause of this phenomenon, we are left very much to conjecture. Superstition discovered a mysterious relation between the outbreak of the Taiping Rebellion and the behavior of the unruly stream in refusing to pay tribute to the Eastern Ocean, bursting over all bounds, and pouring its waters into what the natives call the Northern Sea. They view it only in the light of a portent; but the alleged relation is not to be set aside as altogether imaginary. Dr. D. J. Macgowan, who, in a communi-

---

obstructed by rapids and cascades as not to be practicable for boats of any kind excepting from stage to stage. (*Peking, December*, 1879.)

cation to the *North China Herald*, first drew public attention to this remarkable change in the Yellow River, quotes authority to show that "in the latter part of 1852 the people of Hwaingan found the river fordable, and in the spring of the ensuing year travellers crossed it dry-shod." Mr. Wade, in the Parliamentary Blue-book for 1859–60, cites a Chinese document to the effect that by an inundation in 1855 "the north bank of the river in Honan was carried away, and the river ceased to flow." Now, it was just between these dates that the rebel invasion of the Northern provinces took place; and what more natural supposition can we make than that the *Ho-tuh*, or superintendent of the river works, who has under him a force of sixty-four thousand men, on a *quasi* military footing, should have found other employment for his "navvies" on the approach of the enemy, and neglected the river at a critical juncture? He may even have employed the impetuous stream as a means for checking their advance. A rumor became current at the time that many rebels had been drowned in consequence of the river breaking its banks. That this outbreak was the result of neglect occasioned by the rebel panic is highly probable; but the military use of the river which I have just hinted at is not without a precedent. The Chinese are as well acquainted with this method of extinguishing an enemy as were the heroes of the Dutch Republic. Not to speak of other instances, K'ai-fung-fu has in this way been subjected to at least three destructive inundations. Once by the forces of Ts'in, for the purpose of dislodging the Prince of Wei, who held his court in what was then called Ta-liang; once by the Mongols in their conflict with the Sung dynasty; and again by a general of the Mings, with a view to destroying a body of rebels who were laying siege to the city. The whole population of the city fell victims to the miserable stratagem, and Chinese historians charge the cruel act to the rebel Li-tse-ching; but we prefer the contemporary testimony of Jesuit missionaries.

It is not, perhaps, generally known that the Yellow River, in that immense departure from its late channel which excites the astonishment of the present age, is only returning to a long-forsaken pathway. The highlands of Shantung rise like an island from the level of the great plain; and it appears from Chinese records that the restless river, in finding its way to the sea, has oscillated with something like periodic regularity from one side to the other of this promontory, and at two epochs flowed with a divided current converting it into an immense delta. These vagaries are minutely traced in the 禹貢錐指, a hydrographical work published under the patronage of K'ang-he. From this we learn the curious fact that the river divided its waters between the two principal channels, and insulated the highlands of Shantung for a period of one hundred and forty-six years; and that it was not till the reign of the Mongols, about five hundred years ago, that it became settled in its southern bed. The writer concludes with the expression of an earnest desire that the troublesome stream may be induced to return to its northern course. After the lapse of two centuries, his wish is now gratified.

IV. The canal where I crossed it, to the south of Tung-ch'ang-fu, was nearly dry, and I had not been able to learn whether it was in a working condition above Ts'ing-kiang-p'u. From Kiuhfu to this place it was accordingly my intention to proceed by land; but my cart-driver, taking alarm at rumors of rebels, refused to advance, and I was compelled to seek for some other mode of prosecuting my journey. The canal was suggested, and I made my way in that direction slowly, painfully toiling on, now on foot, now on a wheelbarrow, anon mounted on one of the imperial post-horses, or seated in a mandarin carriage. At length, ascending a hill, I saw the Weishan lake spreading its silvery expanse at my feet. Embosoming an archipelago of green islands, and stretching far away among the hills—to my eye the scene was too pleasing to be real. I distrusted my senses, and thought it a mirage such as often before had cheated my hopes with the apparition of lake and stream; and when my guide assured me that it was no deceptive show, I gave way to transports not unlike those in which the Greeks indulged, when, escaping from the heart of Persia, they caught a distant view of the waters of the Euxine.

Taking passage at the foot of the lake, I glided gently down with the current, and reached Chin-kiang-fu, a distance of nine hundred *li*, in less than a week.

Through this portion of its course the canal deserves the appellation of "Grand." For the first half, extending to Ts'ing-kiang-p'u, it varies from eighty to two hundred feet in width. Seething and foaming as it rushes from the lake, and rolling on with a strong current through the whole of this distance, it has more the appearance of a natural river than of a canal. Near Ts'ing-kiang it parts with enough of its water to form a navigable stream, which enters the sea at Hai-chau. Beyond this point, where it intersects the old bed of the Yellow River, its waters are drawn off by innumerable sluices to irrigate the rice grounds, until it is reduced to about forty feet in breadth and four in depth. Recruited, however, by a timely supply from the Kau-yu lake, it recovers much of its former strength, and flows on to the Yang-tsze-kiang with a velocity that makes toilsome work for the trackers.

To what extent the canal may be practicable for steam-navigation is a question not without interest; and my mind had been occupied with it for some days, when I happily had the opportunity of seeing it subjected to the test of experiment. Just off the city of Kau-yu, where the canal reaches its minimum depth, I met the *Hyson*, a well-known tug-boat from Shanghai, towing a flotilla of war-junks. She would be able to reach the city of Ts'ing-kiang-p'u, but not to go beyond, on account of the locks or water-gates, some of which are only twelve feet in width.

As the canal now is, propellers of three feet draught and ten feet beam, making up in length what they lack in other dimensions, might drive a profitable trade between Chin-kiang and Tsi-ning-chau, a distance of twelve hundred *li;* but the utility of the canal would be greatly enhanced by adding a lock or two in the shallower portions, and increasing the breadth of those that now exist, so as to admit the passage of larger vessels. A little engineering at its point of intersection with the new course of the Yellow River would supply an abundance of water to a portion that is dry, making its facilities for junk-navigation equal to those of its best days; and it would then be possible for steamers of the class that were lately employed in penetrating to the silk districts of the interior to make inland voyages from Shanghai nearly to the gates of Peking.*

---

* To Tungchow, twelve miles distant.

THE DUKE OF K'UNG,

SUCCESSOR OF CONFUCIUS.

The *Peking Gazette* contains the following obituary announcement, in the usual form of an Imperial decree: "The Duke K'ung Siang-k'o, lineal successor of the Holy Sage, has departed this life. Let the proper Board report as to the marks of Imperial favor to be accorded in connection with the funeral rites." *

The Duke was about twenty-six years of age, and a descendant of Confucius at a remove of more than seventy† generations. Of his personal character we know nothing, save that he once admitted a company of foreigners, the Rev. Dr. Williamson and others, into his presence, and treated them with great urbanity. What interests us more, and furnishes the sole reason for chronicling his death, whether in these lines or in the still briefer notice in the *Peking Gazette*, is his representative character. K'ung Siang-k'o was head of the Confucian clan, and as such he enjoyed the dignities and emoluments of a noble of the first class.

Hereditary rank makes so small a figure in the administration of the Chinese government that we sometimes hear it asserted that there is no such thing in China. Now, those who hazard this assertion, not only leave out of view the feudal organization

* This paper was written in 1876 for the *Celestial Empire* by request of the editor. The designation "Successor of Confucius" may not be thought well chosen; but were not the caliphs styled successors of the Prophet? And are not ecclesiastical dignitaries called successors of the apostles?

† The last on the family record, published in the last century, was the seventy-first.

of the Manchu and Mongol races, but forget the sonorous titles prefixed to the names of some of the leading Chinese statesmen of the present day. We can scarcely take up a number of the *Peking Gazette* without being reminded that Li Hung-chang or Tso Tsung-t'ang is an earl or 伯, *peh*, of the first grade; and a few years ago the title of marquis, 侯, *hou*, was made equally prominent in connection with the name of the late eminent Tsêng Kuo-fan. On the decease of the great general, the title descended in due course to his son Tsêng Ki-tsoh,* who writes and signs it in good English in correspondence with his foreign friends. In a word, all the five degrees of hereditary nobility which were in use three thousand years ago are to be found (by searching) among the Chinese of to-day; but with this important difference, that they no longer imply the possession of landed estates or territorial jurisdiction. Leaving the secular peerage of China proper, as well as that of the dominant race, to be treated by some one who has leisure and inclination for the subject, we propose to devote a few paragraphs to what we venture to denominate the sacred heraldry of the Empire.

Ten years ago, in the course of an overland journey from Peking to Shanghai, the writer turned aside to visit the tomb of Confucius. Near the tumulus, his eye was attracted by an inscription informing him that a tree of which the decaying stump was all that remained was planted by the hand of Tsze-K'ung; and another pointed out the place where that devoted disciple had passed six years of his life in a solitary hermitage, near the ashes of his master. The hut which he occupied has long since crumbled to dust, and the sap has ceased to flow through the trunk of that venerable tree; but the family of the Sage still continues to surround the sacred spot, the associations of which are more unfading than the evergreens by which the place is overshadowed. It was an impressive spectacle to see the heads of

* Minister to England, 1880.

the various branches into which the clan is divided performing their semi-monthly devotions before the tablet of their illustrious ancestor. Many of these discharge official duties, and constitute a kind of priesthood in the temple of the Sage; their appointments, whether hereditary or otherwise, being duly recorded in the Red Book, or official register. The chief of the tribe is known as *Yen Sheng K'ung*, the Duke of the Holy Succession—a succession which is older in generations than most aged men are in the reckoning of years. There are Jewish families who can boast a longer pedigree—running back, perhaps, to the return from captivity, B.C. 536; but where, out of China, shall we look for a family whose nobility has a history of twenty centuries?

The first hereditary distinction was conferred on the senior member of the house of K'ung by the founder of the Han dynasty, B.C. 202. The title was at first the vague designation of *keun*, prince, and coupled with the charge of the ancestral temple. This was exchanged for the more distinguishing title of *hou*, marquis, by order of Wu-ti, of the same dynasty. The later Chow, A.D. 550, substituted the title of *k'ung*, duke; but in the next dynasty, that of Suy, it reverted to marquis, and so continued through the three centuries of the Tangs. At the accession of the Sung, the heir of Confucius was again raised to the dignity of duke—a rank which he has retained without material variation for more than eight centuries.

In the topographical and genealogical histories we are favored with biographical sketches of the individual links in this long chain; but through them all there runs a thread of dreary monotony. In earlier ages, the house of K'ung did indeed produce a few men of exceptional eminence in letters and in politics. They are not, however, always found in the line of primogeniture, and in the rare instances in which titled heads have distinguished themselves we have to recognize the stimulating influence of court life, from which they were not yet excluded.

Under the existing *régime*, the succession presents us no name of note; a result more due to want of opportunity than to any deterioration of race, for, according to some observers, the blood of Confucius continues to assert itself in the superior development of his posterity. But what are we to expect when a family is rooted to the soil of a cemetery but that it should become as barren as the cypress that overhangs it?

The Dukes of K'ung are strictly relegated to the vicinity of their sacerdotal charge, and are not at liberty to visit the capital without express permission from the throne.

We recall the late Duke's application for leave to prostrate himself before the sarcophagus of the Emperor Tung-chih, certainly the last and probably the only occasion on which he ever entered the walls of Peking.

The family estate, it must be confessed, is large enough to gratify the ambition and employ the energies of an ordinary mortal, amounting (for it is not all in one place) to an area of not less than 165,000 acres.

And as for honors, the country nobleman has much to console him for the privations of provincial life; the Governor of the province, it is said, being required to approach him with the same forms of homage which he renders to the Son of Heaven. Numerous offices of inferior dignity are conferred on other members of the clan, constituting it a kind of Levitical order; but it is pleasing to remark that these tokens of a nation's undying gratitude are not limited to the lineage of Confucius. Around the grand luminary there moved a cluster of satellites, which drank in his beams and propagated his light.

The chief of these *Yien*, *Tseng*, *Sze*, *Meng*, as the Chinese concisely call them, and a few others, continued to be honored in the same way, though not to the same degree, as the Sage himself. Inseparable attendants of the Sage, in all his temples, at least one of which exists in every district of the Empire, each of them enjoys the honor of a separate shrine, and some of his posterity derive their subsistence from the charge of it. In the city of Chü-fu, a conspicuous inscription points out the spot where Yien-hwei, in the midst of poverty, presented a face ever radiant with joy, because his soul was filled with divine philosophy. Hard by stands a magnificent mausoleum to the man who never wrote a book and never performed any great exploit; but who embodied in his own practice more perfectly than any other the precepts of his Master. In the adjoining district of Tseo-hien stands a temple to Mencius, the St. Paul of Confucianism, who, though he entered the world too late to enjoy the personal teachings of the Great Sage, did more than any other to give them shape and currency. Not far away, in the same city, stands a somewhat dilapidated temple of Tsze-sze, the master of Mencius, and the grandson of Confucius. Though in the direct line, the Chinese have not been willing to merge his name and fame in those of his ancestor; but have taken effectual measures for testifying to all generations their reverence for the author of the *Chung-yung*, or "Golden Mean."

The whole region surrounding the temple of Confucius is dotted over by the tombs of ancient worthies; and it is touching to see with what sacred care their descendants cherish the fire on their altars. Under various designations they have discharged these offices for more than threescore, and in one instance for nearly a hundred, generations; but their present titles date from the Ming dynasty. The founder of the Mings, an unlettered warrior, who never read the Four Books until he was seated on the throne and had Liu-ki for a teacher, conferred certain honors on the descendants of Yien-hwei and Mencius. His successors ordered that representatives of fifteen of the disciples of Confucius should be enrolled in the Hanlin College, and invested with the office of professors and curators of the Five Classics.

Nor is it only the Great Sage and his disciples who enjoy the distinction of a memorial temple, a State ritual, and an hereditary priesthood; all these are accorded to the Duke of Chow, whom Confucius revered as a master and imitated as a model. Chow-kung died more than five hundred years before the birth of Confucius; but the later Sage not only professed to have caught his inspiration from the earlier, but in one of his most touching speeches he gave it as a mark of decaying nature that he had "ceased to dream of Chow-kung."

It is not surprising, therefore, that the family of the virtuous Regent of China's typical dynasty should have some small part in the cloud of incense which China offers to the pioneers of her civilization. Their claim to it was eloquently advocated by one of his descendants when the Emperor Kang-hi visited the "sacred soil of Lu," and promptly recognized by that enlightened monarch. None of these venerated shades is regarded as exercising a tutelar guardianship over the Empire, or over any part of it. Their temples, though vulgar superstitions have gathered round them, are essentially memorial, and the worship wholly commemorative. It is thus that China has sought to mould her children into one family and to secure the stability of society by binding it to the traditions of the past.

The representatives of these families, as we have said, are a priesthood rather than a nobility; but so closely are the two ideas associated in the Chinese mind that a writer of these family histories finds in ancestral worship the origin of feudal dignities. His philosophy is at fault; but it is gratifying to observe that, while the feudal lords of China have gone under in the struggle for existence, the only vestiges of the *ancient nobility* (the secular are all new) are those which cluster round the memories of the wise and good.

TWO CHINESE POEMS.

Note.—As the foregoing pages contain an essay on the prose composition of the Chinese, these verses are added as a specimen of their poetry. Their educated men, as I have elsewhere said, are all poets; and various collections of verses by female writers show that they have their Sapphos and Corinnas. They may also claim to have their Jeanne d'Arcs.

The ballad which celebrates one of their heroines is somewhat abridged by the omission of incidents, some of which are the opposite of poetical.

The tendency of the Chinese to express themselves in verse is exhibited in the occasional issue of official proclamations in rhyme. The latest illustration of this national taste is a couplet which the Marquis of Tseng sent to Peking by telegraph, acknowledging the Imperial mandate requiring him to proceed to Russia:

才疏智淺
聞電戰慄

These lines, as concise as the responses of the Delphic oracle, may be thus rendered:

"My knowledge is scant and my powers are frail,
At the voice of the thunder I tremble and quail.

"Peking, *April* 15, 1880."

歌 扇 秋

LINES INSCRIBED ON A FAN.

Written by Pan Tsieh Yu, a Lady of the Court, and Presented to the Emperor Cheng-ti, of the Han Dynasty, B.C. 18.

Of fresh new silk, all snowy-white,
And round as harvest moon,
A pledge of purity and love,
A small but welcome boon.

While summer lasts, borne in the hand,
Or folded on the breast,
'Twill gently soothe thy burning brow,
And charm thee to thy rest.

But ah! when autumn frosts descend,
And autumn winds blow cold,
No longer sought, no longer loved,
'Twill lie in dust and mould.

This silken fan, then, deign accept,
Sad emblem of my lot,
Caressed and cherished for an hour,
Then speedily forgot.

怨歌行

班婕妤處飛燕之禍求供養
太后於長信宮而作怨歌

新製齊紈素　鮮潔如霜雪
裁爲合歡扇　團團似明月
出入君懷袖　動搖微風發
常恐秋節至　涼飆奪炎熱
棄捐篋笥中　恩情中道絕

木蘭詞

MULAN, THE MAIDEN CHIEF:

A Chinese Ballad of the Liang Dynasty (A.D. 502–556).

An officer being disabled, his daughter puts on his armor, and so disguised leads his troops to the conflict. The original is anonymous and of uncertain date.

"Say, maiden at your spinning-wheel,
Why heave that deep-drawn sigh?
Is 't fear, perchance, or love you feel?
Pray tell—oh, tell me why!"

"Nor fear nor love has moved my soul—
Away such idle thought!
A warrior's glory is the goal
By my ambition sought.

"My Father's cherished life to save,
My country to redeem,
The dangers of the field I'll brave:
I am not what I seem.

"No son has he his troop to lead,
No brother dear have I;
So I must mount my father's steed,
And to the battle hie."

At dawn of day she quits her door,
At evening rests her head
Where loud the mountain torrents roar
And mail-clad soldiers tread.

木蘭辭

木蘭辭無名氏〇一云木蘭作

唧唧復唧唧
木蘭當戶織
不聞機杼聲
唯聞女歎息

問女何所思
問女何所憶
女亦無所思
女亦無所憶

昨夜見軍帖
可汗大點兵
軍書十二卷
卷卷有爺名

阿爺無大兒
木蘭無長兄
願爲市鞍馬
從此替爺征

東市買駿馬
西市買鞍韉
南市買轡頭
北市買長鞭

The northern plains are gained at last,
  The mountains sink from view;
The sun shines cold, and the wintry blast
  It pierces through and through.

A thousand foes around her fall,
  And red blood stains the ground,
But Mulan, who survives it all,
  Returns with glory crowned.

Before the throne they bend the knee
  In the palace of Changan,
Full many a knight of high degree,
  But the bravest is Mulan.

"Nay, Prince," she cries, "my duty 's done,
  No guerdon I desire;
But let me to my home begone,
  To cheer my aged sire."

She nears the door of her father's home,
  A chief with trumpet's blare;
But when she doffs her waving plume,
  She stands a maiden fair.

朝辭爺孃去
暮宿黃河邊
不聞爺孃喚女聲
但聞黃河流水鳴濺濺
旦辭黃河去
暮至黑水頭
不聞爺孃喚女聲
但聞燕山胡騎鳴啾啾
萬里赴戎機
關山度若飛
朔氣傳金柝
寒光照鐵衣
將軍百戰死
壯士十年歸
歸來見天子
天子坐明堂
策勳十二轉
賞賜百千彊
可汗問所欲
木蘭不用尚書郎
願借明駝千里足
送兒還故鄉
爺孃聞女來
出郭相扶將
阿姊聞妹來
當戶理紅妝
小弟聞姊來
磨刀霍霍向豬羊
開我東閣門
坐我西間牀
脫我戰時袍
著我舊時裳
當窗理雲鬢
對鏡帖花黃
出門看火伴
火伴皆驚忙
同行十二年
不知木蘭是女郎
雄兔腳撲朔
雌兔眼迷離
雙兔傍地走
安能辨我是雄雌

MOTLEY'S DUTCH REPUBLIC. The Rise of the Dutch Republic. A History. By John Lothrop Motley, LL.D., D.C.L. With a Portrait of William of Orange. Cheap Edition, 3 vols. in a Box, 8vo, Cloth, with Paper Labels, Uncut Edges and Gilt Tops, $6 00. Sold only in Sets. Original Library Edition, 3 vols., 8vo, Cloth, $10 50; Sheep, $12 00; Half Calf, $17 25.

MOTLEY'S UNITED NETHERLANDS. History of the United Netherlands: from the Death of William the Silent to the Twelve Years' Truce—1584-1609. With a full View of the English-Dutch Struggle against Spain, and of the Origin and Destruction of the Spanish Armada. By John Lothrop Motley, LL.D., D.C.L. Portraits. Cheap Edition, 4 vols. in a Box, 8vo, Cloth, with Paper Labels, Uncut Edges and Gilt Tops, $8 00. Sold only in Sets. Original Library Edition, 4 vols., 8vo, Cloth, $14 00; Sheep, $16 00; Half Calf, $23 00.

MOTLEY'S LIFE AND DEATH OF JOHN OF BARNEVELD. The Life and Death of John of Barneveld, Advocate of Holland: with a View of the Primary Causes and Movements of "The Thirty Years' War." By John Lothrop Motley, LL.D., D.C.L. Illustrated. Cheap Edition, 2 vols. in a Box, 8vo, Cloth, with Paper Labels, Uncut Edges and Gilt Tops, $4 00. Sold only in Sets. Original Library Edition, 2 vols., 8vo, Cloth, $7 00; Sheep, $8 00; Half Calf, $11 50.

GEDDES'S HISTORY OF JOHN DE WITT. History of the Administration of John De Witt, Grand Pensionary of Holland. By James Geddes. Vol. I.—1623-1654. With a Portrait. 8vo, Cloth, $2 50.

SKETCHES AND STUDIES IN SOUTHERN EUROPE. By John Addington Symonds. In Two Volumes. Post 8vo, Cloth, $4 00.

SYMONDS'S GREEK POETS. Studies of the Greek Poets. By John Addington Symonds. 2 vols., Square 16mo, Cloth, $3 50.

BENJAMIN'S CONTEMPORARY ART. Contemporary Art in Europe. By S. G. W. Benjamin. Illustrated. 8vo, Cloth, $3 50.

BENJAMIN'S ART IN AMERICA. Art in America. By S. G. W. Benjamin. Illustrated. 8vo, Cloth, $4 00.

KINGLAKE'S CRIMEAN WAR. The Invasion of the Crimea: its Origin, and an Account of its Progress down to the Death of Lord Raglan. By Alexander William Kinglake. With Maps and Plans. Four Volumes now ready. 12mo, Cloth, $2 00 per vol.

TREVELYAN'S LIFE OF MACAULAY. The Life and Letters of Lord Macaulay. By his Nephew, G. OTTO TREVELYAN, M.P. With Portrait on Steel. Complete in 2 vols., 8vo, Cloth, Uncut Edges and Gilt Tops, $5 00; Sheep, $6 00; Half Calf, $9 50. Popular Edition, two vols. in one, 12mo, Cloth, $1 75.

TREVELYAN'S LIFE OF FOX. The Early History of Charles James Fox. By GEORGE OTTO TREVELYAN. 8vo, Cloth, Uncut Edges and Gilt Tops, $2 50; 4to, Paper, 15 cents.

HUDSON'S HISTORY OF JOURNALISM. Journalism in the United States, from 1690 to 1872. By FREDERIC HUDSON. 8vo, Cloth, $5 00; Half Calf, $7 25.

LAMB'S COMPLETE WORKS. The Works of Charles Lamb. Comprising his Letters, Poems, Essays of Elia, Essays upon Shakspeare, Hogarth, etc., and a Sketch of his Life, with the Final Memorials, by T. NOON TALFOURD. With Portrait. 2 vols., 12mo, Cloth, $3 00.

LAWRENCE'S HISTORICAL STUDIES. Historical Studies. By EUGENE LAWRENCE. Containing the following Essays: The Bishops of Rome.—Leo and Luther.—Loyola and the Jesuits.—Ecumenical Councils.—The Vaudois.—The Huguenots.—The Church of Jerusalem.—Dominic and the Inquisition.—The Conquest of Ireland.—The Greek Church. 8vo, Cloth, Uncut Edges and Gilt Tops, $3 00.

LOSSING'S FIELD-BOOK OF THE REVOLUTION. Pictorial Field-Book of the Revolution; or, Illustrations by Pen and Pencil of the History, Biography, Scenery, Relics, and Traditions of the War for Independence. By BENSON J. LOSSING. 2 vols., 8vo, Cloth, $14 00; Sheep or Roan, $15 00; Half Calf, $18 00.

LOSSING'S FIELD-BOOK OF THE WAR OF 1812. Pictorial Field-Book of the War of 1812; or, Illustrations by Pen and Pencil of the History, Biography, Scenery, Relics, and Traditions of the last War for American Independence. By BENSON J. LOSSING. With several hundred Engravings on Wood by Lossing and Barritt, chiefly from Original Sketches by the Author. 1088 pages, 8vo, Cloth, $7 00; Sheep, $8 50; Roan, $9 00; Half Calf, $10 00.

FORSTER'S LIFE OF DEAN SWIFT. The Early Life of Jonathan Swift (1667–1711). By JOHN FORSTER. With Portrait. 8vo, Cloth, Uncut Edges and Gilt Tops, $2 50.

GREEN'S ENGLISH PEOPLE. History of the English People. By JOHN RICHARD GREEN, M.A. Four Volumes. 8vo, Cloth, $2 50 per volume.

SHORT'S NORTH AMERICANS OF ANTIQUITY. The North Americans of Antiquity. Their Origin, Migrations, and Type of Civilization Considered. By JOHN T. SHORT. Illustrated. 8vo, Cloth, $3 00.

SQUIER'S PERU. Peru: Incidents of Travel and Exploration in the Land of the Incas. By E. GEORGE SQUIER, M.A., F.S.A., late U. S. Commissioner to Peru. With Illustrations. 8vo, Cloth, $5 00.

BLAIKIE'S LIFE OF DAVID LIVINGSTONE. Dr. Livingstone: Memoir of his Personal Life, from his Unpublished Journals and Correspondence. By W. G. BLAIKIE, D.D., LL.D. With Portrait and Map. 8vo, Cloth, $3 50.

MAURY'S PHYSICAL GEOGRAPHY OF THE SEA. The Physical Geography of the Sea, and its Meteorology. By M. F. MAURY, LL.D. 8vo, Cloth, $4 00.

SCHWEINFURTH'S HEART OF AFRICA. The Heart of Africa. Three Years' Travels and Adventures in the Unexplored Regions of the Centre of Africa—from 1868 to 1871. By Dr. GEORG SCHWEINFURTH. Translated by ELLEN E. FREWER. With an Introduction by W. WINWOOD READE. Illustrated. 2 vols., 8vo, Cloth, $8 00.

M'CLINTOCK & STRONG'S CYCLOPÆDIA. Cyclopædia of Biblical, Theological, and Ecclesiastical Literature. Prepared by the Rev. JOHN M'CLINTOCK, D.D., and JAMES STRONG, S.T.D. 9 *vols. now ready.* Royal 8vo. Price per vol., Cloth, $5 00; Sheep, $6 00; Half Morocco, $8 00.

MOHAMMED AND MOHAMMEDANISM: Lectures Delivered at the Royal Institution of Great Britain in February and March, 1874. By R. BOSWORTH SMITH, M.A. With an Appendix containing Emanuel Deutsch's Article on "Islam." 12mo, Cloth, $1 50.

MOSHEIM'S ECCLESIASTICAL HISTORY, Ancient and Modern; in which the Rise, Progress, and Variation of Church Power are considered in their Connection with the State of Learning and Philosophy, and the Political History of Europe during that Period. Translated, with Notes, etc., by A. MACLAINE, D.D. Continued to 1826, by C. COOTE, LL.D. 2 vols., 8vo, Cloth, $4 00; Sheep, $5 00.

HARPER'S NEW CLASSICAL LIBRARY. Literal Translations. The following volumes are now ready. 12mo, Cloth, $1 50 each.

CÆSAR.—VIRGIL.—SALLUST.—HORACE.—CICERO'S ORATIONS.—CICERO'S OFFICES, etc.—CICERO ON ORATORY AND ORATORS.—TACITUS (2 vols.).—TERENCE.—SOPHOCLES.—JUVENAL.—XENOPHON.—HOMER'S ILIAD.—HOMER'S ODYSSEY.—HERODOTUS.—DEMOSTHENES (2 vols.).—THUCYDIDES.—ÆSCHYLUS.—EURIPIDES (2 vols.).—LIVY (2 vols.).—PLATO [Select Dialogues].

VINCENT'S LAND OF THE WHITE ELEPHANT. The Land of the White Elephant: Sights and Scenes in Southeastern Asia. A Personal Narrative of Travel and Adventure in Farther India, embracing the Countries of Burma, Siam, Cambodia, and Cochin-China (1871–2). By FRANK VINCENT, Jr. Illustrated. Crown 8vo, Cloth, $3 50.

LIVINGSTONE'S SOUTH AFRICA. Missionary Travels and Researches in South Africa: including a Sketch of Sixteen Years' Residence in the Interior of Africa, and a Journey from the Cape of Good Hope to Loanda on the West Coast; thence across the Continent, down the River Zambesi, to the Eastern Ocean. By DAVID LIVINGSTONE, LL.D., D.C.L. With Portrait, Maps, and Illustrations. 8vo, Cloth, $4 50; Sheep, $5 00; Half Calf, $6 75.

LIVINGSTONE'S ZAMBESI. Narrative of an Expedition to the Zambesi and its Tributaries, and of the Discovery of the Lakes Shirwa and Nyassa, 1858–1864. By DAVID and CHARLES LIVINGSTONE. Map and Illustrations. 8vo, Cloth, $5 00; Sheep, $5 50; Half Calf, $7 25.

LIVINGSTONE'S LAST JOURNALS. The Last Journals of David Livingstone, in Central Africa, from 1865 to his Death. Continued by a Narrative of his Last Moments and Sufferings, obtained from his Faithful Servants Chuma and Susi. By HORACE WALLER, F.R.G.S., Rector of Twywell, Northampton. With Portrait, Maps, and Illustrations. 8vo, Cloth, $5 00; Sheep, $5 50; Half Calf, $7 25. Cheap Popular Edition, 8vo, Cloth, with Map and Illustrations, $2 50.

NORDHOFF'S COMMUNISTIC SOCIETIES OF THE UNITED STATES. The Communistic Societies of the United States, from Personal Visit and Observation; including Detailed Accounts of the Economists, Zoarites, Shakers, the Amana, Oneida, Bethel, Aurora, Icarian, and other existing Societies. With Particulars of their Religious Creeds and Practices, their Social Theories and Life, Numbers, Industries, and Present Condition. By CHARLES NORDHOFF. Illustrations. 8vo, Cloth, $4 00.

NORDHOFF'S CALIFORNIA. California: for Health, Pleasure, and Residence. A Book for Travellers and Settlers. Illustrated. 8vo, Cloth, $2 50.

NORDHOFF'S NORTHERN CALIFORNIA AND THE SANDWICH ISLANDS. Northern California, Oregon, and the Sandwich Islands. By CHARLES NORDHOFF. Illustrated. 8vo, Cloth, $2 50.

GROTE'S HISTORY OF GREECE. 12 vols., 12mo, Cloth, $18 00; Sheep, $22 80; Half Calf, $39 00.

RECLUS'S EARTH. The Earth: a Descriptive History of the Phenomena of the Life of the Globe. By ÉLISÉE RECLUS. With 234 Maps and Illustrations, and 23 Page Maps printed in Colors. 8vo, Cloth, $5 00.

RECLUS'S OCEAN. The Ocean, Atmosphere, and Life. Being the Second Series of a Descriptive History of the Life of the Globe. By ÉLISÉE RECLUS. Profusely Illustrated with 250 Maps or Figures, and 27 Maps printed in Colors. 8vo, Cloth, $6 00.

SHAKSPEARE. The Dramatic Works of William Shakspeare. With Corrections and Notes. Engravings. 6 vols., 12mo, Cloth, $9 00. 2 vols., 8vo, Cloth, $4 00; Sheep, $5 00. In one vol., 8vo, Sheep, $4 00.

BAKER'S ISMAILÏA. Ismailïa: a Narrative of the Expedition to Central Africa for the Suppression of the Slave-trade, organized by Ismail, Khedive of Egypt. By Sir SAMUEL WHITE BAKER, PASHA, F.R.S., F.R.G.S. With Maps, Portraits, and Illustrations. 8vo, Cloth, $5 00; Half Calf, $7 25.

GRIFFIS'S JAPAN. The Mikado's Empire: Book I. History of Japan, from 660 B.C. to 1872 A.D. Book II. Personal Experiences, Observations, and Studies in Japan, 1870-1874. By WILLIAM ELLIOT GRIFFIS, A.M., late of the Imperial University of Tōkiō, Japan. Copiously Illustrated. 8vo, Cloth, $4 00; Half Calf, $6 25.

SMILES'S HISTORY OF THE HUGUENOTS. The Huguenots: their Settlements, Churches, and Industries in England and Ireland. By SAMUEL SMILES. With an Appendix relating to the Huguenots in America. Crown 8vo, Cloth, $2 00.

SMILES'S HUGUENOTS AFTER THE REVOCATION. The Huguenots in France after the Revocation of the Edict of Nantes; with a Visit to the Country of the Vaudois. By SAMUEL SMILES. Crown 8vo, Cloth, $2 00.

SMILES'S LIFE OF THE STEPHENSONS. The Life of George Stephenson, and of his Son, Robert Stephenson; comprising, also, a History of the Invention and Introduction of the Railway Locomotive. By SAMUEL SMILES. With Steel Portraits and numerous Illustrations. 8vo, Cloth, $3 00.

RAWLINSON'S MANUAL OF ANCIENT HISTORY. A Manual of Ancient History, from the Earliest Times to the Fall of the Western Empire. Comprising the History of Chaldæa, Assyria, Media, Babylonia, Lydia, Phœnicia, Syria, Judæa, Egypt, Carthage, Persia, Greece, Macedonia, Parthia, and Rome. By GEORGE RAWLINSON, M.A., Camden Professor of Ancient History in the University of Oxford. 12mo, Cloth, $1 25.

SCHLIEMANN'S ILIOS. Ilios, the City and Country of the Trojans. A Narrative of the Most Recent Discoveries and Researches made on the Plain of Troy. With Illustrations representing nearly 2000 Types of the Objects found in the Excavations of the Seven Cities on the Site of Ilios. By Dr. HENRY SCHLIEMANN. Maps, Plans, and Illustrations. Imperial 8vo, Illuminated Cloth, $12 00.

ALISON'S HISTORY OF EUROPE. FIRST SERIES: From the Commencement of the French Revolution, in 1789, to the Restoration of the Bourbons in 1815. [In addition to the Notes on Chapter LXXVI., which correct the errors of the original work concerning the United States, a copious Analytical Index has been appended to this American Edition.] SECOND SERIES: From the Fall of Napoleon, in 1815, to the Accession of Louis Napoleon, in 1852. 8 vols., 8vo, Cloth, $16 00; Sheep, $20 00; Half Calf, $34 00.

NORTON'S STUDIES OF CHURCH-BUILDING. Historical Studies of Church-Building in the Middle Ages. Venice, Siena, Florence. By CHARLES ELIOT NORTON. 8vo, Cloth, $3 00.

BOSWELL'S JOHNSON. The Life of Samuel Johnson, LL.D., including a Journal of a Tour to the Hebrides. By JAMES BOSWELL. Edited by J. W. CROKER, LL.D., F.R.S. With a Portrait of Boswell. 2 vols., 8vo, Cloth, $4 00; Sheep, $5 00; Half Calf, $8 50.

ADDISON'S COMPLETE WORKS. The Works of Joseph Addison, embracing the whole of the *Spectator*. 3 vols., 8vo, Cloth, $6 00; Sheep, $7 50; Half Calf, $12 75.

SAMUEL JOHNSON: HIS WORDS AND HIS WAYS; what he Said, what he Did, and what Men Thought and Spoke concerning him. Edited by E. T. MASON. 12mo, Cloth, $1 50.

JOHNSON'S COMPLETE WORKS. The Works of Samuel Johnson, LL.D. With an Essay on his Life and Genius, by A. MURPHY. 2 vols., 8vo, Cloth, $4 00; Sheep, $5 00; Half Calf, $8 50.

THE VOYAGE OF THE "CHALLENGER." The Atlantic: an Account of the General Results of the Voyage during 1873, and the Early Part of 1876. By Sir WYVILLE THOMSON, K.C.B., F.R.S. With numerous Illustrations, Colored Maps, and Charts, and Portrait of the Author. 2 vols., 8vo, Cloth, $12 00.

BLUNT'S BEDOUIN TRIBES OF THE EUPHRATES. Bedouin Tribes of the Euphrates. By LADY ANNE BLUNT. Edited, with a Preface and some Account of the Arabs and their Horses, by W. S. B. Map and Sketches by the Author. 8vo, Cloth, $2 50.

BOURNE'S LOCKE. The Life of John Locke. By H. R. Fox Bourne. 2 vols., 8vo, Cloth, Uncut Edges and Gilt Tops, $5 00.

BROUGHAM'S AUTOBIOGRAPHY. Life and Times of Henry, Lord Brougham. Written by Himself. 3 vols., 12mo, Cloth, $6 00.

THOMPSON'S PAPACY AND THE CIVIL POWER. The Papacy and the Civil Power. By the Hon. R. W. Thompson, Secretary of the U. S. Navy. Crown 8vo, Cloth, $3 00.

ENGLISH CORRESPONDENCE. Four Centuries of English Letters. Selections from the Correspondence of One Hundred and Fifty Writers from the Period of the Paston Letters to the Present Day. Edited by W. Baptiste Scoones. 12mo, Cloth, $2 00.

THE POETS AND POETRY OF SCOTLAND: From the Earliest to the Present Time. Comprising Characteristic Selections from the Works of the more Noteworthy Scottish Poets, with Biographical and Critical Notices. By James Grant Wilson. With Portraits on Steel. 2 vols., 8vo, Cloth, $10 00; Sheep, $12 00; Half Calf, $14 50; Full Morocco, $18 00.

THE STUDENT'S SERIES. Maps and Illustrations. 12mo, Cloth.
France.—Gibbon.—Greece.—Rome (by Liddell).—Old Testament History.—New Testament History.—Strickland's Queens of England (Abridged).—Ancient History of the East.—Hallam's Middle Ages.—Hallam's Constitutional History of England.—Lyell's Elements of Geology.—Merivale's General History of Rome.—Cox's General History of Greece.—Classical Dictionary. $1 25 per volume.

Lewis's History of Germany.—Ecclesiastical History.—Hume's England. $1 50 per volume.

CRUISE OF THE "CHALLENGER." Voyages over many Seas, Scenes in many Lands. By W. J. J. Spry, R.N. With Map and Illustrations. Crown 8vo, Cloth, $2 00.

DARWIN'S VOYAGE OF A NATURALIST. Voyage of a Naturalist. Journal of Researches into the Natural History and Geology of the Countries visited during the Voyage of H.M.S. *Beagle* round the World. By Charles Darwin. 2 vols., 12mo, Cloth, $2 00.

CAMERON'S ACROSS AFRICA. Across Africa. By Verney Lovett Cameron. Map and Illustrations. 8vo, Cloth, $5 00.

BARTH'S NORTH AND CENTRAL AFRICA. Travels and Discoveries in North and Central Africa: being a Journal of an Expedition undertaken under the Auspices of H.B.M.'s Government, in the Years 1849–1855. By Henry Barth, Ph.D., D.C.L. Illustrated. 3 vols., 8vo, Cloth, $12 00; Sheep, $13 50; Half Calf, $18 75.

www.ingramcontent.com/pod-product-compliance
Lightning Source LLC
Chambersburg PA
CBHW021152230426
43667CB00006B/354

* 9 7 8 3 7 4 4 7 1 8 0 4 2 *